P9-CRL-833

ARRIVALS

ARRIVALS

Stories *from the* History of Ontario

John Bentley Mays

PENGUIN
CANADA

PENGUIN CANADA
Published by the Penguin Group
Penguin Books, a division of Pearson Canada, 10 Alcorn Avenue, Toronto, Ontario,
Canada M4V 3B2
Penguin Books Ltd, 80 Strand, London WC2R ORL, England
Penguin Putnam Inc., 375 Hudson Street, New York, New York 10014, U.S.A.
Penguin Books Australia Ltd, 250 Camberwell Road, Camberwell, Victoria 3124,
Australia
Penguin Books India (P) Ltd, 11, Community Centre, Panchsheel Park,
New Delhi – 110 017, India
Penguin Books (NZ) Ltd, cnr Rosedale and Airborne Roads, Albany, Auckland 1310,
New Zealand
Penguin Books (South Africa) (Pty) Ltd, 24 Sturdee Avenue, Rosebank 2196,
South Africa

Penguin Books Ltd, Registered Offices: 80 Strand, London WC2R ORL, England

First published 2002

3 5 7 9 10 8 6 4 2

Copyright © John Bentley Mays, 2002
Illustrations © Marie Day, 2002

Author representation: Westwood Creative Artists
94 Harbord Street, Toronto, Ontario M5S 1G6

Printed and bound in Canada on acid free paper ∞

NATIONAL LIBRARY OF CANADA CATALOGUING IN PUBLICATION DATA

Mays, John Bentley
Arrivals : stories from the history of Ontario / John Bentley Mays.

ISBN 0-14-301340-8

1. Ontario—History. 2. Ontario—History—Biography.
I. Title.

FC3061.M39 2002   971.3   C2002-901232-5
F1058.M39 2002

Visit Penguin Books' website at **www.penguin.ca**

This book is dedicated to the memory of Greg Curnoe

We shall not cease from exploration
And the end of all our exploring
Will be to arrive where we started
And know the place for the first time.

—T. S. Eliot, "Little Gidding"

CONTENTS

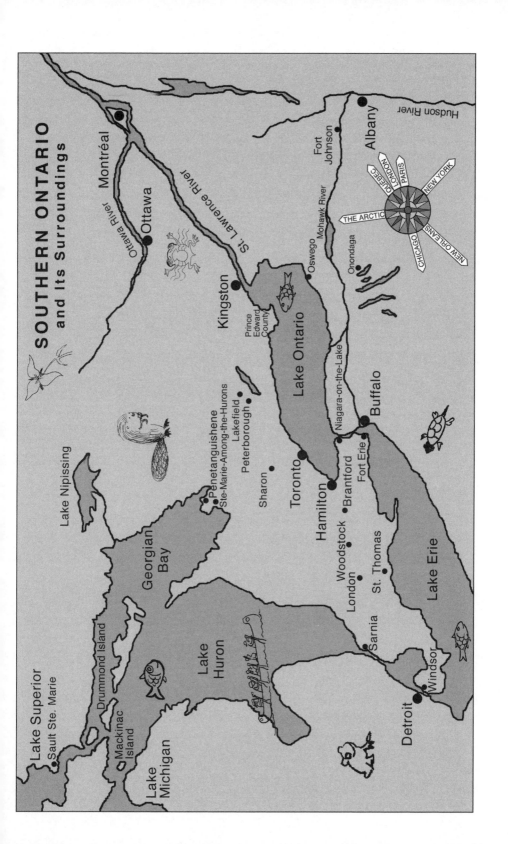

I
ORIGINS

1
HOW THE STORIES CAME

THIS IS A BOOK OF STORIES ABOUT PEOPLE who have come to
Ontario from elsewhere and done something interesting, horrible or
wonderful here since the withdrawal of the continental ice sheet, about
eleven thousand years ago.

Though I would love to tell their tales, I have left out movie star
Marie Dressler, architect Frank Gehry and the sensational radio
evangelist Aimee Semple McPherson, along with many others who
grew up in Ontario, but made their fortunes and fame elsewhere.
Nor are there very many politicians here, or other important people.
I have chosen to write only about men and women who engaged my
interest. Among others, there are mastodon stalkers, Alexander
Graham Bell, a professional murderer and a diplomat from the
court of Louis XIV who hit on a novel (and unintentionally hilari-
ous) way to show *les sauvages* what the Chinese looked like. There
are several notable members of Ontario's ancient nations in this
book, and some very earnest Catholic missionaries, whose biggest
complaint about the Indians, as far as I can tell, was that they
weren't modern enough.

Many Americans have come to Ontario—a few to loot and plunder, most to farm. There are some stories here about things that aren't people—the most famous elephant in the world, who did not get out of Ontario alive, and several visions handed down by celestial messengers, one a beautiful naked boy who visited a renegade Quaker north of Toronto.

Many newcomers in this book created things. The long-distance telephone call and the radio were thought up by Ontarians in a couple of charming Victorian villages near each other. Ontario has always offered a comfortable home to brilliant, half-mad modern visionaries fascinated by telecommunications, electricity, waves and vibrations, that sort of thing. The most famous is Marshall McLuhan. Another was a psychiatrist who became the first biographer of Walt Whitman. The great American poet had hardly arrived in Ontario before deciding it was an especially wonderful place. "If the most significant trait of modern civilization is benevolence (as a leading statesman has said)," wrote the poet,

> it is doubtful whether this is anywhere illustrated to fuller degree than in the province of Ontario. All the maimed, insane, idiotic, blind, deaf and dumb, needy, sick and old, minor criminals, fallen women, foundlings, have advanced and ample profusion of houses and care and oversight, at least fully equal to anything of the kind in any of the United States—probably indeed superior to them. In Ontario for its eighty-eight electoral ridings, there are four Insane Asylums, an Idiot Asylum, one Institution for the Blind, one for the Deaf and Dumb, one for Foundlings, a Reformatory for Girls, one for Women, and no end of homes for the old and infirm, for waifs, and for the sick.

LIKE MOST OF THE PEOPLE IN THIS BOOK, I was born elsewhere. I came from the United States to Ontario at the end of the 1960s, and almost at once learned, to my surprise, that many Canadians believed Canada to be boring, and Ontario *very* boring. Some thirty years later, when I began writing this book, I found that people still thought Ontario to be boring. This influential opinion, which has been especially popular among Toronto writers, artists and intellectuals, has always struck me as absurd—but, I hasten to add, many new Ontarians have had sound reasons for not knowing much about the place. Though I am not one of them, most newcomers have come here to escape famine, war, persecution, genocide, the hopelessness of poverty—all infinitely worse than boredom. Immigrants who have escaped peril and reached safe harbour tend not to think much about the place they've come to. Their grandchildren might. But not the original newcomers. They want to know where the next meal is coming from.

That said, the idea that Ontario is boring has proven durable enough to merit a book, this one, to contradict it. In fairness, I should add that people who regard themselves as colonials usually tend to view their homeland as tiresomely peripheral. And, to be fair to Ontarians who so regard themselves, this place has indeed always been a colony, or protectorate, or dependency, or outpost of one or more great powers headquartered outside the political boundaries one finds drawn on maps.

The earliest power for which records exist is the so-called Iroquois Confederacy. For centuries before the Europeans arrived, and for some 250 years afterwards, the ancient nations that farmed and hunted in the luxuriant forests north of Lake Ontario were subjects of this great League, the most impressive political organization north of Mexico, headquartered in what is now New York State.

After the French came, in the early sixteenth century, their king claimed all Ontario, and most of North America for France.

Another sovereign, this one enthroned in London, fought the king in Versailles to a standstill in the eighteenth century, after many years of hot and cold war, and seized a vast swatch of eastern North America as booty—only to lose the most densely populated and heavily industrialized parts of it soon thereafter, when thirteen of his colonies broke away and became the United States.

The Americans, as the citizens of the republic are inexactly called, stopped invading Canada and resigned themselves to the idea of a monarchy on North American soil only toward the end of the nineteenth century. But as the twentieth century progressed, the American Republic took Ontario, and Canada, under its mighty wing.

If you've been keeping count, that adds up to four strong political interests—Confederacy, France, England, the United States—that have viewed Ontario, either in part or in whole, at the same or at different times, as their bailiwick during the last thousand years. Only one of them, the British, thought it prudent to populate the territory with large numbers of their offspring and establish the welcome of immigrants as permanent policy.

There would be no way to exclude the shifting international contexts from my stories of Ontario, even if I wanted to, which I definitely do not. Though the whole world comes into my stories, to write a history of the world lies beyond my ability or intention. But if you are interested, at the end of this book you will find a list of Ontario and international dates that frame all that is to come.

THE ONLY WAY TO KNOW ONTARIO, or any place, is to look at the ground under one's feet and start thinking about it.

The first time I made a discovery of this sort was some years ago, when visiting Niagara Falls with European friends. (Every visitor to Toronto travels down to see the cataract, or thinks he's been cheated.) As I was standing there, being genuinely bored by all that noisy water, I began to think about that place, recalling stories I'd absent-mindedly picked up over the years. After the Civil War, Jefferson Davis, deposed president of the Confederate States of America, liked to visit Niagara-on-the-Lake because it wasn't the U.S.A., where he was despised. He was welcome here because numerous Canadians had fought on the side of the Rebels. As it happened, Niagara-on-the-Lake, where his friends lived, was once ruled by an aboriginal nation, now vanished, which loved parrots and alligators, though they never saw them. They also adored Catholic missionaries, whom they did get to see. The first European to glimpse Niagara Falls was a rambling Parisian scamp who told the oldest stories we have about southern Ontario, most of them lies. The first European to write down and publish his impressions 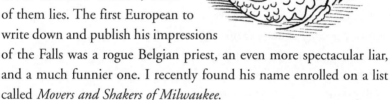 of the Falls was a rogue Belgian priest, an even more spectacular liar, and a much funnier one. I recently found his name enrolled on a list called *Movers and Shakers of Milwaukee.*

A FEW THINGS ABOUT THIS BOOK may strike readers as odd. I make no apology for them, though you should know what they are beforehand.

One has to do with the many voices that can be heard in these pages. Whenever their words have been available, I have tried to let people tell things their own ways. When printed as originally written by the authors, the texts have been followed exactly, except for some silent changes in spelling or punctuation, and some abridgements. My goal in every case has been to make the text legible and free of stumbling blocks to understanding what is being said. For this light tampering, I beg forgiveness in advance from both my authors and readers.

When the available texts are translated paraphrases or digests, as in the case of the aboriginal histories of Ontario that open this book, I have played with wording and phrasing, keeping this reworking always strictly at the service of the voice I hear speaking through the printed words.

I can hardly stress too strongly the importance of those voices, most of which belonged to venerable storytellers from the ancient nations, reciting to anthropologists the great oral literatures of their people. The stories they tell are the oldest surviving histories of Ontario. The first Europeans to arrive in Ontario, and generations after them, believed other stories. One was that the world, including Ontario, was made in seven days quite recently, and that the Sun went around the Earth each day. The story about the Sun changed a couple of hundred years ago. The story about seven days was overturned more recently. The basic stories of what we are, where we come from, where we are going, will almost certainly change again. The tales about the creation of Ontario in the first chapters are blendings of what various people have believed and now believe, presented here with prejudice toward none of them. In the course of writing this book, the Woman Who Fell from the Stars has become as real to me as Walt Whitman, and more real than Étienne Brûlé. That's the way things are.

Another thing you should know has to do with what's meant by the word "Ontario." It changes to fit the story I am telling. For about half this book it is a region of Canada, a country half as old as the United States, and heir to British institutions and traditions imposed midway through the European presence here. Ontario's population is also largely English-speaking, but that's changing as new immigrants continue to arrive from elsewhere. They've been doing so for the last eleven thousand years, rearranging matters to suit themselves, and speaking many languages. The language most often heard in my Toronto neighbourhood is Portuguese. But one can live and die in Ontario speaking only Italian or Chinese or Tibetan or French or Cree. It's always been like that here, from the beginning.

If the children of today's immigrants or newcomers in the future are so inclined, Ontario may some day become an American state. Or it may turn into an independent country with a seat in the United Nations. Or it could disappear altogether, at least as a political entity. Whatever its destiny, Ontario will quite literally start disappearing in about twenty thousand years, when the next Ice Age begins in earnest.

For the time being, however, Ontario certainly exists, though it is hard to say exactly what and where it is. The borders one sees neatly inscribed on maps are the arbitrary work of politicians and were settled quite recently, and may change again before this book is old. Of course, they are *true* boundaries in the same sense that the statement "Ontario is older than Italy" is true. It *is* true, factually and absolutely—though the truth of the statement is trivial and irrelevant. Even the political outline of Ontario has always been like Alice, getting bigger and smaller and bigger again. But unlike Alice, and like a lady on a bad diet, Ontario has occasionally shrunk this way while bulging that way, all of it rather often and unpredictably.

At times, of course, boundaries become powerfully real, as Josiah Henson, a fugitive slave from the American South, found when he crossed the Niagara frontier from America and danger to Canada and safety. But most of my stories have less to do with the political entity inscribed on maps—as seen from heaven, in other words—than with what happened on, alongside or because of three defining systems of waterways: the St. Lawrence River, the Great Lakes and the Ottawa River. Ontario, as the word is used here, is the sequence of the civilizations that have arisen, flourished, fallen, disappeared or changed on the shorelines of these great water-roads. Ontario is the human matrix in which the tales told here emerged, and where they were remembered until someone wrote them down, and occasionally after.

The final thing to watch out for are names, especially those of the ancient Ontario nations.

Like all the old peoples of America, they have been known as Indians since they discovered Europeans at the gates of their towns some five hundred years ago. Many people called "Indians" now dislike the term. But it is surely nothing worse than an immense geographical mistake, and I have used it when unable to do otherwise. The word "aboriginal," in my view, raises real questions. The ancient societies encountered by the Europeans had not been in Ontario *ab origine*. Like the Europeans themselves, they wandered in at various times, displacing earlier peoples, then being chased to various parts of the province, or out of it altogether, by still other newcomers. Because neither corresponds to reality, I have sought to use the words "Indian" and "aboriginal" as sparingly as possible.

The most obnoxious names of Ontario's ancient peoples are the most common, and appear here not at all. Most names such as "Iroquois" and "Huron" are racist slurs devised by enemies. I have decided to call the ancient peoples of Ontario, instead, what they called themselves, wherever possible and sensible. Thus, the Iroquois— a word with especially nasty connotations—become the People of the Long House or the Great Peace, or the League or the Confederacy. The Huron here become the Wendat, or People of the Peninsula (which Wendat means). We do not know what the once-powerful Ontario nation we recall as the Neutral called themselves, because they no longer exist. Neutral will have to do. If finding the Huron called Wendat seems uncomfortable or strange, that's something you will simply have to get used to. It's high time we all did.

You already know a Wendat word. It's "Toronto." From high antiquity through the French period in Ontario, Toronto was exactly what it means in Wendat: a gathering place. Here, traders assembled and set out on a system of trails and water-routes that provided a shortcut between Lake Ontario and Lake Huron. Laying out his new Upper Canadian capital city in 1793, Lieutenant-Governor John Graves Simcoe found the name Toronto barbarous, and decided to call the town York. So it remained until incorporation in 1834, when the old, enduringly popular name Toronto was restored. Just remember that York and Toronto are the same place, and you will not become confused.

The name of the *first* capital of Upper Canada is more stubbornly baffling. When he arrived in Upper Canada in 1791, Simcoe took up his governorship at a place that I have decided to call, everywhere and always in this book, by its modern name, Niagara-on-the-Lake. But for the record, you should know that it was Newark from the 1780s to 1793, when it became Niagara. Throughout the nineteenth century, people were always mixing up the towns of Niagara and

Niagara Falls. But a common-sense solution prevailed; and by 1900, and ever since, everybody has known the older city as Niagara-on-the-Lake (which it is, in fact).

Unless clearly otherwise indicated, the word "Québec" refers not to the latter-day Canadian province but to the tiny French outpost on the lower St. Lawrence River that became an important city in the history of La Nouvelle France, the vast vanished commonwealth that once included Ontario, and Detroit and New Orleans and my father's cotton plantation in northwest Louisiana. Had history taken a somewhat different (and altogether possible) twist, I might have been born exactly when and where I was, though it would have been a sub-tropical *département* of La Nouvelle France, not an American state. I would have grown up speaking French, like most everyone else in the world, and perhaps a little English patois for communicating with the British colonials on the east side of the Appalachians.

THIS BOOK IS DEDICATED to the memory of the London, Ontario, artist Greg Curnoe. I did not know him. We spoke once, twenty years ago, when a touring retrospective of his paintings, copybook scribblings, drawings, rubber-stamp prints, assemblages and so forth came to the Art Gallery of Ontario and I reviewed it. I do not recall seeing him again before his death ten years later.

In 1990, a minor question about the boundaries of his London property made necessary a check of land transfers, deeds and such. This kind of thing happens all the time in old towns. But when it happened to Greg Curnoe, the event touched off an obsessive drive to know everything—not merely what was needed to settle the boundary dispute, but absolutely *everything* that had ever transpired on the site of 38 Weston Street, his home. The project that resulted consists of two parts, the first called *Deeds/Abstracts*. It is a two-hundred-page chronology of every discoverable occurrence on the site of the artist's home, beginning shortly after the withdrawal of the continental ice sheet until December 12, 1991, when Curnoe wrote down something he'd learned about a man who belonged to a local horseshoe club. This compilation is drawn from every imaginable source: personal experience, local legend, land records, genealogies and family histories, geological accounts, ethnographies, treaties and every recorded instance of a serious flood on the Thames River, which twists through London.

Deeds/nations, the second half, is an alphabetical listing of every aboriginal person, with everything known about each person appended to his or her name, who lived in the London area between 1750 and 1850. The bond between the project's two parts lies in the artist's street address. The chronology is an enormous heap of facts about the place; the "directory" gives us the names of aboriginal inhabitants who sold or treated away the land of which the property is a tiny part. Curnoe jotted down an entry in the huge two-part manuscript shortly after midnight on November 14, 1992. He died in a cycling accident a few hours later.

This collection of stories is dedicated to him because I hope people will recall his art forever, long after this book has been forgotten. His work in pictures and language embodied the most profound investigation of Ontario attempted so far, and is a superb example of the intensive, particular study of *where we are.* Most of the people who have arrived here have thought they were somewhere else—an island created by magical creatures, the east coast of China, a mysterious kingdom where gold lay on the ground like gravel, a blank place that could be easily turned into a new France or new Britain. Gradually they began to understand that they had arrived in a land thick with stories. Because Greg Curnoe understood that Ontario is the sum of its stories, he understood everything.

Among the things Greg also knew is that the old stories that count will tend to persist in the archive of collective memory, written down or remembered, waiting to be told when the time is right. The time is right to tell some stories—though a great many remain to be told. No complete narrative history of this fascinating province exists. Robert

Bothwell's *Short History of Ontario*, my constant companion on this journey, is a handy beginning. But, like my book, it is only a beginning.

There is a great need for a thorough history, if those who live here are ever to know where they are. I recall one evening in the spring of 1999, when some terrorized people, airlifted in a big-bellied military plane across the Atlantic Ocean from the Balkan horror, were deposited at Canadian Forces Base Trenton, in southern Ontario near the U.S. frontier. Their arrival was televised nationally. The weary newcomers stepping off the plane knew they'd come to Canada, of course, but none had been told exactly where they were. As it happened, their point of entry was a very short distance from the border-crossing where many British colonials, disinclined to become republicans, had fled terror and misery into Ontario two hundred years before. I was thrilled by the coincidence. I still am. Clearly, that night in May was not the time to tell the immigrants how rich in the history of freedom that lovely little patch of Lake Ontario coastland was and long has been. Perhaps the time is now right. I hope they find this book someday, and the yet-unwritten history that tells the whole tale.

IN 1883, A STORYTELLER OF THE SENECA NATION named Henry Jacob told Jeremiah Curtin, who knew sixty languages, how the stories came. It went like this.

A long time ago, before there were any stories, a boy everybody called Orphan lived in a village of the Seneca. They called him Orphan because he *was* one.

Fortunately, Orphan was looked after by a good woman of the village, so he grew up to be a healthy, busy lad. One day the woman said it was high time Orphan learned how to hunt, so she sent him into the forest armed with a bow and some arrows and a buckskin bag full of parched corn for lunch and instructions to kill every bird he found. As things turned out, Orphan was very good at killing birds, so he did it all morning and well into the afternoon. By the time the sun began dropping below the horizon, he had a respectable string of birds to show the woman who looked after him.

She was understandably pleased by Orphan's success on his first day out, so the next morning she dispatched him into the woods with the same equipment and instructions. That day, he thought, "If I do exactly as my mother says, killing all the birds I can find, then some day I will be good enough at this to hunt down big animals." First, of course, he had to learn to hunt birds, and with each passing day he got better at it.

On his tenth day out, Orphan headed off from home as usual, but went deeper into the forest than he had ever gone before. About noon, he saw a clearing through the woods and, in the sunny middle of it, a high, smooth rock, flat on top. Orphan strode out of the forest darkness and jumped up on the rock, and got down to business, making arrows.

That was when he heard a voice, right beside him.

"Shall I tell you stories?" the voice said.

After looking around and seeing nobody, Orphan became annoyed, stopped work on the arrows and began to keep a sharp lookout for the man who had hidden himself nearby and was now playing tricks on him.

Then the voice spoke again, apparently out of nowhere, asking the same question: "Shall I tell you stories?"

That's when Orphan realized no man was talking. It was the large, flat rock he sat on. The trouble was, Orphan had no idea what Rock was talking about. He had never heard of a story, nor even heard the word. Nobody had, because they did not exist. So he asked the stone, "What's a story? What do you mean when you propose to tell me stories?"

To that, Rock replied, "A story is about what happened a long time ago. Give me your birds, and I'll tell you stories. Then you'll know what I'm talking about . . ."

After deciding Rock had made him a fair offer, birds for stories,

Orphan promised to hand over his kill—and immediately Rock began telling what happened a long time ago. He would finish one story, then begin another. Orphan was fascinated, and sat, head down, while Rock told one story after another, until nightfall.

"That's enough for today," said Rock at last. "Come back tomorrow. If anybody asks why you've returned to the village with so few birds, tell them it's just because you've gotten really good at this, and killed all the birds in the neighbourhood and you now have to go much deeper into the woods just to find something to kill."

Which is what Orphan told the woman who looked after him, when she wondered aloud why he'd come home with just a little handful of dead birds.

For the next several days, it kept going on this way. The boy would go out in the morning, kill a few birds to give Rock, listen to the stories, then come back home to the village, nearly empty-handed.

One day Rock said, "Tomorrow everybody in your village has to come out here and listen to my stories. Go back and tell your headman to make every man come here, bringing something to eat. Now clear this place of brush and weeds and trash so everybody can sit on the ground near me."

That evening, Orphan gave Rock's message to the headman, who sent a runner to each family in the village, telling them what he wanted them to do. The next day, after everybody had settled down, Rock spoke. This is what he said.

"Now I'm going to tell you stories of what happened a long time ago. There was a world before this one. Everything I am going to tell you happened there. Not everybody will remember everything, so remember what you can—every word I say, or at least some of my words. Some of you will forget everything. Do the best you can. In the future, you have to tell these stories to each other—so listen."

Each villager bowed his head and attended carefully to every word Rock said. When the sun began to set and the time came to stop, Rock told them all, "That's enough for today. Come tomorrow and bring some more meat and bread."

This went on for several days, and so it was, Henry Jacob told Jeremiah Curtin, that Rock taught them everything they knew about the world that came before this one.

"You must treasure these stories as long as the world endures," said Rock in his closing speech to the assembled villagers. "You must tell them to your children and grandchildren, who must tell them to their descendants forever." To treasure and to transmit—these now become the work of humankind. Some people, of course, will remember the stories better than others. That is, as Rock reminded his listeners, to be expected. But the work of telling must go on, lest those alive forget.

I CANNOT CLAIM TO KNOW EVERYTHING that has happened in Ontario, that has constituted it as a unique moment and place within the world. I cannot claim knowledge of more than a fraction of that accomplishment, but part of what I have learned is in this book.

Now I'm going to tell you some stories of what happened here a long time ago, and not so long ago, and quite recently—but most of these things took place a long time before you got here.

2
THE WOMAN WHO FELL FROM THE STARS

THERE ARE THREE INTERESTING TALES about how Ontario came to be and looks as it does today.

The oldest one passed down among the Europeans and their descendants in North America was written down a couple of thousand years ago and became known as the Book of Genesis. It is in the Bible, sacred to Jews, Christians and Muslims, and has to do with how the Unpronounceable Name made everything that exists, including our first parents, Adam and Eve, out of nothing in six days, then rested.

A much newer story was invented by Charles Darwin and Louis Agassiz and people who thought as they did, and spans millions and millions of years. Nobody can imagine millions of years (or millions of anything), and the story lacks an Unpronounceable Name or Raven or Sky God or other creator, which perhaps explains why it so much more bleak than the one in the Bible. It nevertheless happens to be the most popular one in circulation nowadays. This is not because it is any more self-evidently true than any other story. It's because people these days, for reasons I am not going to pursue, tend to like stories without Unpronounceable Names or gods or magic in them, and stories of creation that explain everything except what creation stories are supposed to explain: how it all began.

A third story of creation was told by the Wendat of southern Ontario and, in more or less the same version, by the once-powerful People of the Long House, who ruled much of eastern North America until about 250 years ago. This third story is both beautiful and explains everything. Like all creation stories, it was probably sung long before it was said, and said long before it was written down. We have only remnants of the song. The best we've got are plot summaries given by elderly storytellers of the old nations, who were perhaps too tired and old to sing all the songs to story-listeners and story-gatherers descended from the European peoples.

The oldest rendition of the Wendat story we have has come down to us from Father Jean de Brébeuf, the famous Jesuit, who heard it in 1636. He found the Wendat tale, and the Wendat themselves, very annoying indeed—not because they were pagans, but because they did not take quickly to the newest science and technology.

The Wendat found a more sympathetic listener in the restlessly busy, eager Horatio Hale, who, like Jeremiah Curtin, was a Harvard graduate coming of age in a time when everything that was once considered permanent seemed to be decaying, disappearing, falling apart.

Hale came from a family with literary interests and little talent. (His mother's most memorable contribution to literature was the poem "Mary Had a Little Lamb.") But keen interest and a lack of personal flair served Hale well, when he decided, while still an undergraduate, to devote his life to writing down the traditions of America's ancient nations in the language they spoke, before the traditions were forgotten or the nations themselves disappeared. In 1872 and 1874, Hale visited a tiny Wendat community (now vanished) on the east bank of the Detroit River and was fortunate to find a storyteller named Alexander Clarke who remembered a great deal. Better yet, Clarke remembered the tales in the Wendat language, which not many people other than he and Horatio Hale could speak and understand. Here is the gist of what the Wendat told about the beginning.

IN THE TIMELESS TIME BEFORE EVERYTHING, everything was just water, going on forever, but teeming with all kinds of fish, with snails and loons and all other creatures that love the waters and call them home.

The arising of the land and trouble both began high above the sea, among the stars, when some man pushed his wife through a crack in the sky-floor, and sent her hurtling down toward the infinite ocean. But Alexander Clarke recalled another version of what happened. The sky-woman, whom Father Brébeuf calls "Aataentsic," was working her field, when her dog followed a bear down a hole that unfortunately opened into the empty sky. In despair over the loss of her good dog, Ataentsic flung herself down the hole after him. There are some other variations. The important point is that the woman fell from the stars, and that was the beginning.

Being one of those long-ago people, hence like us and unlike us at the same time, Aataentsic fell slowly—so slowly, in fact, that two loons on the wing saw the woman dropping down and decided to save her from death by drowning. The loons raced to the spot where they figured the falling woman would hit the water, to catch her on their backs, all the while calling out for the other dwellers in the great sea to help them.

The sea creatures heard the loons' far-sent cry and swiftly answered the summons, arriving just as Ataentsic dropped onto the downy backs of the tightly circling birds. Being light and quick in their flight over the waters and spindly-legged and little—certainly not as strong as the large animals who were to inhabit the land later on, when there was a land to live on—the kindly loons could not hold up the woman for very long. So Snapping Turtle got the job.

His hard mossy back was certainly broad and strong enough for Aataentsic to stand on, but Snapping Turtle knew his back was no place for a woman. For one thing, it was too small. For another, Snapping Turtle, like a loon, was a citizen of the waters, and the woman a creature of the sky.

So, as was the custom in those days, a great council of the sea creatures was convened to decide how to save the woman who had fallen from the stars. After talking it over, the council decided the woman needed land to live on. All the deep divers among the creatures knew dirt lay underneath the boundless ocean, so Snapping Turtle ordered them to plunge into the depths and bring up some dirt to make land for the woman to live on.

Beaver, Muskrat and others took up the dredge work, some almost perishing in the attempt, all failing to accomplish the task. Then Snapping Turtle, who had been ordering the others to dive for dirt, found a little dirt in his own mouth, and gave it to the woman. After she had trimmed his shell all round with the dirt, the fringe began to grow outward—ever further outward from the centre, until grasses and trees took root and flourished. So it was that Snapping Turtle gave Ataentsic a suitable home on his own hard back, which still undergirds the land.

WITH A LITTLE IMAGINATION, anyone can see the bumps and jags of Snapping Turtle's back in Ontario's rocks, where the earth has been washed away, leaving the earth's bones bare. It's the best way to discover where Ontario is located, by thinking of it at ground level.

There is a view of it from space, of course, and we are accustomed to seeing that one on maps. Then there is the way we actually experience it, approaching from its western or southern or eastern boundaries, and that's the way I want to talk about where Ontario is. It is the way the explorers found and saw it.

Arriving in Ontario from the southwest or south involves crossing water: the short tumultuous Niagara River carrying the waters north from Lake Erie into Lake Ontario. These immense, shallow bodies of water began to be filled with cold, fresh water thirteen thousand years ago, as the continental glaciers began to melt. The most ancient visitors known to have come to Ontario arrived eleven thousand years ago by following the reforested shorelines on foot or by boat, finding amenable hunting grounds by Lake Huron and Georgian Bay. Eleven millennia later, most people who arrive in Ontario still come from the south and southwest, and visit or settle in the southern ranges of the land.

Flying into Toronto by night from the United States, one beholds the western end of Lake Ontario as a diadem of gems, with the brightest clusters of brilliance where Niagara-on-the-Lake, Toronto and Hamilton now stand.

Approaching from the north, through the vast wastelands of forest, rocks and barrens, is the most formidable and strangest route. Very few people, at any time, have done so. And when, exactly, the south-bound traveller comes into Ontario from the north is itself a disputed matter. Until the mid-nineteenth century, when it was given to Canada, the gigantic wilderness of rocks, deep ponds and bush that compose most of what's now called Ontario was called Rupert's Land, and belonged to the Hudson's Bay Company. Yet if you must come to Ontario from the north, perhaps it is best to start out on the cruel grey waters, recalling that strange, obsessively driven Englishman Henry Hudson, whose grave Hudson Bay is. Hudson, his son and other crew members were cast adrift there by mutineers in 1610. Their death is not only the northern introduction to Ontario—the first fact imprinted on this terrain by a European—but also a bleak reminder of what drove the Europeans to seek and find this place at all: the hope that through that terrible northern wasteland lay the fabled water-road to China.

A less haunted boundary and more visible one lies between the ultimate north and not-so-northern expanses of Ontario. It is the great
Arctic Watershed. North of this line, zigzagging unevenly east-west
across 2,250 kilometres of wilderness from Sault Ste. Marie eastward
to the Québec border of Ontario, all the water flows back north, the
direction from which you came, into Hudson Bay.

When standing on the Arctic Watershed, what old explorers called
"the height of land," you are very near the beginning of the world.
The oldest rocks are on Highway 11—Yonge Street, the longest street
in the world—16 kilometres west of Nipigon. There, a granite ridge
formed inside the earth 2.5 billion years ago lies exposed after constant
grinding down by rain and ice and the advance and recession of
glaciers. It is a stack of pages from the history of the world. More than
a million years ago, molten stone flowed over the incredibly old,
underlying levels and created the nearby Palisades of the Pijitawabik,
stone towers looming 152 metres in some places above the surface of
Lake Nipigon, its shoreline cleft with deep, steep-sided valleys.

For most of the way south of the Arctic Watershed to the low plains
just short of Lake Ontario, you are navigating the streams and lakes of
the Shield Plateau, the roots of once-gigantic mountains now worn
down to stumps. This vast, gently sloping tableland stands about 300
metres above sea level throughout most of Ontario, while ridges and
peaks on Snapping Turtle's back can jut up several metres higher in
many places. The highest point in Ontario is Ogidaki Mountain, rising
665 metres just north of Sault Ste. Marie, presiding over the tens of
thousands of lakes, swamps and bogs of northern Ontario.

The route from the east is, for Europeans, the oldest. Early in the
sixteenth century, Jacques Cartier looked east from Mount Royal, up
the great northwestern river—the Ottawa—that he was destined never
to explore but that was to become the French road of empire into the
continental interior.

The French found that the 1,120 kilometres of the Ottawa led them
not to China but instead to the large northern lakes and Georgian Bay,
to the Wendat and other people ready to hunt and trade with them. It

provided the roadbed for their huge rafts of timber and canoes loaded with beaver pelts, sent downriver to Montréal, thence to the markets of Europe. And for centuries after the moment Cartier glimpsed it, and dreamed of marvels and treasures lining its shores upstream, the Ottawa was the passage connecting the two parts of La Nouvelle France, the older now the provinces of Québec and Ontario, the newer sprawling down the Mississippi Valley. And the Ottawa was the main street, arcing northward over the southern Ontario landscape, forested and loamy after the glaciers retreated, but made forbidding for centuries by the vigilance and ferocity of the People of the Long House.

SO MUCH FOR HOW THE LAND EMERGED. It remains to tell how the problems came.

When the woman was shoved from the sky, the Wendat say, she was pregnant with twin brothers who were already quarrelling so loudly in her womb that the woman could hear them.

The argument had to do with the way the twins, named Good Mind and Flint, were to come out into the world. Good Mind said he did not mind making his way out by the usual route babies take. Flint was determined not to emerge in that fashion, so he cut his way out of the womb, killing his mother. Once buried, the dead woman gave to humankind all the goodness she had brought with her from the stars. The pumpkin vine sprang from the earth over her buried head; the corn sprouted from her breasts, and from her arms and legs came the beans and all other green things that are good to eat.

Good Mind and Flint were star-folk destined to shape the land on Snapping Turtle's back. They were therefore not people like us, except in one regard. They argued all the time and could get along together no better in the world than they had in their mother's womb. So, sensibly, they parted company, each taking a different part of the land as his own, then set about peopling the territories with their thought-children. Flint's mind being vile, his creations were vile: snakes and panthers, gigantic wolves and bears, mosquitoes as big as turkeys. Another mind-child Flint created was Huge Toad, who drank up all the fresh water in the world.

In the sector of the world he had chosen, Good Mind was creating gentle, useful animals. Among them was Partridge, who one day let Good Mind know he was heading off to Flint's territory. What with Huge Toad guzzling down all the fresh water, Good Mind's land was stricken with drought, and Partridge heard there was good water over in Flint's domain. Good Mind did not stop Partridge, but watched carefully where the bird flew and followed him from the decent land into the dark realm Flint was peopling with his evil thoughts.

One after another, the immense snakes, ravenous beasts, titanic mosquitoes and other things Flint had made were shrunk by Good Mind. (These annoying things were not eradicated, of course—just made smaller, hence more tolerable.)

The last bit of Flint's vicious handiwork to be overcome was Huge Toad, which Good Mind slashed open, letting the fresh water flow back into the riverbeds and lakes.

Clearly the land was not big enough for both Good Mind and Flint. So the brothers finally met face to face and decided to fight a duel to the death, to determine which would be master of Snapping Turtle's back, now extending to the horizon. This being a duel, a certain decorum had to be observed and strict regulations agreed to. One rule stipulated that each combatant had to tell the other what weapon could kill him. Accordingly, Good Mind declared the one thing that could destroy him: a decisive blow with a bag of beans or corn, seeds of all goodness that humankind requires. Flint replied by naming the weapon he most feared: the horn of a deer or some other wild beast.

So the duel began, with Flint getting the first shot at Good Mind with a bean-bag. The hit was almost fatal, but Good Mind revived enough to strike back at Flint with a deer's horn, killing him.

Thus Flint's active career of mischief came to an end, but not before he had left the Turtle's Back peppered with problems. Some, like snakes and bears, Good Mind had made smaller. Other issues did not yield to such simple solutions. When the brothers had been busily completing the world, Flint would occasionally disrupt something Good Mind had created. As designed by Good Mind, each river, for example, was to have a two-way flow, so someone could paddle easily either way with equivalent ease. Flint decided to change that. To make travel harder for those who used the water-routes, he made every river flow either upstream or downstream. Moreover, he put in rapids and cataracts and other obstacles—again, as a way to disrupt Good Mind's plan that getting around should be easy for the first people who came here.

3
WAYS UP AND DOWN

WHEN THE OLD TIME ENDED and human time in Ontario began, Good Mind had disappeared, while leaving the world to work itself out more or less as he intended.

Huge Toad—a much more interesting name for it than the "Wisconsinian glacier"—had indeed swallowed all the fresh water he could hold about twenty thousand years ago, after soaking it up and locking it down as ice for the previous ninety thousand years.

Now, under the benign reign of Good Mind's design (albeit flecked with traces of Flint's mischief) Huge Toad was dying, his waters being released to carve valleys and fill immense, beautiful, pebble-shored lakes, of which our Great Lakes are the last, low puddles. And as Huge Toad's waters were freed, he shrank, and his great white body, that had long squatted heavily and cold on the land, began to recede, showing again the grey, rocky back of Snapping Turtle beneath.

And as it had been in the Old Time, when Aataentsic fell from the stars, so again the vast turtle-back became mossy, then loamy, and finally shadowed by trees, seeding themselves a few kilometres farther north each spring. The animals came back north, as well—Good

Mind's deer in the forests and fantastically huge herds of migrating caribou, and also Flint's sabre-toothed tigers. As Good Mind had intended, Ontario was readying itself for the visit of the first humans, who probably arrived from a southerly direction one cool day eleven thousand springs ago.

The ice sheets were leaving behind tundra, then fields of gravel. Next came the firs and pines, which gave way gradually to the deciduous forests. The creatures that liked the glacial edges—the mastodon, caribou and Arctic fox—retreated with the ice, and began to disappear. The ones that died out altogether were not helped more than a bit toward extinction by people. The best guess is that no more than about two hundred humans ever lived on this land at any given time during those early millennia. But they came and went with the seasons, vigorously tracking the caribou, plotting ways to topple the shy, gigantic elephants that grazed on the mosses gradually getting a toehold on the glacial gravel, fishing with spears tipped with tiny stone points.

They left souvenirs of their passing in at least two places. One lay between the west side of Georgian Bay and the Parkhill area on the south side of Lake Huron, the other was on the northern shores of Lake Iroquois, as the greater lake that would eventually shrink and become Lake Ontario was known. The first visitors are today called Paleo-Indians, though they may not have been Indians, or Wendat or Long House People or anybody else we know.

Of course, we only know them (as people eleven thousand years in the future will know us) from the things they made or used that did not decay—chiefly tools and appliances. They were likely excellent at making clothes for themselves from skin, at thinking one step ahead of the animals they hunted, and all else they did, just because they were certainly expert stoneworkers. They were also choosy about materials. The raw stone preferred by the Parkhill people, for example, came from two hundred kilometres away from their campsite. It was the best they could find, and they got it.

Almost without exception the earliest people camped out by the shorelines of the old glacial lakes. These folk chose these sites because chilly winds blustering across the lakes kept the forests from becoming very dense along the shorelines. Seeing grazing animals at long distance, fishing, wildfowling—all these would have been good reasons to visit and dwell there for a time. But it is strange to learn that archaeologists now call what the first Ontarians did "subsistence activities." Those first people feasted royally on the abundance of post-glacial Ontario and killed their prey with exquisite, elegantly fluted stone tools. The waters were their roads between worlds, their larder was the forest, close at hand and teeming with game.

About three thousand years ago, perhaps because the climate was becoming more suitable year-round, the earliest visitors, or others, settled down and began making pottery. Their earlier skill at crafting lovely hunting tools went into decline, perhaps because they were learning to gather or even cultivate green foodstuffs.

But before that happened, and the world changed for them, they inadvertently left behind a clue about what they believed. The place they did so is called Caradoc, and is found at the southeast edge of Strathroy, Ontario, on a small hill by a swampy stream. Many stone fragments have been found, but no waste—suggesting this was not a place of manufacture. There is no evidence that anything happened at this place other than the deliberate breaking of unfinished tools, with a single whack. The scientists who have studied this site have found in it traces of sacred significance, and this conclusion is hard not to believe. Our tools hold us close to earth, and to the needs and activities of earth. To kill them has always been understood as an act of liberation. Perhaps the tools were killed as sacrifices to gods long forgotten, for the liberation of souls from bondage to the earth and the ceaseless cycle of eating and hunting, procreating and being born and dying. Perhaps there is a whisper of the answer in the Wendat histories of the world, where we learn of Flint's chopping his way out of his mother's womb.

But where did these first hunters learn of Flint, or of the gods, or of hunting? While we do not know where the knowledge of hunting, cooking and making tools came from, a story told among the Algonkian people of Ontario gives us a hint.

In different spots along that great band of civilization that encircles the northern part of the globe, Nanabozho goes by different names and always has a local birthplace—though anybody can see that it's old Nanabozho the storytellers of Siberia or Lake Huron are singing and talking about.

More than a century ago, another listener of stories, A. F. Chamberlain, gathered all the tales he could find about the great gift-giver. Here is the story as it can be made out from the ways it was told among the ancient northern peoples of Ontario. (These folk I will call Real People, to distinguish them, as they did themselves, from the spirit people and other kinds of people who used to live here long ago.)

The hunting points that were used or ceremonially broken were brought here by Real People when they arrived along the cold shores of the old lakes on Snapping Turtle's back. Before they got here, however, they had nothing—tools, weapons, not even clothes, because they had no way to kill the animals for hide and thong. I can't tell you how they survived, though it must have been quite an ordeal, being mostly hairless (as all humans are) and living in a place like Ontario.

Then a remarkable thing happened. One of those miserable people, a Real Woman, had sex with one of the beautiful creatures who live among the stars. She conceived four sons by this star-man. In a baleful reprise of the fate of the Woman Who Fell from the Stars, the human woman died in childbirth. But her four sons survived. One of them was Nanabozho, who was to be remembered forever among the Real People as a friend and teacher. Another of the woman's sons became lord of the Land of Souls, while the third became Rabbit, a magnificent and mysterious man who lives in the Utter North. The last son was yet another Flint Man, and it was this boy upon whom the blame for the mother's death came to rest.

Made of earth but with star-fire in his heart, Nanabozho very quickly grew to manhood, becoming one of those rather fearful, wondrous grown-ups whom we admire but are happy to see living only in stories. For while Real People had to slog across the swamps and

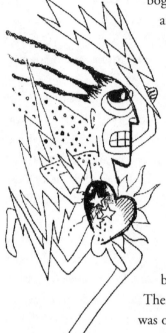

bogs and streams, he could step across anything, however wide, in one long step. His voice was as terrible as thunder, and he could grasp lightning in his fist. He did not like obstacles. This dislike was obviously something he passed along to Real People, who have been discontented with obstacles ever since. But so long as Nanabozho stalked around the world, grabbing lightning from the sky and so forth, he did not give the Real People anything.

Nanabozho, it's worth remembering, lived on the shifting, ambiguous line between the Old Time and our time. There were Real People around; his mother was one of them. But perhaps because he had a sky-man for a father, he was able (as we ordinary folk obviously are not) to change into whatever he liked, whether animal or plant, little rock or big mountain, and talk with anything that was alive. That was before the Flood came and ended the Old Time once and for all. After the Flood, Nanabozho invited the Real People to dwell on his land. For some reason, the animals who lived there planned to inflict some harm on the Real People. Offended, Nanabozho punished the animals by condemning them to eternal silence. That's why the Real People were the only creatures on earth that could speak when they came to Nanabozho's land, and still are.

In the Old Time, a great many things had been different from the way they were to be, among them the coming and going of winter and summer.

Among Nanabozho's first gifts to the Real People were the seasons and the weathers. He saw to it that the winter came, blanketing the ground with snow and damming the streams with ice, so that the Real

People could pursue the animals for food. And he arranged for summer to come, and rain and bright sunshine, so that the earth could yield melons, maize and tobacco.

But most important was the gift of fire, without which the Real People would be creatures hardly worth calling people of any sort. This he did by hacking apart the body of Flint Man and scattering the fire-making flints over the earth for the Real People to find. Fire transforms raw flesh into cooked meat, hard seed into soft porridge. All his gifts, in fact, had to do with transformation. He taught the Real People how to take a chunk of dense rock or length of bone and turn it into light points that would fly through the air and kill things a great way off. He taught them how to make traps and axes, so that the hide of trees could be stripped away and made into canoes. He learned from a spider how to spin a web and decided that was something the Real People should know, so he instructed them in the fine craft of making fishnets. He gave them paint for their faces and for writing on rocks, and the knowledge of the herbs that kill and those that heal.

With the beavers' help, he dammed up the rivers and scooped out Lake Superior. Wherever he went, he left huge rocks behind to mark his passage, and they are mountains. To the Real People, the beautiful rocks and islands along the shore of Lake Superior are all traces of something Nanabozho did, or somewhere he had been. Now the Real People really had everything they needed to keep themselves and their families alive through each of the seasons that marvellous Nanabozho had given them.

THE EUROPEANS BROUGHT OTHER STORIES of how the poor, ignorant ordinary people became the Real People, able to hunt and till the land. The attempts of Christian missionaries to show the ancient Algonkian peoples a different way to the stars was resisted with more firm resolution than it was in any other old Ontario nation. At the heart of the resistance was the Grand Medicine Society, or Medewiwin, which already had a way up and a way down, a presiding genius who was both god and man, a giver of wonderful gifts.

After Nanabozho had given the ignorant people the skills they needed to live fruitfully and well on his land, he found an otter, shot into its body a little shell, then taught it the secrets of finding and following the line between earth and heaven. Thus did he create the rite; next he created the sacred architecture, which took the form of a tent to be dedicated to celebrations of the otter's secrets. The members of the Medewiwin learned the otter's secrets gradually from venerable teachers, who used the power that came down from heaven to help and heal.

A certain Mr. Hiram Calkins has left a record of the enactment of a Medewiwin rite by a remarkable high priest named Black Nail. He usually began his work of calling down the powers of heaven after dark, reports Mr. Calkins,

in a wigwam just large enough to admit of his standing erect. This lodge or wigwam is tightly covered with mats, so as entirely to exclude all sight and the prying curiosity of all outsiders.

Having no light within the lodge, the acts and utterances of the medicine man or conjurer are regarded as mysterious, and credulously received by the wondering crowd surrounding the tent.

He first prepares himself in his family wigwam by stripping off all his clothing, when he emerges singing, and the Indians outside join him in the song with their drums, and accompany him to the lodge, which he enters alone. Upon entering, the lodge commences shaking violently, which is supposed by the Indians outside to be caused by the spirits. The shaking of the lodge produces a great noise by the rattling of bells and deer's hoofs fastened to the poles of the lodge at the top, and at the same time three voices are distinctly heard intermingled with this noise. One is a very heavy hoarse voice, which the Indians are made to believe is that of the Great Spirit; another is a very fine voice, represented to be that of a Small Spirit, while the third is that of the medicine man himself . . . The ceremony lasts about three hours, when he comes out in a high state of perspiration, supposed by the superstitious Indians to be produced by mental excitement.

Looking through Mr. Calkins's nineteenth-century account of what he clearly thought was so much pagan mumbo-jumbo, we can see shadows and flashes of the same rites the Greeks beheld at Eleusis, or in the Dionysian rites, thousands of years before.

The problem the Christian missionaries faced was that Nanabozho had taught the Real People a perfectly workable idea of how things were and worked and how we could enter into harmony with that celestial operation. He gave them the sacred drum and rattle, for restoring the rhythm that had been lost or moved out of phase with the greater harmonics of the cosmos. He gave them tobacco, a beautiful plant which, when burned, carried prayers upward like incense. And the last gift was the dog, companion and food. Two of these gifts, the drum and the rattle, were tools of heaven; the tobacco and the dog came from the earth.

And one other thing Nanabozho gave humankind: the ability to laugh at ourselves and our pretensions. He sometimes came to us as creator, but often as clown; and that is why the legends of Big-Time Rabbit are also part of his story among the Real People.

There has never been much agreement about what happened to Nanabozho in the end. But his burial place is believed to be east of Thunder Bay, along the north shore of Lake Superior, or perhaps on Michipicoten Island.

Then there are people who claim he's alive—that the sounds of nature, the spring and winter and the wonderful events of nature are all signs of his life. There are even some people who think he lives alone on a great ice floe in the far north, wishing not to be disturbed by anyone.

In any case, he doesn't work in Ontario any more. The fact that people make tools, speak, make music, seek the divine are simply facts of life. The problem, of course, is that only recently has anybody considered these things anything other than remarkable gifts, continually flowing from the largesse at the centre of reality.

All that remains of him are his gifts of language and music, toolmaking and the rites of seeking the divine. And we know Nanabozho in the beauty of song, where he dwells forever.

4
FLINT'S WORK

THE TERRIBLE TROUBLES OF THE OLD NATIONS of Ontario had not begun along with the beginning of everything else, but came later, and along with the most unlikely thing: the beautiful spring bloom, the summer green, the cob of maize.

The greatest gift of Good Mind to the people began as a tall wild grass growing in wind-riffled, isolated patches in the Sierra Madre of Mexico. The Mexicans gave the grass the fragrant name of *teosinte* and, as the peoples of the western Mediterranean had done with wheat centuries before, small bands of wandering hunters began to experiment with this grass, and turned it into corn perhaps four thousand years ago.

In only a few centuries, the wonder had reached both Mexican coasts, prompting storytellers to invent stories about its irrepressible glory. It could not be held by any group of people as private property. According to one of the oldest tales told among the Mexicans, Fox followed Ant into a large mountain and discovered there a stash of maize. He ate it, and very much liked his dinner. He liked it so much, in fact, that he decided to keep the whole thing a secret—until a big, loud fart betrayed his fantastic discovery.

"What's that noise?" everybody said. "Where's it coming from?" Whereupon the people found the maize Fox wanted to keep for himself. In a more august myth told among the imperious Maya, the most important constellation in the night sky is the shining knop of the maize pod, and the stalk is the axis of the cosmos itself—the column up and down which the spirits of humanity, and the immense cosmic powers running between the gods and the earth ascend and descend.

It took a long time for this marvel to reach Ontario and, for thousands of years before it did, the various peoples who passed through the forests or settled along the shorelines of the lakes hunted the wild things. But settlement in Mexico, and in every place, brought concentrations of power and wealth, and the knowledge of lands beyond, and trade. And so the knowledge of corn began to spread northward from Mexico along the ever-lengthening trade routes that soon extended beyond the edges of dry mountains into the vast forest that covered most of the continent. As far as anyone can tell, it was about 1,500 winters ago—at a time in European history when hordes advancing from the East were destroying the last laws and settled village ways of old Rome throughout the Western Empire, and a fabled figure remembered as Arthur was battling to save old Celtic Christendom from pagan Saxons sweeping westward through the province of Britannia—that the scattered hunting bands around Lake Ontario received the gift of maize by trade from far away.

The women of the travelling bands, left at home in the summer camps while the men were off hunting in the forests for the ever-scarcer game animals, recognized the value of what they had received, and grasped the process by which useless teosinte had become this marvellous food. They patiently experimented with other weeds, and eventually invented beans, sunflowers, squash and tobacco. It was fire that changed everything. For countless millennia, the fire had driven back the fearful night and the wild animals, creating a circle of light. The same light could transform raw, inedible flesh to edible meat. And now, with the winters about as short and severe as they are today, and with long seasons of warmth in which the transfigured weeds could grow, the mental fire, the light of stars, that Nanabozho had given to the people of Ontario ended the need to travel with the herds, and made the women the powerful anchors of the people. The women, like the fire, were about to change history.

Reading the traces they left on the ground—the burnt spot where they built fire, and the scars of long-abandoned fields, and postholes of their dwelling places—we learn that the men continued to hunt and fish along the large lakes and in the forests for a long time after farming began. Men, it seems, wanted to ramble and hunt even after hunting had become no longer really necessary, and the animals were far away. Perhaps men are like that, and will always be that way—never really as comfortable as women with the routines of settled life that come with the maize and beans and other fruits of the cultivated earth. Perhaps wandering stays in men longer, is a thing more dear, and women are more ready to give it up. Wherever the truth lies in such matters, the corn fields gathered the people around them in new ways, enabling them to stay in their camps year-round, then build sturdy houses instead of temporary shelters, and finally towns that grew from year to year.

But as everywhere else in the world where agriculture emerged and settlement emerged, there arose a notion of property, mine and yours, ours and theirs. Ours had to be co-ordinated; growing corn or any crop involves organization and discipline, hence headfolk and underlings. And *ours* had to be protected from the depredations of *them,* whomever *they* might be—other towns with exhausted or more barren fields, or folk who could no longer sustain themselves on hunted food, but had not yet got the knack of cultivating, or perhaps simply had no inclination to settle down. And so it was, for the first time in the immensely long journey of the human family, that the wonderful tools that had extended our power by allowing mastery of the wild beasts were now turned against other people.

By about a thousand years ago, the nations around Lake Ontario were fortifying their villages with stockades and ditches. The postholes in the ground are traces of that fear of attack and need for protection from human enemies. Around the same time, as the towns grew, they began to recognize themselves as distinct nations, separated from each other by language or need and quarantined by uninhabited forests or stockades. The time of great hostilities had begun in Ontario, and also the time in which strange new states of mind emerged that nobody had ever known before the corn came—minds fixed on tyranny and conquest, discontented until their power extended over the lives and powers of others. Politics was born at the same time as settled food production, storage and surplus. When the famine times came, the stored surplus had to be defended, and there had to be men to defend it; hence the rising of a warrior class. But the warrior class had to take orders from someone, and thus arose an élite of enforcers, without the kindness and co-operative spirit of the old times.

To the ancient peoples of Ontario, such states of mind were strange, and they would never become accustomed to them. The greatest cycle of stories of the Long House People was all to do with this problem, how it cursed the people in former times, and how a near-miraculous cure was brought to all the eastern forests of the continent through the genius of one man, born on the beautiful near-island in Lake Ontario called Prince Edward County. His name was Dekanawida. In company with a princely headman called Hiawatha, the madness of the time, incarnate in a monstrous tyrant called Entangled—because his hair was a hideous tangle of snakes—was overcome.

Like the falling of the woman from heaven, the marvellous event now to be described happened a long time ago, but certainly not as far back as the Old Time. There are many ways of telling this story, but the one here was told by Chief Ska-na-wa'-ti and fire-keeper John Buck, of the Six Nations Reserve in Ontario, to J. N. B. Hewitt. It goes like this.

The Great Tree of Peace, in whose shadow the peoples found harmony after wars that went on and on, was rooted in the sorrows of Hiawatha, a man much admired among the Onondaga. These were a people who would later become founders of the Long House People and first beneficiaries of the Great Peace.

Along with all the People who lived in villages around Lake Ontario, Hiawatha's life had always been made miserable by the appalling wizard named Entangled. This wretch had a disposition very much like Flint's. He ruined everything beautiful and good for no apparent reason, and frustrated the ambitions of anyone who wished to make peace among the quarrelling peoples. Everybody wanted to be rid of him, but nothing they thought or did passed unnoticed by his countless murderous spies.

If important leaders of the People picked a remote place by the water to unbank the council fires and talk over what to do about the malignant magician, they would arrive to find Entangled already there, muttering spells to raise a storm. Suddenly, the winds would rush out of nowhere, tipping the canoes on the lake, drowning everyone. This sort of depressing thing happened so often that the People had a saying, when anything went wrong: "Entangled has again ruined our plans."

Then came a day when a large number of the People tried to meet, once again, to design a way to oust the wizard and free themselves from his tyranny. As usual, Entangled had found out about the council, and so pitched up in the middle of it. "Look up!" shouted the sorcerer. "Something alive is falling. What can it be?"

Even though they should have known better than to listen to this deceiver, the headfolk of the peoples looked up and saw a beautiful, birdlike item plunging through the air toward the treetops. And bewitchment fell upon them all.

As Entangled knew, but the People did not, the beautiful thing was falling right toward the place where Hiawatha's pregnant daughter was gathering wood for the council fire. The girl suddenly saw a horde of people running toward her, their faces turned skyward. It was the last thing the unfortunate young woman would ever see. For as the sorcerer knew, the People would converge at the spot the beautiful thing was falling toward, heedless of whatever was on the ground. And so it happened that Hiawatha's daughter was trampled to death.

Hiawatha had lost all his other children to Entangled's malice. Now the last of his offspring had perished at Entangled's hands, plunging the noble Onondaga into deepest despair. "Entangled has again ruined our plans!" he cried—then left that place, dazed and maddened by the tragedies that had befallen him.

Hiawatha wandered through deserted forests and fields of growing corn. Occasionally he would sit down and sing. At other times, he would find someone to tell his story to.

"Entangled is insane, angry and raging," he would tell anyone who would listen. "My three children are dead, destroyed by him. That's why I came away from that place, and that is the reason I wander."

But why did the coming of so lovely a gift as corn bring about the terrors that Hiawatha and his people faced?

Long before Hiawatha set out on his wandering way, the striving nations that eventually joined to create the League of the Long House had been living around Lake Ontario. But they did not come from there.

According to the most solemn traditions, all the people who spoke the Long House language had once lived to the northeast, in the St. Lawrence Valley, where they were brutally dominated by Algonkian-speaking neighbours. But if they were cruel rulers, they also gave to the future Long House People the gift that would enable them to flourish: the art of planting the precious corn.

To escape the dominion of the Algonkian, the Long House People embarked on a great migration. Some went along the northern shore of Lake Ontario, and became the Wendat. Another group founded the large nation known to us only as the "Neutral," because they chose neutrality in the incessant wars that later arose between the Long House People and the Wendat. Others travelled southward, along the lower edge of Lake Ontario, and even farther abroad, to the wide valleys of the southern Atlantic seaboard. Thereafter—at some time in history unknown—they settled into the regions they would later dominate and divided into warring villages. Thus began the great sorrows of the People.

Of the Long House People, the Onondaga seem to have been the first created by a merger of warring villages, joining as an alternative to fighting, as the two founding tribes of Rome did. But the alliance that gave rise to the Onondaga only incited the still-fragmented peoples around Lake Ontario to greater hostilities, and more exhausting and destructive warfare. Tyrants like Entangled flourished.

Complete destruction was at hand. And all the lands around Lake Ontario might have become a wasteland, devoid of human population and thought, had not it been for Hiawatha's madness and the wanderings that led him to Dekanawida.

IN THE MISERY OF HIS EXILE, Hiawatha crossed the barren land to the nation of the Canienga. There, in the early dawn, he sat down on a fallen tree trunk, in a fearful state. A woman found him when she came down to the spring to draw water, but she was terrified by his dishevelled appearance. Remarkably, he had around his neck a string of white shell beads. When she reported this strange apparition to the chief of the Canienga, he welcomed the madman into his cabin. He had heard of the greatness of Hiawatha, as well as the depth of the despair and madness wrought in Hiawatha by the machinations of the wizard Entangled. But he listened carefully to everything the sad man had to say.

After he had heard Hiawatha's tragic story, the man said, "Where does this Entangled live?"

"At the foot of a fume of smoke that rises until it touches the sky, so I understand," Hiawatha replied.

"I will tell the headmen about this. Perhaps they will have something to say about it."

The man who spoke, named Dekanawida, was able to convene a council so cleverly that even Entangled's sneakiest scout did not learn of it. At the end of this meeting of the headmen, they were of one opinion. "It's time to get down to work," they said. "We must go to the place Entangled dwells. Then we must straighten out his wild mind, and rebuild it, so that he will once again possess the mind of a normal man."

But before setting out upon this potentially lethal journey, Dekanawida decreed that everyone should give thanks, offering up Six Songs that the People of the Long House have sung ever since, when they gather to remember the wonderful gift of Dekanawida and the triumph of Hiawatha.

Again Dekanawida gave orders; and two spies departed in the direction of Entangled's dwelling place. Sometimes skulking quietly through the woodlands, at other times taking the form of crows and skipping through the branches—always querying the people they met along the way about Entangled's exact whereabouts—the spies eventually spotted what they were looking for. The astonishing column of smoke that ascended from the opening in Entangled's longhouse billowed upward until it touched the sky.

Once within the house, the two spies asked if they'd come to the right place, only to be shushed into silence by the terrified slaves of the magician. The servants then whispered they knew something, and nodded in the direction of the sorcerer, until the spies beheld him and were paralyzed by the sight.

In the shadows of his longhouse sat this creature of immense evil—his hair so many twisting, hissing snakes; his hands, a turtle's rough talons; his huge feet, bear-clawed and twisted. He was clothed only in

his own wrinkled fore-
skin, stretched and
folded around his
horrible body.

Once over the
initial shock of seeing
the sorcerer as he
had become through
cruelty—inhuman,
horrifying—the spies
quickly became crows again
and sped back to the council fire,
where they reported everything to
Dekanawida. Everyone agreed that
the time had come to travel together
to the place where Entangled dwelt
and change his mind back into
something human, rebuilding it
sensibly. So Hiawatha and the other
leaders of the People set out with Dekanawida in the direction of the
longhouse from which the terrible column of smoke arose forever
and ever.

As planned, they stopped at the edge of cleared fields near the
Sorcerer's longhouse and kindled a little fire. To get Entangled's
attention, they sang the Six Songs. It worked. At soon as he heard the
beautiful music, the dreadful magician's demeanour began to gladden
and brighten.

Then the headmen entered the longhouse and, like the spies, were
shushed by the frightened slaves. They, too, were horrified by the sight
of what Entangled's vicious disposition had turned him into. But
encouraged by Dekanawida, they sang the Six Songs of thanksgiving in
the presence of Entangled, who was pleased and moved by what he
heard, and perhaps made a little more sane—but nothing changed his
appearance. So the visitors continued to sing the songs of beauty, while

Dekanawida passed his hands over every misshapen and perverse part of the sorcerer's body. As Dekanawida worked, Entangled's bear-clawed paws became a man's feet, the twisting snakes became ordinary hair, his hideous hands were restored.

"One thing remains to be fixed," said Dekanawida, looking at Entangled's enormously long penis. Whereupon he tried chopping the penis of Entangled back to normal size, but nothing he did would work. So the visitors said, "Though it won't submit, it will no longer have the power to kill anybody. So leave it be."

And this is what happened when Dekanawida and his allies turned Entangled back into a Real Person (as the People of the Long House called human beings), by first pleasing him with songs, then gently taming the wildness in his mind and rebuilding it.

With the restoration of Entangled to his right mind, the long night of affliction he had visited upon the People of the Long House came to an end. But as Dekanawida quickly realized, the magician had been as much symptom as cause of the troubles riddling the various communities of the Real People. In his malicious madness, he had prevented the building of the council fires. But even had they been free to meet and talk, the headmen of the people would almost immediately have set about plotting how to inflict themselves on some weaker neighbour. Fear of Entangled had merely superseded greed, not eliminated it. And now that the terror of Entangled was eliminated, greed for land and corn again threatened to overwhelm the People, depriving them of their right minds.

Still, most of the headmen thought that, with the killing of the sorcerer, the world had been restored to balance. "We have restored Entangled!" they cried in triumph. "Everything will now prosper naturally, peacefully."

FOR DEKANAWIDA, the wisest man among them, the restoration of order in the world was one thing, maintaining it was quite another. So as Dekanawida expected, things turned out more or less unchanged, and the People went back to fighting among themselves, even without the excuse of the terrible wizard. So he decided it was high time to do something about that, and what he did was one of the most remarkable things that happened in Ontario during the reign of the Long House People.

5
THE GREAT PEACE

ONE NIGHT YEARS BEFORE, a woman living near the Bay of Quinte, a beautiful, deep inlet on the northern shoreline of Lake Ontario, had been visited in a dream by a divine messenger. This messenger told her that her daughter, still so small that she lived at home, would soon give birth to a son, whom she was to call Dekanawida. When he had become a grown man, he would bring to all people the words of peace, and power from the ones who dwell among the stars.

As the messenger predicted, the girl had been delivered of a son, and she named him Dekanawida, which means "Two River Currents Flowing Together." That's because he was predestined to join the various streams of the Long House People into one mighty river.

Once the boy had grown up, he had told his mother and grandmother, "It's time for me to do my duty in the world. That's why I'm now going to build my canoe."

When his canoe of white stone was finished, Dekanawida and his mother and grandmother dragged it to the water's edge, whereupon the young man climbed in, waved goodbye to his beloved ones and paddled away swiftly in an easterly direction.

Before long, he spotted a band of Seneca hunters across the water, on the far shore, and quickly paddled over to them. Stepping on the sandy shore, Dekanawida asked them what they were doing. The first Seneca said they were hunting, which is what men did for a living in those days. But the second Seneca who spoke told Dekanawida about the terrible strife dividing their home village.

"When you get back home," Dekanawida told the hunters, "you will find all is at peace, because the Great Law of Peace and Power will have come to those people. The strife will be ended. Tell your headman that Dekanawida has brought the good news. But now it's time for me to continue on eastward."

The Seneca hunters were amazed at the white stone canoe, but they returned to their town and duly reported to their headman all that Dekanawida had said. Peace prevailed.

Meanwhile, Dekanawida had dragged his marvellous canoe up on to the eastern shore of Lake Ontario and left it there, walking overland until he came to a town and called on the headman.

"Have you heard that Peace and Power have come to earth?" he asked.

"That's certainly the rumour," answered the headman. "I have been thinking about it so much that I can't sleep."

Then Dekanawida explained, "The thing that has kept you awake is now standing before you. From this day forward, you will be known as Hiawatha. [Which means "The Man Who Has Misplaced Something, But Knows Where to Find It." Or it may mean "River-Maker."] You will help me bring peace to all the nations, and thus staunch the bloodshed that afflicts them."

So Dekanawida and Hiawatha brought together the various nations of the Long House and spoke to them in words that would be recalled and retold forever after. With this speech, the great confederacy of the Long House People was founded.

The basic message of Dekanawida, the Great Binding Law, was that the People were to join together and stop killing each other, thus ending the terror that had afflicted the People for as long as anybody could remember. Though speaking roughly the same language, the

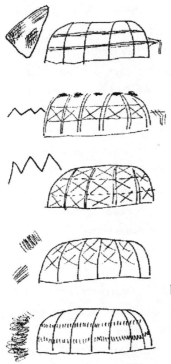

people fighting each other were the Mohawk (Possessors of the Flint), Onondaga (People on the Hills), Seneca (Great Hill People), Oneida (Granite People) and Cayuga (People at the Mucky Land). The Tuscarora, or Shirt-Wearing People, became the sixth nation of the Confederacy many years later. The original five were the ones who accepted the law, but, as Dekanawida always insisted, the great law was for all humankind.

Once Entangled's mind had been rebuilt and these people had been persuaded that it was better to establish rules among themselves than slaughter each other into nothingness, the five first members came together in council to receive the Great Binding Law. What they heard began like this:

We rejoice in what we have accomplished. Now we declare the common good and the laws to be our next great objectives . . . This is something that should be set right, so the nations can live in peace and tranquility, without fear of bloodshed.

The headmen, especially, must be patient, uncomplaining and courageous in upholding right and equity. Everything must be done for the sole object of peace and quietness. We are to carry this Great Law with us everywhere, showing it to the nations.

All of them, without exception, hate the People of the Long House, for—we may as well face the fact—wars are going on everywhere among us and we are slaughtering each other.

So we have uprooted a tall pine tree, at the roots of which runs a swift river; and into that river we have cast down the causes of wars and tumults. Our descendants will see them no more, for we have set back the great pine tree where it stood.

And we have set ourselves in the beautiful shade of an immense Tree with long leaves, one that we ourselves have erected upon the earth. We will rest there. And all the nations will look upon the Tree and desire to put their minds in its shade, dwelling there in peace and tranquility. We have put our minds into this one place.

On top of the Tree of the Law of nations will sit Eagle, who can see forever. He will keep a sharp lookout in every direction and will warn us if death or destruction is coming our way. Sometimes we may be in wretched shape. Eagle's gift of far sight will have power to help us. And a council-fire in honour of this Law will be kindled everywhere, even for the Cherokee and the Wendat, and for the Seven Nations living toward the sunrise, so they can work on behalf of this law—then, in turn, light the fires among nations living even farther east.

By the time of the american revolution, when the wars among themselves and between themselves and the Europeans and other ancient peoples, had brought them to the brink of perishing altogether, a great many Long House People had even forgotten how to speak the language the old stories were told in. While not an especially happy thought, this is the normal way of things. And ordinarily, it just happens without much fuss and languages simply disappear, with few traces or none. But in the middle years of the nineteenth century, the leaders of the Long House League, or what was left of it, fell to worrying that their ancient literatures and histories were in danger of being lost forever. The worrying prompted them to compare the versions of the old narratives kept by various tellers and to devise a conclusive text that could be kept on file, if, as indeed seemed possible, everybody forgot everything.

Highest among everything the League leaders wished to conserve and protect was the body of narratives, songs, prayers and rites that had to do with the foundation of the League itself. To that end, a traditional record-keeper from each of the five founding nations of the Long House People—Mohawk, Oneida, Cayuga, Seneca and Onondaga—and someone from the sixth partner, the Tuscarora, who were provisionally annexed in 1722, were asked to dictate to scribes what they had received from their ancestors about this all-important topic. There were, of course, several versions of the tales of Entangled and Hiawatha and Dekanawida, and what Dekanawida accomplished, but everything was written down. An authoritative rendition was solemnly approved by the highest Council of the League on July 3, 1900.

The important thing they wished to preserve was what Dekanawida saw and sought to remedy. The problem was really not whether or not Entangled, or any other leader, went berserk, became a tyrant or whatever. People do that kind of thing from time to time. But there was nothing in place, no system of restraints, to prevent such a man from emerging and making life miserable for his own and other people. That was the challenge to which Dekanawida turned his formidable mind, after Entangled had been set right. (In commemoration of this critical moment in the formation of the League, and by way of thanksgiving, the speaker of the Long House councils was always called "Entangled.")

Dekanawida persuaded the various nations to gather themselves and he delivered to them, first, an acknowledgement of blood-guilt and general exhortation to embrace the Great Binding Law, a long and elaborate constitution given to provide practical instructions for the maintenance of the Great Peace. The address began this way.

I am Dekanawida and with the Five Nations' Confederate Leaders I plant the Tree of Great Peace . . .

The Smoke of the Confederate Council Fire shall ever ascend and pierce the sky so that other nations who may be allies may see the Council Fire of the Great Peace.

Whenever the Confederate Leaders shall assemble for the purpose of holding a council, the Onondaga Leaders shall open it by expressing their gratitude to their cousin Leaders and greeting them, and they shall make an address and offer thanks to the earth where men dwell, to the streams of water, the pools, the springs and the lakes, to the maize and the fruits, to the medicinal herbs and trees, to the forest trees for their usefulness, to the animals that serve as food and give their pelts for clothing, to the great winds and the lesser winds, to the Thunderers, to the Sun, the mighty warrior, to the Moon, to the messengers of the Creator who reveal his wishes and to the Great Creator who dwells in the heavens above, who gives all the things useful to men and who is the source and the ruler of health and life.

Next, Dekanawida delivered a carefully detailed set of rules to govern every aspect of the League's political culture, from the process by which leaders would be elected (by the female elders of the nations) to the most minute questions of procedure and precedence. Here are only a few clauses of the long and supremely important document, as preserved at last in 1900. In them it is possible to witness the care of Dekanawida. It is also possible to see the flaws that were to afflict the League and, as we shall see in later chapters, undermine its immense nobility.

But of all that, more later. We return to Dekanawida's decrees on the procedures of the high council of the League, imagining ourselves standing in the shadows at the back of the longhouse in which the leaders of the people have gathered.

The Leaders of the Confederacy of the Five Nations shall be mentors of the people for all time. The thickness of their skin shall be seven spans—which is to say that they shall be proof against anger, offensive actions and criticism. Their hearts shall be full of peace and good will and their minds filled with a yearning for the welfare of the people of the Confederacy. With endless patience they shall carry out their duty and their firmness shall be tempered with a tenderness for their people. Neither anger nor fury shall find lodgment in their minds and all their words and actions shall be marked by calm deliberation. . . .

Look and listen for the welfare of the whole people and have always in view not only the present but also the coming generations, even those whose faces are yet beneath the surface of the ground—the unborn of the future Nation. . . .

The lineal descent of the people of the Five Nations shall run in the female line. Women shall be considered the progenitors of the Nation. They shall own the land and the soil.

When peace shall have been established by the termination of the war against a foreign nation, then the War Chief shall cause all the weapons of war to be taken from the nation. Then shall the Great Peace be established and that nation shall observe all the rules of the Great Peace for all time to come.

Whenever a foreign nation is conquered or has by their own will accepted the Great Peace their own system of internal government may continue, but they must cease all warfare against other nations.

Whenever a war against a foreign nation is pushed until that nation is almost exterminated because of its refusal to accept the Great Peace and if that nation shall by its obstinacy become exterminated, all their rights, property and territory shall become the property of the Five Nations . . .

I, Dekanawida, and the Union Leaders, now uproot the tallest pine tree and into the cavity thereby made we cast all weapons of war. Into the depths of the earth, down into the deep under-earth currents of water flowing to unknown regions we cast all the weapons of strife. We bury them from sight and we plant again the tree. Thus shall the Great Peace be established and hostilities shall no longer be known between the Five Nations but peace to the United People.

THERE IS NO DOUBT TODAY that Dekanawida and Hiawatha existed, and that Dekanawida delivered the Binding Law as it was remembered and transcribed in 1900. But apart from a shared certainty that the crisis and proclamation of the League happened before the Europeans arrived, there has never been much agreement about the date these things took place.

The League was old by the time the Europeans came. Other smaller confederacies around Lake Ontario—the Neutral, for example, and Wendat—had been created in imitation of the great one. The Great Peace had not extended as far as the ends of the earth, as Dekanawida had hoped. Nor was it working perfectly even among those who had come under the Tree and ratified the Binding Law. But the background is true. The small, beleaguered groups of similar speech that came together in the Long House League had lived farther northeast a thousand years ago, harassed and brutalized by their Algonkian neighbours. They had left that country to find peace, only to fall into the wars, feuds, revenges and terrorist campaigns among themselves that, Dekanawida frankly admits in his exhortation, had given them a terrible reputation among all other nations. Then came the creation of the League, which changed everything.

Several dates for this event have been suggested by scholars who have studied the problem closely. One conjecture would place the League's foundation at eight hundred years ago, with good reason. A more popular date is 1451, in the Christian way of figuring dates. It has been fixed by correlating references to a solar eclipse mentioned in the tradition with known dates when the narrow black blot could have passed over the League's territory. From the old stories, and the

number of names on the traditional roster of "Entangleds" (or speakers of council), 1451 is probably the best date for the *ending* of the process by which the Binding Law was adopted.

But it hardly makes any difference. The League constitution is old and magnificent, noble and deeply flawed. No more so than the American Constitution, perhaps, but with a similar looseness that led with apparent inevitability to terrible consequences: in the United States, a devastating civil war that could have extinguished the American republic; in the League, to instability that plunged it often into disarray, and a military policy that could only weaken Dekanawida's dream of extending the Great Peace to all humankind.

But the dream remains embedded in the addresses passed down from the genesis of the League. And the greatness of Dekanawida is no more diminished by his flaws than Thomas Jefferson's greatness by his errors of judgement as revolutionary, president, statesman. Dekanawida and Jefferson share many things, but most poignantly of all a hope for peace to be insured by a document understandable by everyone, and a lofty, wrong-headed optimism about the capacity and willingness of human beings to behave themselves. And if what has come down to us about these men is true, they also shared a keen awareness of their own importance in history, and a deep humility in the face of that fact.

According to the ancient oral traditions of the Long House, messengers were dispatched from the founding council of the League, to take the Great Peace to the world. As the Seneca told the tale,

wherever the council fire was lit, the Great Law of the League was received. After all this magnificent work was finished, Dekanawida declared that his name must never be included among those of the League's leaders.

"Nobody shall be appointed to succeed me," he continued. "Having founded this League of the Long House People— something no other man could have done—I now disappear from the sight of humankind."

Whereupon Dekanawida died, and was buried in a grave lined and covered with hemlock boughs.

6
SPEAKING A LITTLE DIFFERENTLY

LONG BEFORE THE FIRST EUROPEANS ARRIVED in southern Ontario, the Great Peace had been offered by the League to the Wendat, and declined.

Rather than risk the appalling consequences of refusal, as spelled out in Dekanawida's Binding Law, the Wendat and the League, which now controlled trade over a vast part of eastern North America, agreed to regard that part of Ontario lying south of Lake Simcoe as a kind of League protectorate. The Wendat idea, it appears, was to play at being compliant enough to avoid annihilation while keeping actual subservience to a minimum, and having whatever truck and trade they liked with Algonkian and other nations the League feared and hated.

As things turned out, the arrangement suited neither the leaders of the League nor the Wendat, which is the reason the first Europeans in the parts found the League and their northern neighbours locked in a conflict that had already become prolonged, deadly and costly. Because the French adventurers could not resist taking sides, or perhaps merely because they could not avoid doing so, the Wendat-League struggle was destined to become the decisive background for everything that was to happen here in Ontario, from that day until this. But the later parts of this story, which involve the French and English, are really best kept for later. This chapter is less about the grim wars of empire than the manner in which an old Ontario nation greeted the first newcomers from Europe—with delight.

Across the Niagara Peninsula, between the Falls—old Ontario's western frontier with lands under direct Long House domination—and Lake Simcoe, where the Wendat lived, there dwelt a political alliance of some forty farming villages that were neither League nor Wendat but shared a common culture and a language easily understandable by both adjoining powers. They were as warlike and touchy as their neighbours, but for their own reasons they wanted no part of the protracted, bloody trade squabbles between League and Wendat.

So instead of sending their warriors out to battle for one side or the other, they chose Switzerland's traditional position: aloof, above-the-fray neutrality in the midst of violent warfare all round. This stance struck the fancy of the French, who dubbed them the *"Nation du Neutre,"* and Neutral is the name by which they are known today. The Wendat called them "Attiwandaron," meaning "people who speak a little differently from the way we do," and the League's name for these people means more or less the same thing. Nobody knows what they called themselves, for the Neutral, and the slightly eccentric manner of speaking that impressed their neighbours, have vanished from the face of the earth.

The Neutral may well have discovered Europe in the person of a young rascal named Étienne Brûlé—we shall meet him again—who paddled along the north shore of Lake Ontario between Niagara-on-the-Lake and present-day Hamilton, sightseeing, in 1615. Whether the first European the Neutral ever saw or not, he brought back to the headquarters of New France in Montréal stories about some fascinating people he'd run into during his voyage along the northern shore of Lake Ontario. As everybody knew, Brûlé was inclined to say the wildest things. But he had learned the languages of the people he met—hence his frequent denomination as "the interpreter." And the tales he told intrigued the far more earnest young men, all consecrated devotees of the God of the French, who were even then about to begin a journey that would take them inland along the Ottawa River, then down into the League protectorate of southern Ontario. Their agenda: to tell all the people they met about their God and what he required of them, to get the hunters to settle down and become civilized, and buy French—roughly in that order. They were decent young men, these Franciscans; they were also men of their rather intense time, when being Christian and being civilized were virtually inseparable ideas. They can't be blamed for believing that.

In the summer of 1627, one of these men, Father Joseph de la Roche Dallion, wrote an excited letter to a friend in Paris, all to do with a remarkable event in his mission into the wilderness. This note contains virtually the only memories that remain of the people he visited. He begins:

> I received a letter from our reverend Father Joseph le Caron, by which he encouraged me to pass on to a nation we call Neutral, of which the interpreter told wonders. Encouraged, then, by so good a Father and the grand account given me of these people, I started out for their country, starting out from the Huron with this design October 18, 1626 . . .
>
> On the sixth day we arrived at the first village, where we were very well received, thanks to our Lord, and then at four other villages, which envied each other in bringing us food—some venison, others squashes, *neinthoaouy* [parched corn], and the best they had.
>
> All were astonished to see me dressed as I was, and to see that I desired nothing of theirs, except that I invited them (by signs) to lift their eyes to heaven, make the sign of the cross, and receive the Faith of Jesus Christ. What filled them with wonder was to see me retire at certain hours in the day to pray to God and attend to my spiritual affairs . . .

Roche Dallion was obviously a greenhorn when it came to encountering old Ontario's nations. Unless they arrived on the scene obviously in cahoots with some enemy nation, the first Europeans encountered by Ontario's older dwellers were always met with mixed fascination and awe. Through the grateful priest's recollection, we can catch a whisper of the thoughts going through the minds of his hosts.

What on earth do we have here! A man like us, more or less, except that he is shrouded chin to toe in dark-stained woven material—But why? And he is weaponless to boot! That must mean he is far too important a man to hunt for his food, so a feast is definitely in order. But while he seems happy enough with the meat and bread we serve up, he won't take the girl we offer him for the night. Nobody here ever heard of anything like that. But if he does go off into the forest, he does so alone, because (as he tells us) his gods are calling him. What kind of gods are these, who live in the forest? Important ones! Given the fact that everybody we've ever met looks and acts more or less like us, there's just no doubt about it: he's the most interesting thing we've ever seen.

Delighted by their interest in him, and their readiness to do all the things his god wanted them to, Roche Dallion asked everybody to come together in council, where, he reports to his Parisian friend, the Neutral sat "in profound (very strict) silence while the chief harangues." The headman of the village (who, as it happens, was also the highest official in the Neutral league) next invited the interesting newcomer to speak.

Then I told them, as well as I could, that I came on behalf of the French to contract alliance and friendship with them, and to invite them to come to trade. I also begged them to allow me to remain in their country to instruct them in the law of our God, which is the only means of going to Paradise. They accepted all my offers, and showed me that they were very agreeable.

Roche Dallion had heard the nations of the interior liked nice trinkets, and he had brought some along, which he now passed out to all those gathered in council.

> In return, they adopted me, as they say—that is to say, they declared me a citizen and child of the country, and gave me in trust—a mark of great affection—to Souharisson, who was my father and host; for according to [one's] age, they are accustomed to call us cousin, brother, son, uncle, or nephew.
>
> This man is the chief of the greatest credit and authority that has ever been in all these nations; for he is not only chief of his village, but of all those of his nation, composed of twenty-eight towns, cities and villages, made like those in Huron country, and also of several little hamlets of seven or eight cabins . . .
>
> It is unexampled in the other nations to have so absolute a chief. He acquired this honor and power by his courage, and by having been repeatedly at war with seventeen nations which are his enemies, and taken heads or brought in prisoners from them all . . .
>
> After this cordial welcome our Frenchmen returned, and I remained, the happiest man in the world, hoping to do something to advance God's glory. . . .
>
> I did my best to learn their manners and way of living. During my stay I visited them in their cabins to know and instruct them. I found them tractable enough, and I often made the little children, who are very bright, naked, and disheveled, make the sign of the holy cross. I remarked that in all this country I met no humpback, one-eyed or deformed persons.

Roche Dallion was not too young to remember the days when his beautiful land had been ripped apart by wars of religion, Catholic against Protestant, leaving France littered with the victims of famine and poverty and stalked by hollow-eyed men driven mad or grievously wounded by detonations in the name of God.

Still vivid in his mind on the day he set sail for New France, as well, was the surrender of France to the Protestant heretics by the Edict of Nantes, and the years of strife that marred the nation after the king who executed the Edict was murdered in 1610 by a Catholic fanatic. True, Protestantism was in retreat or its advance had come to a standstill throughout Europe. But France—or at least the only France this young priest had known—seemed ever to be teetering on the brink of yet another outbreak of unspeakable horror.

But now he had come to a place in which his gospel was the sole religion preached and heard, and in which peace prevailed, so that the hearing and teaching might go on.

> The country of the Neutral nation is incomparably larger, more beautiful, and better than any other of all these [other] countries. There is an incredible number of stags, great abundance of moose or elk, beaver, wild-cats, and black squirrels larger than the French; a great quantity of wild geese, turkeys, cranes and other animals, which are there all winter, which is not long and rigorous as in [Lower] Canada.

Now the adopted, honoured son of the magnificent Souharisson, with all the Neutral eager to hear the wonderful stories he brought from far away, living in a peaceable, abundant land, Roche Dallion should be forgiven for believing he had seen that persistent dream of medieval travellers come true and had walked into the outskirts of the Earthly Paradise.

For the Neutral, the visitor must have seemed more marvellous than even the young missionary himself imagined. A stranger usually meant trouble, but this one came without weapons. The usual message brought by a runner from another place was the coming of sudden death, war with either the League or the Wendat, or both, some new campaign of violence threatening yet again to engulf the Neutral. But this strangely clothed messenger brought fascinating stories and beautiful little things from farther away than any Neutral had ever travelled, or even heard of or imagined. The Neutral loved and cherished such objects, even as they cherished the small island of peace they had created in the great, never-ending storm of war.

But as it happened, greed, not war, destroyed the paradisiacal life of Father Roche Dallion.

In the first winter after his arrival among the Neutral, the Wendat began to suspect that the priest's venture might have the effect of strengthening diplomatic and trade links of all the other non-League nations on the north side of Lake Ontario. That, in turn, would effectively have cut the Wendat out of the business of fur brokering between the Neutral, in the Niagara Peninsula, and the Wendat settlements on the lower St. Lawrence. The Wendat knew the Neutral well, and knew their weakness for good tall tales. So they stealthily began to spread malicious rumours among the Neutral about their honoured adopted kinsman. They said he was a "great magician," as Roche Dallion tells his Parisian friend,

> that I had tainted the air of their country and poisoned many; that if they did not kill me soon I should set fire to their villages and kill all their children . . . I was, as they said, a great *Atatanite*— that is their word to mean "he who performs sacrileges," whom they hold in great horror. . . .

In fact, so the Wendat rumours went, the French as a whole were loathsome—an "unapproachable, rude, sad, melancholy people,"

> who live only on snakes and poison; that we eat thunder . . . that we all had a tail like animals; that the women have only one nipple in the centre of the

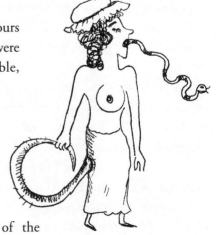

breast; that they bear five or six children at a time, adding a thousand other absurdities to make us hated by them and prevented their trading with us, that they might have the trade with these nations themselves exclusively, which is very profitable for them.

The Wendat campaign of lies succeeded. Father Roche Dallion sadly left his Neutral friends one wintry day in 1627 and made his way up to the mission headquarters at Ste-Marie-Among-the-Hurons, on the south end of Georgian Bay. In 1639, the Jesuit priests Jean de Brébeuf and Joseph Marie Chaumonot reached the land of the Neutral and found local opinion of the French unimproved. "They were convinced," wrote the missionaries, "that we were sorcerers, imposters come to take possession of their country, after having made them perish by our spells, which were shut up in our ink-stands, in our books, etc."

The Neutral's apprehension about the French neither hastened nor postponed the doom hurtling toward them, and that overwhelmed them some ten years after the disappointed Jesuits Brébeuf and Chaumonot left their territory in the Niagara Peninsula. In the 1640s conflict over control of the beaver trade, simmering between the League and its competitors from Niagara-on-the-Lake to Montréal for decades, flared up everywhere and intensely, closing what little gap that might have remained for neutrality in the war zone. Armed with guns bought from the Dutch in New York, the League swept into what is now southern Ontario and Michigan, and southwestern Québec, on a rampage of unbridled savagery. The nations they did not destroy utterly were absorbed according to the rules of the Binding Law and impressed into military service or scattered into the forests to find refuge with whomever would take them, or to die. The Neutral suffered every fate at the hands of the League—a few adopted, some dispersed, but most men, women and children ruthlessly annihilated according to the genocidal mandate installed in the otherwise exalted and noble Binding Law of Dekanawida.

By EVERY ACCOUNT, the Neutral were quite as ready to use violent aggression and sadistic tortures as their neighbours and their European contemporaries, when it suited their purposes. Their "neutrality" was a temporary diplomatic expedient, adhered to strictly so long as it maintained their sovereignty over the Niagara Peninsula and abandoned when the League threw itself against the Wendat.

Several years ago, a property owner in Grimsby, a small town between Hamilton and Niagara-on-the-Lake, not far back from the north shore of Lake Ontario, decided to erect an apartment building on his land. But before the bulldozers rumbled onto the site, he allowed a thorough scientific excavation of the place, which had long been known to local weekend souvenir pickers as a rich source of doodads, beads, bits of bone and other stuff. What the archaeologists discovered was the burial ground of a Neutral village, planted with the bodies of folk of every age, all from the 1640s. A Neutral settlement tended to last about a decade, before the land round about became exhausted and the citizens moved on. For these Neutral, however, the decade of their residence at Grimsby would be the last years of the very existence of their people.

Like mourners everywhere, from highest antiquity, the Neutral buried their dead with cherished and lovely things. Copper beads, trinkets of shell, little carvings—such things are found in great abundance among the bones of those laid with great care to final rest in Grimsby some 350 years ago. They tell us not only what the Neutral loved, but they whisper to us messages about the people who loved them. Many objects have their origin in places far away, beyond the direct knowledge of any Neutral, in that zone from which mysteries emerge, along with such strange creatures as Joseph de la Roche Dallion, who fascinated these people.

Found with an infant no more than two months old was a strand of tiny copper beads, crafted from metal mined and smelted in Minnesota and shipped over the water-roads that had served Ontario's people since the ice melted off the land. Also along the trade routes leading to southern Ontario came the beautiful chips of conch shell found at Grimsby, made from a marine snail found in the warmer, southerly waters of the Atlantic Ocean. There are beads of turquoise mined almost as far away as Mexico, and, perhaps most wonderful of all, a pipe carved from local Ontario clay in the shape of a parrot.

It's safe to say that no Neutral had ever seen a parrot. But at some time in the past, a parrot carving from the Gulf of Mexico must have made its way into the hands of a Neutral, who admired it and decided to copy it in local stone, simply because it was wonderful. And when time came for burying, the little copied parrot went into the grave. Whether the person buried was the carver, or simply someone who loved the carving, we cannot know. What we may be certain of is that someone living decided his or her dead should not be buried without this lovely thing from another world, an infinite distance away from Ontario. They were charmed by the things and people that came to them across that vast expanse of time and space.

Writing of this vanished nation, the nineteenth-century historian James H. Coyne recalls what's known about the Neutral, and what was said of them by such observers as the Jesuit Jérôme Lalement, who came after the Franciscan priest Roche Dallion.

The Neutrals were distinguished for the multitude and quality of their madmen, who were a privileged class. Hence it was common for bad Indians to assume the character of maniacs in order to perpetrate crimes without fear of punishment. The Jesuits suffered very much from their malice. Some old men told them that the Neutrals used to carry on war "towards" a certain western nation, who would seem to have lived on the Gulf of Mexico, where the "porcelain, which are the pearls of the country," was obtained from a kind of oysters [sic]. It is an undoubted fact that a traffic was carried on with tribes as far south as the Gulf of Mexico, from which shells used for wampum were obtained by successive interchanges of commodities with intervening tribes. They also had some vague notion of alligators, which are apparently referred to by the description "certain aquatic animals, large and swifter than elk," against which these same people had "a kind of war," the details of which are somewhat amusing, as given by Lalement.

II
STRIFE OF EMPIRES

7
ROADS TO CHINA

No MATTER WHERE ONTARIANS HAVE COME FROM during the last five hundred years—Europe or Asia or Africa or on any island or continent beyond the Americas—we arrived through gates thrown open by one visionary.

That astonishing man, Christopher Columbus, inhabits our imaginations oddly. Though his name is embedded in the names of nations and cities on two continents, he stands in deeper shadow than Alexander the Great, Augustus Caesar, even William Shakespeare. His name brings to mind the date 1492, and his famously mistaken idea that he had found an island in the Indian Ocean. These commonplaces hide Columbus, turning him into a man without relevance to the present—except as perpetrator of some vague, vast crime against America's aboriginal peoples. Yet few men in the history of the world have so radically changed the way humankind understands itself and its condition in the universe.

He stepped onto the stage of history at a moment of European amazement and confusion. The feudal world of medieval Europe was collapsing violently into so many pious crusades and trade wars and dynastic feuds. At the same time, the Renaissance of learning and art promised marvels of a different sort: a revived Roman architecture to symbolize the coming peace, prosperity and stability of mercantile society; a new realistic painting that recalled and exalted the beauty of ordinary humanity.

The most devastating revelation of the age—that our world revolves around the sun—still lay a generation later than the first Columbian expedition, and would shake European thought to its foundations only after 1543, with the publication of the Polish astronomer Nicolaus Copernicus's *De Revolutionibus Orbium Coelestium.* But in 1492, Leonardo da Vinci, a contemporary of Columbus, did the first drawings for a bicycle, thereby creating a machine as novel as anything the astronomers would discover in heaven. Columbus, at the same moment, was unintentionally inventing a new kind of human being. After 1492, any knowledgeable European would know that there were worlds unpredicted by Holy Scripture and unknown to the geographers of antiquity. Jacques Cartier, the first European to imagine the place now called Ontario, is unthinkable without Columbus. So is Samuel de Champlain, who was whisked by the dream of radical newness from monastic contemplation to the building of New France, innocent and fresh, free of the wars that had racked Old France. Étienne Brûlé, the lad who first paced off the extent and saw the beauty of Ontario, is among the new men of the new age: rootless, curious, secular, ready to cast off centuries-old traditions without a second thought, able to manoeuvre in a profane universe where the things that mattered were savvy, guile, charm, intelligence.

That Columbus was one of the most original and remarkable men of his own or any age dawned upon Europe with the publication of his announcement *Concerning the Islands Recently Discovered in the Indian Sea,* addressed by the author to "the magnificent lord Raphael Sanxis," treasurer to Ferdinand, King of Spain.

It was among the first instantly popular works to be printed with movable type, and perhaps the most influential non-religious tract of its time. Eleven editions appeared in 1493 across western Europe, in

Spain, Italy, France, Switzerland and the Netherlands. More followed in the years to come, as the stock was exhausted by eager readers. The words of Columbus excerpted here are better than any paraphrase, if what's wanted is a sense of what appeared to those who saw in it the first light of a new dawn.

"In thirty-three days," he begins,

I passed from the Canary Islands to the Indies, with the fleet which the most illustrious king and queen, our sovereigns, gave to me. There I found very many islands, filled with people innumerable, and of them all I have taken possession for their highnesses, by proclamation made and with the royal standard unfurled, and no opposition was offered to me . . .

When I came to Juana, I followed its coast to the westward, and I found it to be so extensive that I thought that it must be the mainland, the province of Cathay. And since there were neither towns nor villages on the seashore, but small hamlets only, with the people of which I could not have speech, because they all fled immediately, I went forward on the same course, thinking that I could not fail to find great cities and towns . . . I understood sufficiently from other Indians, whom I had already taken, that this land was nothing but an island . . . This island and all the others are very fertile to a limitless degree, and this island is extremely so. In it there are many harbours on the coast of the sea, beyond comparison with others that I know in Christendom, and many rivers, good and large, which is marvellous. Its lands are high; there are in it many sierras and very lofty mountains, beyond comparison with that of Teneriffe. All are most beautiful, of a thousand shapes; all are accessible and are filled with trees of a thousand kinds and tall, so that they seem to touch the sky. I am told they never lose their foliage, and this I can believe, for I saw them as green and lovely as they are in Spain in May, and some of them were flowering, some bearing fruit . . .

They do not hold any creed nor are they idolaters; only they all believe that power and good are in the heavens and are very firmly convinced that I, with these ships and men, came from the heavens, and in this belief they everywhere received me after they had mastered their fear. This belief was not the result of ignorance, for they are, on the contrary, of a very acute intelligence and they are men who navigate all those seas, so that it is amazing how good an account they give of everything. It is because they have never seen people clothed or ships of such a kind . . . They were the first to announce this wherever I went, and the others went running from house to house, and to the neighbouring towns, with loud cries of, "Come! Come! See the men from Heaven!" So all, men and women alike, when their minds are set at rest concerning us, came, not one, small or great, remaining behind, and they all brought something to eat and drink, which they gave with extraordinary affection.

Before Columbus set out to seek a route to China uncontrolled by the sultans and sheiks of the East, he navigated the Mediterranean, visited the coastlands of Africa and Ireland and learned to read the language of clouds and winds better than any man of his time. He then set himself up at the Spanish court, to lobby for his "enterprise of the Indies."

It seemed at first to be a doomed ambition. After years of lounging about, trying to catch the ear of this or that potentate, a committee of the Spanish Crown declared "that the claims and promises of Captain Colon are vain and worthy of rejection. . . . The Western Sea is infinite and unnavigable. The Antipodes are not livable, and his ideas are impracticable."

They were right, of course, as far as anyone knew, including Columbus. And they were backed by formidable authorities: the Bible, Aristotle, the greatest thinkers of the ancient and medieval periods. They had the relations of Marco Polo and other adventurers, who had seen the marvels and brought back credible accounts of what lay at the edges of the world, which grew more fabulous the farther away from Europe one went.

Meanwhile, in distant China—the goal of all this visionary thinking and economic dreaming—the Son of Heaven probably thought little about Europe. If he did, it was a sort of Wild West frontier at the edges of the world, peopled by filthy semi-barbarians who wanted nothing other than to buy things. The Arab merchants who came to the Chinese imperial court were men graced with admirable virtues: elegance of manner and expression, simplicity and rigour of learning, harsh justice and a serene, aristocratic theology. The proposals of Columbus involved a journey to the greatest empire on earth, rich, vast and peaceful, with treasuries of wisdom that beggared the imagination of poor, war-exhausted Europe.

The brilliant mind of Christopher Columbus and the drives at work in it are known to us only in flashes, and in deeds, and in the reflections of others. There is the conventional wisdom, conveniently summarized by author and critic Robert Hughes. "Sometime between 1478 and 1484, the full plan of self-aggrandizement and discovery took shape in his mind," Hughes wrote. "He would win glory, riches, and a title of nobility by opening a trade route to the untapped wealth of the Orient. No reward could be too great for the man who did that."

All this was certainly true. But to make it the whole story is to read back into the mind of Columbus the dominant motivations of our own day. Like the late medieval nations from which Columbus emerged, we, too, are driven by wealth, security, fame. But there was far more in it for Columbus. "With a hand that could be felt," Columbus wrote, "the Lord opened my mind to the fact that it would be possible . . . and he opened my will to desire to accomplish that project . . . The Lord purposed that there should be something miraculous in this matter of the voyage to the Indies." I see no reason to doubt that he believed every word of it.

Not only had God provided for the possibility of such a voyage, but He had also mandated it. "Who can doubt that this fire was not merely mine, but also the Holy Spirit who encouraged me with a radiance of marvelous illumination from his sacred Scriptures . . . urging me to press forward?"

Once he had arrived in the New World, he began to understand his mission in ways difficult to grasp today. It was for him a unified task—spreading the Christian gospel, winning an empire for a sovereign, as strategies of establishing a polity of justice and hope where there had been none. Unless one can imagine such a strategy to be utterly sincere, then the Europeans who first recognized and claimed Ontario for their sovereigns—Cartier and Champlain and the missionaries, especially—will remain forever incomprehensible.

Columbus also had a different way of reading books, hence of reading history and his times. His learning combined Scripture and the Christian teachers of antiquity with astronomy, geography and prophecy with his theology. His mental world was the distillation of what the German writer Alexander von Humboldt called "everything sublime and bizarre that the Middle Ages produced."

For him, the end of the warring and difficult old world and the beginning of a new age of grace and knowledge were at hand. As he wrote in 1500, "God made me the messenger of the new heaven and the new earth of which he spoke in the Apocalypse of St. John [Rev. 21:1] after having spoken of it through the mouth of Isaiah; and he showed me the spot where to find it."

> This is enough. And [praise to] the eternal God, Our Lord, Who gives to all those who walk in His way triumph over things which appear to be impossible, and this was notably one. For, although men have talked or have written of these lands, all was conjectural, without suggestion of ocular evidence, but amounted only to this, that those who heard for the most part listened and judged rather by hearsay than from even a small something tangible. So that, since Our Redeemer has given the victory to our most illustrious king and queen, and to their renowned kingdoms, in so great a matter, for this all Christendom ought to feel delight and make great feasts and

give solemn thanks to the Holy Trinity, with many solemn prayers for the great exaltation which they shall have in the turning of so many peoples to our holy faith, and afterwards for the temporal benefits, because not only Spain but all Christendom will have hence refreshment and gain.

Done in the caravel, off the Canary Islands, on the fifteenth of February, in the year one thousand four hundred and ninety-three.

At your orders.

THE ADMIRAL.

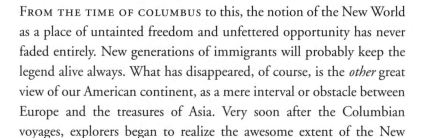

FROM THE TIME OF COLUMBUS to this, the notion of the New World as a place of untainted freedom and unfettered opportunity has never faded entirely. New generations of immigrants will probably keep the legend alive always. What has disappeared, of course, is the *other* great view of our American continent, as a mere interval or obstacle between Europe and the treasures of Asia. Very soon after the Columbian voyages, explorers began to realize the awesome extent of the New Land they had found. After his transoceanic trip of 1524, the Florentine explorer Giovanni da Verrazzano wrote:

> My intention on this voyage was to reach Cathay and the extreme eastern coast of Asia, but I did not expect to find such an obstacle of new land as I have found. The ancients believed that our Western Ocean was joined to the Eastern Ocean of India without any land between . . . Land has been found by modern man which was unknown to the ancients, another world with respect to the one they knew, which appears to be larger than our Europe, than Africa, and almost larger than Asia, if we estimate its size correctly. . . .

In 1520, Ferdinand Magellan had found a southern passage to the East, around the dangerous, storm-wracked tip of South America.

But this discovery effectively closed the southern Atlantic to everyone but Portugal, whose king would have sent armies against any nation that dared launch ships in that direction. So adventurers in other European nations began to imagine the most fantastic project of early modern times, and the one that led directly—one could even say remorselessly—to the search for Ontario: the discovery of an internal route from the Atlantic to the Pacific.

In 1497, the Venetian sailor John Cabot had been dispatched by King Henry VII of England to find this more direct route to the Spice Islands. He discovered Newfoundland instead. Then in 1508, John Cabot's son Sebastian followed the Atlantic coastline of the New Land from the Arctic Circle south, as far as Cape Hatteras, perhaps even Florida—searching for the mouth of the Northwest Passage (as this fabled waterway became known), without success.

The notion that the New Land might be marvellous in itself—and the even more bizarre idea that it might actually serve as a new dwelling place for the peoples of Europe—long remained unthinkable by European minds. Well into the seventeenth century, after Ontario had been discovered and explored by the Europeans, Samuel de Champlain, founder of La Nouvelle France, still did not realize where he was, and where he was not. In about 1620, Champlain heard from inland voyagers that some people living far up the Ottawa River knew all about China, because they lived near it. Champlain apparently dispatched Jean Nicollet, the French ambassador for the commercial interests in New France, to visit the Chinese and the Indian nation with which they did business.

Nicollet surely gave the matter careful thought. We can imagine him wondering, How should a person of his social stature best meet the Chinese? With what decorum, and what proof that he did, in fact, fully appreciate the greatness of Cathay? Nicollet seems to have hit upon an elaborate plan involving a dispatch back to France for the necessary supplies. I am sure he believed that, despite all the trouble involved in preparation, the plan would be a stunning success.

Fully prepared, Nicollet and his interpreters and guides then set off on the long canoe voyage up the Ottawa River, across the hard portages, up Lake Huron and into Lake Superior, and beyond, until they at last neared the village he'd been told was quite close to China. To these people, called Fox by the Europeans, Nicollet sent a Wendat member of the crew "to bear tidings of the peace, which word was especially well received when they heard that it was a European who carried the message."

At last they met, the first Fox and the Wonderful Man (as the Indians called Nicollet), within sight of the village. Once a suitable number of Fox had come out to see this marvel—they had never before encountered a European—Nicollet grasped two guns and flung off his cloak, revealing what he thought would most deeply impress them and instantly communicate what he wanted: a magnificent robe of China damask, strewn with flowers and birds of many colours. "No sooner did they perceive him," the narrative continues, "than the women and children fled, at the sight of a man who carried thunder in both hands,—for thus they called the two pistols that he held."

As so often happened when the Indians met Europeans for the first time, the initial shock gave way to fascination. What manner of man could this be, the Fox wondered, who would greet them in a gorgeous, shimmering gown decorated with birds and flowers? A very great one, without doubt. So they prepared a series of grand feasts for Nicollet, and "at one of these banquets they served at least sixscore Beavers."

At some point during these festivities, Nicollet got to the point. Of course, the Fox had no idea what this spectacularly attired Wonderful Man wanted or where the Chinese were. But being polite, they probably told him: Quite close. Just over there, a little farther west. You've come to the right place. But we unfortunately live just a bit too far east of China. Keep going, and you're bound to find it.

Disappointed, Nicollet returned to Montréal, without having made contact with the Chinese of western Ontario—but not without leaving us a very funny story of how driven these men were to do so, and how very close they thought they had come. Their belief that the St. Lawrence and the Ottawa Rivers might be the beginning of the inward passage to China led to the finding of Ontario. But it was never Ontario they sought. It was always the road to China.

8
FABULOUS SAGUENAY

Jacques cartier's journey toward Ontario began when he made landfall in Newfoundland in the late summer of 1534, after only twenty days at sea. He saw nothing that Europeans had not seen before. Fishermen from his native Brittany had been fishing for cod off the Newfoundland coast, as far south as Prince Edward Island, for years. Nor were the Indian nations that lived along the Atlantic coast strangers. They liked the French, and especially the doodads and fabrics that Frenchmen and others always hauled over the eastern ocean to barter away for food; and the French liked them.

When asked the way to China, Cartier's Indian hosts of course had no idea what he was talking about. But when queried about the source of the fresh water issuing from within the western wilderness, they knew the general direction to point him. Cartier took a cruise around the huge bay in search of the influx, but was chased into a tiny inlet by bad weather on August 10, 1534, the feast day of St. Lawrence, an early Christian martyr. Cartier named the tiny refuge after the saint. It was by one of those accidents in the history of exploration that the entire gulf, and the great river that fed it, eventually became known as the St. Lawrence.

Undaunted by the stormy weather on the Gulf of St. Lawrence, Cartier followed the fresh water inland and upstream on his second voyage, in 1535, between a broad wedge of shorelines ever narrowing as he travelled west. On this trip, he found a band of Wendat living on the site of present-day Québec, who insisted he go no further, and tried to scare him off with an elaborate show of three shamans dressed as demons. Cartier wintered over at Québec that year, and heard wonderful stories from his Wendat hosts. As for the Great River that Cartier sought, the Wendat really didn't know, but they told him that if he kept going *thataway*, more or less toward the sunset, he would come to a place with gold all over the ground, to be had for the price of a stoop.

So now Cartier had two reasons for making the inward voyage. One was to discover the Great River, if he were not already sailing inland upon its waters. The other was to discover the northern El Dorado of which the Wendat spoke. He got as far west as the large Indian town of Hochelaga, on the site of present-day Montréal. The history of the Europeans in Ontario begins the day Cartier was guided to the top of the extinct volcano the French would call Mount Royal by the citizens of Hochelaga.

> On reaching the summit we had a view of the land for more than thirty leagues round about. Towards the north there is a range of mountains, running east and west, and another range to the south.
>
> Between these ranges lies the finest land it is possible to see, being arable, level and flat. And in the midst of this flat region one saw the river extending beyond the spot where we had left our longboats. At this point there is the most violent rapid possible to see, which we were unable to pass. And as far as the eye can reach, one sees that river, large, wide and broad, which came from the south-west and flowed near three fine conical mountains, which we estimated to be some fifteen leagues away. And it was told us and made clear by signs by our three local Indian guides, that there were three more such rapids in

that river, like the one where lay our longboats; but through lack of an interpreter we could not make out what the distance was from one to the other. They then explained to us by signs that after passing these rapids, one could navigate along that river for more than three moons.

And they showed us furthermore that along the mountains to the north, there is a large river, which comes from the west like the said river. We thought this river must be the one that flows past the kingdom and province of the Saguenay; and without asking any questions or making any sign, they seized the . . . Captain's whistle, which was made of silver, and a dagger-handle of yellow copper-gilt like gold, that hung at the side of one of the sailors, and gave us to understand that these came from up that river [Ottawa], where lived *Agojuda,* which means bad people, who were armed to the teeth, showing us the style of their armour, which is made of cords and wood, laced and plaited together.

They also seemed to say that these *Agojuda* waged war continually, one tribe against the other, but though not understanding their language, we could not make out what the distance was to that country. . . .

On our return from Hochelaga [to Québec] with the bark and the longboats, we had intercourse and came and went among the tribes nearest to our ships in peace and friendship, except for a few quarrels now and then with some bad boys, at which the others were very angry and much annoyed.

And we learned from Chief Donnacona, from Taignoagny, Dom Agaya and the others that the above mentioned river, named "the river of the Saguenay," reaches to the kingdom of the Saguenay, which lies more than a moon's journey from its mouth, towards the west-north-west . . .

And they gave us to understand, that in that country, the natives go clothed and dressed in woolens like ourselves; that there are many towns and tribes composed of honest folk who possess great store of gold and copper. Furthermore they told us that the whole region from the first-mentioned river up as far as Hochelaga and the kingdom of the Saguenay is an island . . . [By following this river, one reaches] two or three large, very broad lakes until one reaches a fresh-water sea, of which there is no mention of anyone having seen the bounds, as the people of the kingdom of the Saguenay had informed them; for they themselves, they told us, had never been there. . . .

And moreover [Cartier] had quite made up his mind to take Chief Donnacona to France, that he might relate and tell to the king all he had seen in the west of the wonders of the world; for

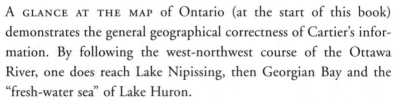

he assured us that he had been to the land of the Saguenay where there are immense quantities of gold, rubies and other rich things, and that the men there are white as in France and go clothed in woolens.

He told us also that he had visited another region where the people, possessing no anus, never eat nor digest, but simply make water through the penis.

A GLANCE AT THE MAP of Ontario (at the start of this book) demonstrates the general geographical correctness of Cartier's information. By following the west-northwest course of the Ottawa River, one does reach Lake Nipissing, then Georgian Bay and the "fresh-water sea" of Lake Huron.

To find Saguenay, however, requires some new imagining of the map. Nowadays, that name belongs to a minor river running from Lac St-Jean alongside the town of Chicoutimi, before debouching into the broadening St. Lawrence. The name is believed to derive from a word used by people the French called Montagnais: *saki-nip,* "water which issues forth."

But with a little work, we can say the word "Saguenay," and hear in it what Cartier heard: echoes of glory, promises of reward at home, and riches beyond measure, all lying just beyond his reach in the land we now call Ontario. Perhaps worried that the story wouldn't be believed by his near-bankrupt king, and knowing that, if he couldn't deliver China, he was still obliged to bring back *something,* Cartier did have his translators kidnapped and taken back to France in 1536.

King Francis I was impressed, and fell to wondering what everybody else wondered: whether Saguenay would turn out to be as glorious as what the Spanish had found farther south. The king pored over the records with a Portuguese pilot he'd taken on.

"On two charts belonging to the king, which are well-painted and illuminated but not very accurate," the Portuguese noted in his diary, "Francis I showed me a river in the land of Cod whither he has sent twice. On this matter he is very intent, and what he wishes to do would make men marvel. Jacques Cartier on his last voyage brought back three Indians, two of whom are dead, but the survivor is chief of three or four towns, according to the king of France; for all I write I heard from his own lips." He then adds that "beyond the falls"—meaning the Lachine Rapids, at Montréal—"the King of France says the Indian King told him there is a large city called Saguenay, where there are many mines of gold and silver in great abundance, and men who dress and wear shoes like we do; and that there is abundance of clove, nutmegs, and pepper."

Moreover, "the river contains an abundance of good fish, and at its mouth there are oranges and pomegranates. . . . Greatly praising the rich novelty of the land and telling these and other tales; and that there are men who fly, having wings on their arms like bats, although they fly but little, from the ground to a tree, and from tree to tree to the ground. And the said Jacques brought to the King a sample of gold, ten or twelve stones shaped like small goose quills, and says it is fine gold and comes from the said city of Saguenay."

In October, 1541, King Francis issued the formal commission to "our dear and well-beloved Jacques Cartier, who has discovered great tracts of the countries of Canada and Hochelaga which form the confines of Asia on the west, which countries he found productive of good commodities." It was an order to find the "land of Saguenay." Cartier was to do the actual exploration, while Francis I appointed Jean-François de la Rocque, Sieur de Roberval, official leader of the expedition of conquest in 1541.

Whereupon Cartier went back, with 6 ships, 120 sailors, 150 mechanics, among them 10 master masons, 2 goldsmiths "skilled in handling precious stones," 4 artillerymen, 6 priests, 3 barbers and 2 apothecaries, to claim the kingdom of spice and gold. While heading inland, Cartier pitched camp on the northern bank of the St. Lawrence and picked up some glittering crystals he took for diamonds and something that looked like gold.

Meanwhile the Wendat, who then lived along the river, had run out of patience with the French, their fantasies and foolishness about Saguenay. To make sure their guests got the message that they were no longer wanted, Wendat warriors hatcheted more than thirty Frenchmen to death in the winter of 1641. More died of scurvy. The expedition, begun with such promise, was collapsing.

Cartier returned to Newfoundland, where Roberval was stationed, in exactly what state of mind we shall never know. According to Newfoundland fishermen formally deposed in Spain in 1542, Cartier told Roberval that he had eleven barrels of gold ore and almost a bushel of precious stones, rubies and diamonds, seven casks of silver, and seven containers of "pearls and rubies." He almost certainly told Roberval nothing of the kind. In any case, Cartier stole back to Brittany and retired in obscurity on his estates at St-Malo, where he died in 1557.

We know nothing of Cartier during those years of retirement. But there is a hint of the frustrated dreams that may have preoccupied the old man in a letter by Jacques Noel, Cartier's grandnephew, who had a map that once belonged to his seagoing relation, with certain descriptions written on it. *"By the people of Canada and Hochelaga it was said, That here is the land of Saguenay, which is rich and wealthy in precious stones,"* quotes young Jacques. "And about an hundred leagues under the same I found written these two lines in the said Carde inclining toward the Southwest. *'Here in this Countrey are Cinamon and Cloves, which they call in their language Canodeta.'"*

Cartier belonged to the earliest wave of New World explorers, who were not yet free of the fantasy of finding China or finding gold, or finding both. But along with European explorers of his generation, he was finding that millennia of geographical lore to be a tissue of forgeries. Ancient wisdom about *terra incognita* had taught them to expect ferocious pygmies who did battle with storks, men with eight toes on each foot and dog-headed folk who snarled and barked all the time about nothing. There were supposed to be odd bodies in the tropical zones who survived the fiery sunshine by lying on their backs and using their single enormous foot as a parasol, and grotesque animals stitched together from scraps left over at the world's Creation—a scrawny haunch of this, a heavy wing of that, the lethal fangs of some other creature, the switching tail of yet another. But discovering that the New World's people were more or less like Europeans posed a problem. What if they were really human? At this distance, it is hard for us to grasp how radical the latter contention was—so radical, in fact, that the Catholic Church held a solemn theological conclave at Valladolid in 1550 to decide whether the talking, bipedal New World folk were human, hence capable of salvation and exempt from enslavement. The decision was a firm *yes*. Not only were the denizens of the New Land human but they had to be treated as human and could under no circumstances be enslaved. (The missionaries rejoiced, though the Spanish and Portuguese colonialists, like white Southern Americans later on, conveniently ignored the last bit.) This decree of the Church was more than a validation of Columbus's intuition about the people he had met. It was among the great recognitions in European history of the essential unity and equality of all humankind.

For the first generations of explorers, being men steeped in the beliefs of antiquity and Scripture, the absence of fabulous humanoids must have come as a disappointment, and perhaps (at least to the more thoughtful among them) an existential shock. They could have known nothing, of course, about the very astonishing creatures that had lived in Ontario in the past. Immense elephants, each weighing up to eight tonnes, had foraged for scraggly weeds and mosses on the cold rocky aprons of the receding glaciers. Sabre-toothed tigers, which weren't really tigers, but a kind of big, short-legged, very dangerous cat, had been ambushing unwary little animals in the wild terrain for a million years before joining the great elephants in oblivion.

And as the ice sheets withdrew ever farther north and the trees found a toehold in the turf of what is now Ontario, a race of monster rodents came lumbering back up north, following the treeline. These behemoths had been on our native ground eons earlier. With the return of warmth, they were coming home. Though not exactly like anything alive today, this rat was a sort of beaver, bigger than a bear and weighing half a tonne. A front tooth almost a foot long has been dug up in Ohio. She was either the ancestor of Canada's Official Mammal (also that of the American states of Oregon and New York) or a titanic relation that died out, leaving a hefty little cousin, whom scientists dubbed *Castor canadensis,* to take over the job of damming the streams and flooding the forests of the continent north of Mexico.

By the time Cartier arrived, the animals of Canada were more or less like ones he had known in Europe. The Canadian beavers would not have been exactly familiar, though they would hardly have struck Cartier as strange. The last of their European cousins were being wiped out by the time the first adventurers cruised by the cold, stony north-eastern edge of Canada and pitched camp. A few beaver still lived in Norway. There is an unconfirmed report that a colony of beaver lived somewhere in Germany as recently as the 1820s. But while never more exciting or exotic in historic times than it is now, the Canadian beaver was not unknown to the newcomers. The French did not have to make up a new word for it.

The voyagers who followed Cartier, leaving the great waterways and forging into the bush, might have cursed the beaver occasionally for damming up an otherwise navigable rivulet. They surely were aware of the chewing and damming and obsessive things beaver do—felling trees, building dams, flooding whole districts of low-lying forest land. For a time, the handful of Frenchmen exploring New France did not realize that a source of unthinkably great riches was busily chewing down trees. Blinded by the hope of marvels, China and gold, Cartier did not recognize that Canada's true and illimitable riches lay in the streams and ponds all around him. It was gold that gnawed, gold that slapped the ground with a scaly tail, gold that built mud bunkers from chewed-down trees and was literally everywhere, in every wooded pond and stream from the Atlantic to the Pacific. The discovery of *this* lode was yet to come.

Meanwhile, the "diamonds" Cartier took back to France turned out to be so much worthless quartz, and his "gold" so many scraps of iron pyrite. But Cartier's glittering stones did enrich the French language with a new proverb: "Phoney as a Canadian diamond."

9
CHAMPLAIN'S KNEE

THE SEARCH FOR THE ROAD TO CHINA began and ended in different ways for different men—with hope declining into disillusionment, in a reckless rush stopped by death, in vexation at the start and at the end.

The Englishman John Davis sought the Northwest Passage for his Virgin Queen along the northern coast of Labrador on three voyages between 1585 and 1587, though "none took him to the Pacific," he notes ruefully in his report. At the entrance to Hudson Bay, Davis encountered a tidal rush of water that sounded "loathsomely crying like the rage of the waters under the London bridge." He named it the Furious Overfall. Though he had not found the great northern route to China, Davis wrote, "the passage is most probable, the execution easie."

We know nothing of the motives of Henry Hudson, probably the first European to die in what is now Ontario—only his remorseless dedication to finding a northern route around the American continents. Between 1607 and his murder by mutineers in 1611, he tried four times to forge a route, thrice through the Arctic Ocean, once—his last voyage—through the vast, icy waste of Hudson Bay. Other visionaries and adventurers, spiritual heirs of Christopher Columbus, continued to explore the waterways that cut through the inner forests of North America in search of the great western waterway.

By the beginning of the seventeenth century, explorers continued to hurl themselves into the unknown vastness of the New World. But a new man—strategist, planner, militant for Crown and Cross—was on the scene, shaping the future course of civilization on the waterways leading inward. Of the Europeans who appear early in the story of Ontario, none more perfectly embodies this revolutionary new presence than Samuel de Champlain.

Beginning with his *Des Sauvages, ou, Voyage de Samuel Champlain* (1603) and continuing through subsequent volumes, the author seeks to locate his project in the great history of adventure.

The inclinations of men differ according to their varied dispositions; and each one in his calling has his particular end in view.

Some aim at gain, some at glory, some at the public weal. The greater number are engaged in trade, and especially that which is transacted on the sea. Hence arise the principal support of the people, the opulence and honour of states. This is what raised ancient Rome to the sovereignty and mastery over the entire world, and the Venetians to a grandeur equal to that of powerful kings. It has in all times caused maritime towns to abound in riches, among which Alexandria and Tyre are distinguished, and numerous others, which fill up the regions of the interior with the objects of beauty and rarity obtained from foreign nations.

For this reason, many princes have striven to find a northerly route to China, in order to facilitate commerce with the Orientals, in the belief that this route would be shorter and less dangerous . . .

So many voyages and discoveries without result, and attended with so much hardship and expense, have caused us French in late years to attempt a permanent settlement in those lands which we call New France, in the hope of thus realizing more easily this object; since the voyage in search of the desired passage commences on the other side of the ocean, and is made along the coast of this region. These considerations had induced the Marquis de la Roche, in 1598, to take a commission from the king for making a settlement in the above region.

With this object, he landed men and supplies on Sable Island; but, as the conditions which had been accorded to him by his Majesty were not fulfilled, he was obliged to abandon his undertaking, and leave his men there. A year after, Captain Chauvin accepted another commission to transport settlers to the same region; but, as this was shortly after revoked, he prosecuted the matter no farther.

After the above, notwithstanding all these accidents and disappointments, Sieur de Monts desired to attempt what had been given up in despair . . . [proposing] to his Majesty a means for covering these expenses, without drawing any thing from the royal revenues; viz., by granting to him the monopoly of the fur-trade in this land. . . .

Eventually Sieur de Monts chose a spot, the future Québec, to be the site of a permanent outpost—the first such settlement by the French in the New World, the true beginning of New France, the establishment of an economic focus.

He was also influenced by the hope of greater advantages in case of settling in the interior, where the people are civilized, and where it is easier to plant the Christian faith and establish such order as is necessary for the protection of a country, than along the sea-shore, where *les sauvages* generally dwell. From this course, he believed the king would derive an inestimable profit; for it is easy to suppose that Europeans will seek out this advantage rather than those of a jealous and intractable disposition to be found on the shores, and the barbarous tribes.

CHAMPLAIN, LIKE COLUMBUS, STANDS ASTRIDE the chasm that separates the medieval from the modern world; but Champlain's forward foot was planted on the modern side of the great chasm.

No contemporary portrait of him has survived, if any was ever painted. The next best thing appears at the opening of Samuel Eliot Morison's biography. "As one who has lived with Champlain for many years," writes Morison, "I may be permitted to give my own idea of him. A well-built man of medium stature, blond and bearded, a natural leader who inspired loyalty and commanded obedience. A man of unusually rugged constitution, never complaining of discomforts in his voyages or on his canoe and other overland journeys, sleeping in the open with no covering and over evergreen boughs between his body and the snow, eating the natives' often loathsome food. A proud man among his fellows, demanding the respect due to his position, but humble before God." In his *Treatise on Seamanship,* Champlain describes himself: "an upright, God-fearing man, not dainty about food or drink, robust and alert, with good sea legs."

This Champlain, or one quite like the Champlain described by Morison and the captain himself, was born on the Bay of Biscay, near La Rochelle, around the year 1570. His father, Antoine, was a mariner, and he seemed destined from the beginning to be a traveller. But Champlain loved God and the Church, and might have become a priest in foreign parts, had he not, at age twenty, joined one of the bloody crusades of French Catholics against their domestic Protestant enemies. But this experience of land battle left him longing to return to the sea, and to a life of service beyond the seas. As he wrote in 1613, in an early account of his travels:

> Navigation has always seemed to me to occupy the first place. By this art we obtain a knowledge of different countries, regions, and realms. By this we attract and bring to our own land all kinds of riches; by it the idolatry of paganism is overthrown, and Christianity proclaimed throughout all the regions of the earth. This is the art . . . which led me to explore the coasts of a portion of America, especially those of New France, where I have always desired to see the lily flourish, together with the only religion catholic, Apostolic and Roman.

He came out to the new land from France in 1603, seeking the northern route to China. But the French were attracted by the fur trade up the St. Lawrence, and had established their first provisional settlement at Québec. He returned again from France in 1607, at the command of King Henri IV of France, on a very different quest: to establish his monopoly on the beaver trade, for France had discovered the beauty and utility of beaver and the fact that the western lands could supply their wants plentifully.

Champlain's first months on this continent were hard enough to disillusion anyone less stalwart. In the terrible winter of 1608, when camped out where Québec now stands, he saw eight of the twenty-eight men he had brought from France dead from scurvy, and the rest afflicted by it.

Though discouraged by the cold, disease and deaths, Champlain was determined to cultivate the friendship of the Wendat who visited Québec. They knew of places far inland, up the Ottawa River, where the Indians hunted and harvested the beaver in huge numbers. So he accepted their invitation to bring his guns and armour, come up the Ottawa with them and make common cause with them and their Algonkian allies.

He knew that by going up the St. Lawrence River with the Wendat, he was entering an area that had long been a war zone. The Wendat assured him that their enemies were quite worthy of destruction and would be easy to destroy. Champlain could not have known that the enemy of which the Wendat spoke was the great League of the Long House, governors of eastern North America from Ontario south to the Carolinas, and the most formidable force the Europeans would encounter in their settlement of North America.

This first voyage into southern Ontario was to be an occasion that would determine the history of the French in Canada for decades to come.

That August in 1615, Champlain set out to assist his Wendat friends in besieging a League town in what is now New York State. On their journey there, they passed by Lake Simcoe and proceeded by way of Sturgeon Lake. Following the Trent River they reached the Bay of Quinte—"the entrance to the grand river St. Lawrence," wrote Champlain (and already familiar to us as the birthplace of Dekanawida). Crossing Lake Ontario they penetrated the woods and passed over the Oswego River, to the League settlement that so concerned the Wendat. In the conflict, Champlain was hit in the knee by an arrow and painfully wounded. The Wendat were forced to retreat, and the war party found its way eventually to a Wendat encampment near present-day Kingston. There, Champlain spent the winter.

On the face of it, the campaign of 1615 was a minor episode in the French expansion inland. Yet by pressing the case of the Wendat in the violently disputed territory of southern Ontario, Champlain was consolidating the hatred of the League for the French, and effectively turning the Lake Ontario basin into a no-passage zone for both the French and the Wendat. The beaver were already becoming the stakes for which a terrible military scenario in southern Ontario would be played out, through the seventeenth century and well into the next. Meanwhile, farther north a happier relation between French and Indians was being forged.

IN ONTARIO TODAY, they name public schools and parks after Étienne Brûlé, a sidekick of Samuel de Champlain. You have to wonder what the children and grown-ups who study or play in these places would think if they really knew the kind of man such respectable places are dedicated to.

Brûlé was probably born near Paris around 1592, and became every parent's nightmare by the time he could talk. At age sixteen, he landed a job in New France as a sort of errand boy for Champlain. The year was 1608. The most recent attempt by the English to get a toehold in the New World was tottering toward disaster on the Atlantic coast at the mouth of Virginia's James River. My first ancestor on these shores came out that year as a chaplain to these adventurers, who believed they could make a fortune raising silk worms and tropical fruit. William Mays may have come close to meeting Étienne Brûlé a few years later, after the Virginia Company had given up on those hopeless worms and started growing vastly more profitable tobacco.

But I'm getting ahead of the story. Almost as soon as young Étienne came ashore in La Nouvelle France, he began putting his own plans in motion, which did not include being Champlain's boot boy. He asked for and got permission to decamp and set out up the Ottawa River, "as well to pass his time," Champlain writes mildly, "as to see the country and learn [the aboriginal] language and mode of life." Champlain went along with this respectable-sounding scheme because Brûlé convinced him that a trip inland would outfit him as a skilled interpreter, hence a useful instrument in the imperial enterprise to which his employer was devoted, body and soul.

He returned to Québec from this first inland adventure in the summer of 1611, fluent in the languages of the Algonkian people who lived along the Ottawa, then busied himself around Champlain's head-quarters for a couple of years. This young man with restless feet was soon off again up the Ottawa River, with dreams in his head far more colourful than those he had treasured on this first voyage of discovery. He was gone four years that time. When Brûlé got back to home base this time, Champlain was planning one of those ambitious, doomed military campaigns that histories of New France are full of. Brûlé seemed like exactly the right man to sally forth into what was to become a major offensive against the League. The point of this trip was to forge an alliance between the French-Wendat forces and the Susquehannah, who lived at the north end of Chesapeake Bay and hated the League.

If I leave out lots of details about this expedition and others like it, it's only because anything happening all the time—such as the endless tussles between the League and its neighbours over control of the Ontario fur trade—isn't as interesting as things that happen once, or unique people who start something radically new. Brûlé was one such event, and one such person.

Like so many other political missions, pious escapades or just plain follies launched by the French faced with a fantastically vast inland they knew nothing about but wanted to own every inch of, the 1615 trip of Brûlé did not work out as planned. On his round trip from Québec, to the rendezvous point with the Susquehannah at a place called Carantouan, in what's now upstate New York, Brûlé and his Wendat scouts led the French party up the Ottawa River to Lake Huron. From this place—"the Sweetwater Sea" of the Wendat—he then circled back down across Lake Ontario, led by his Wendat allies toward the site of a palisaded town of the Long House League lying south of Lake Oneida, in what is now New York State. He travelled with his Wendat comrades down the ancient forty-five-kilometre trade track from Lake Simcoe to Lake Ontario, lying more or less along the route of Yonge Street. In September, 1615, he arrived at the mouth of the Humber River and saw Lake Ontario. On this trip, he may have gotten through Pennsylvania to the north end of Chesapeake Bay. On his other voyages into the wilderness, he may have seen Lake Superior.

He certainly let on that he saw and experienced marvellous things. When quizzed by Champlain about his failure to carry out a military mission to the League villages south of Lake Ontario, Brûlé came up with the following story.

When he reached his destination, the villagers were told that a "man of iron," as they called the French, had arrived. (This may not have been complimentary. The iron pots and weapons of the French may have seemed ugly and common to the old nations, who treasured copper, a beautiful metal.) Curious, as always, about Europeans, the villagers came in a great rush to meet him. The headmen were suspicious, but Brûlé, always the charmer, persuaded them that the French he represented wanted only friendship. The chief was inclined to believe Brûlé and see where further talks with him might lead. The chief's unhappy compatriots grew impatient, turned on the hapless Frenchman, ripped out his nails with their teeth, burnt him with blazing branches and committed other horrors on him. When his tormentors had almost done in Brûlé, one of them noticed a religious medal he always wore round his neck. At which point, Brûlé sternly warned them that, should they steal the medal and kill him, horrid death would fall on them all at once.

Undeterred, the impious torturers made ready to rip the medal from Brûlé's neck, when lo! Divine Providence came to the rescue. As Champlain retold Brûlé's story:

> God, showing him mercy, was pleased not to allow it, but in his providence caused the heavens to change suddenly from the serene and fair state they were in to darkness, and to become filled with great and thick clouds, upon which followed thunders and lightnings so violent and long continued that it was something strange and awful. This storm caused the savages such terror, it being not only unusual but unlike anything they had ever heard, that their attention was diverted and they forgot the evil purpose they had towards Brûlé, their prisoner. They accordingly left him without even unbinding him, as they did not dare to approach him. This gave the sufferer an opportunity to use gentle words, and he appealed to them and remonstrated with them on the harm they were doing him without cause, and set forth to them how our God was enraged at them for having so abused him. The captain [or chief] then approached Brûlé, unbound him, and took him to his house, where he took care of him and treated his wounds. After this there were no dances, banquets or merry-makings to which Brûlé was not invited.

After a few days of such carryings-on, miraculously cured of his tortures as well as redeemed from the hands of his enemies by the

Lord, Brûlé decided to take leave of his new-found friends and come home to headquarters.

That the warriors of the League often inflicted unspeakable torments on their enemies and competitors—a use of terror to inspire submission that worked—was well known to the French. Throughout the reign of the French in Ontario, their enemies never inflicted upon them any torture more horrible than what the Europeans inflicted on each other, while waging war or hunting out heresies, or merely wrenching a confession out of some hapless crook. That God was on the side of the French and their king, and ready to help even an adventurer like Brûlé in his moment of most dire need, was an obvious truth to the rigorously devout Champlain. He believed every word of Brûlé's story. But like most of Brûlé's stories, this one should be taken with a pinch of salt. It was merely the kind of hero-story Champlain wanted to hear from his emissary into the wilderness.

Brûlé, as the historical plaques along Ontario roadways tell us, was quite likely "the first European to see This-or-That"—even "the discoverer of This-or-That," though this expression is, rightly, not used much any more. After all, people of various nations had been discovering all kinds of places and things in Ontario for thousands of years before the Europeans arrived. Brûlé's claim to having been the first European to explore Ontario and see Lake Ontario, or whatever we wish to call the lake at that point in its history, is the reason they name schools after him.

It's worth remembering that Brûlé did not know he was discovering Lake Ontario or discovering anything other than something he had not seen before. He certainly did not think of himself as a great explorer. It was a tourist's interest in learning new things that drove him. He taught himself the languages of the nations who hunted the forests and shorelines he visited because he wanted food, shelter, sex. Brûlé did not share the abounding, irrepressible curiosity about flora and fauna typical of the Renaissance newcomers, such as Columbus. Complicated philosophical questions, such as the ones about whether the old nations of the New World were human or not, probably never crossed his mind. And unlike Cartier before him and René Robert Cavelier, Sieur de La Salle after him, Brûlé was not driven to look for the route to China or gold on the ground. He didn't want to convert anybody to Christianity. Unlike some contemporaries, he did not try to make the earlier Ontario nations dress up in the French style. On the contrary, he dressed and talked and acted as they did so convincingly that Champlain was disgusted. He also horrified the Jesuits whom Champlain was importing to Christianize *les sauvages*.

Brûlé knew he had a king, of course—everybody had one in those days—but he probably never did anything out of respect for the king, or for Champlain, beyond what was necessary to get what he wanted out of the old imperialists he worked for. By every account, what Brûlé wanted more than anything was simply the pleasure of going places. Unlike most travellers, however, he never went home, because, like generations of Europeans after him, he decided he had found an earthly paradise. His spiritual descendants and kinsmen are Paul Gauguin, Lafcadio Hearn, the first settlers in California and the voyageurs.

Because Brûlé's style of tourism is so well established in Western history, it's somewhat hard to imagine a time when it was new. For the thousand years before Brûlé's time, Europeans had not done much long-distance travelling, apart from the crusades and the odd pilgrimage to the Holy Land. The streets of medieval towns were dark and dangerous, so people did not go out after dark. The medieval forests were thick with wolves and thieves. The great old Roman roads that once criss-crossed the world between Damascus and Spain, between Sicily and the Scottish border, had gone to ruin with the collapse of imperial rule. A few very remarkable medieval people, such as Marco Polo (and, for that matter, Columbus), had gone on missions officially intended to establish trade links between Europe and China.

But most Europeans stayed home. The ones who could read enjoyed best-sellers full of lies and fabulous fantasies about exotic places, such as the hugely popular fourteenth-century *Voyages of Sir John Mandeville,* a forgery composed by person or persons unknown. Then came Gutenberg and, around the same time, Columbus's writings.

Like modern newspaper readers picking up a story about somebody accomplishing some great adventure or making a million dollars with an invention, the vast majority of Europeans who read about the Columbian expeditions were content to sigh with envy, and disinclined to sign on to the next ship. But such writing changed their view of the world, its possibilities and limits. Brûlé was one of the few who seemed to have been interested in staying on the road. And everyone who has taken to the road just because it is there is a spiritual kinsman of Étienne Brûlé's.

Brûlé should perhaps also be honoured because he severed so many ties with old Europe that he became, without meaning to do so, the first Canadian. The men and women who were descended from Europeans but born here, rarely, or perhaps never, thought about Europe. They were the fur traders, sent into the wilderness by Champlain in the name of God and King, who then found themselves at home there, doing things for themselves. In the great inland forests that lined the rivers and lakes, they got wives from the older nations, and their children were the first Europeans to know nothing of Europe. These fur-trapping lads, breaking with traditions as old as European Christendom, prefigured the radical individualism, free-booting spirit and independence of the frontier. But they also revolutionized the nature of North American business. With the immense upswing in volume and tightening organization in the beaver trade around 1600, "a remarkable period of intrigue and diplomacy among Indian tribes" was initiated, according to an historian of the period. "Indian middlemen were able to exercise greater bargaining power over more remote tribes with the use of European weapons." The Europeans who traded with these middlemen and spent their working lives in the great beaver system questioned and rejected civilization, as currently defined by men of Champlain's cast of mind. And they set an agenda for all those who would come after. Brûlé probably knew he was not like other men; Champlain certainly did.

10

BLACK ROBES

THE FRENCH DID NOT NEED TO SETTLE large populations or build impressive fortresses far inland, if one of the two key trade routes for fur—the Ottawa River or Lake Ontario—could be kept open and secure, and free of interference from either the English to the north or the League to the south. Because of Champlain's alliance with weaker, northern nations, the Ottawa became the great road of the fur trade, and the stories of Ontario during the era of French domination were created on a northerly arc extending upward from Montréal along the Ottawa River to Lake Huron and Lake Superior, and down into the Mississippi basin.

In the early seventeenth century, the durable beaver system—with its wars, unlikely alliances, trade fairs and busy exchanges—came quickly into existence, and along with it the French settlement of Ontario. The key point in the far north was the Sault, the juncture through which the waters of Lake Superior emptied through rapids into Lake Huron and where the northern missions and trading stations were established. Quickly a seasonal trade fair emerged on the tiny island of Mackinac, between Lake Huron and Lake Michigan, near the larger island of Blanc Bois. Here, French trappers met the various nations that came to sell pelts, and a famously wild, raucous seasonal trade fair developed that would have shocked the missionaries whom Champlain hoped would civilize the southern Wendat.

Champlain's system required a little military effort; he expected missionary work. But its major contribution to future Ontario history was the drawing of young men from France and New France westward—men like Étienne Brûlé, of a new, wild kind. Some of the coureurs de bois went out to the beaver ponds, and lived and hunted among the native tribes. Other, less hardy men, according to a contemporary witness, merely went "as far as the Long Sault . . . to meet the Indians and French who come down, in order to obtain, exclusively, their peltries, for which they carry goods to them, and sometimes nothing but Brandy contrary to the King's prohibition, with which they intoxicate and ruin them . . ."

These men were happy to live away in the forests, marrying the daughters of the nations they found there, becoming parts of the nations even more fully than the happy Father Joseph de la Roche Dallion. The coureurs de bois, the lawless, happy-go-lucky first exploiters of Ontario, represented one kind of young European the older peoples of Ontario were to meet; the missionaries, another. (Of both the coureurs de bois and the missionaries, two manifestations of the same centrifugal force casting Europeans to the four winds in the seventeenth century, more later in this book.)

The Mackinac Island fair stood at the western end of Champlain's system, Ville-Marie de Montréal at the eastern—simply because it was not possible, for military reasons, to sustain a French settlement and fairground any farther west. Each year, down the Ottawa River would float huge canoes piled high with beaver pelts. These goods would be traded for kettles, knives, trinkets and liquor amidst scenes remembered as something between high spirits and pandemonium. A pattern was being established for the enduring colonization of New France: the settlement as interface between suppliers to the north and consumers to the south, with a fairground that, as one writer has said, "grew in

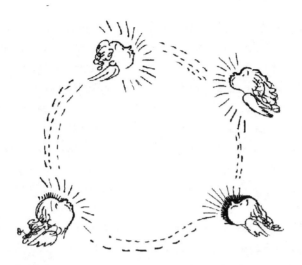

importance, picturesqueness and violence as years went by, and became the most fantastic feature of the Canadian fur trade."

In Champlain's day and long afterward, Ville-Marie was mostly empty between fairs. But just as the French ships were arriving,

> the settlement was astir with life: traders and seamen and clerks come up the river from Quebec, Indians come down from the friendly tribes along the upper lakes bringing fleets of canoes weighted low in the water with beaver and bear-skins. During the weeks of the annual trading, Villemarie hummed with business and excitement. The Indians made themselves gaudy with French beads and sham gold lace, and drunk with fiery brandy. Even the habitants bought all they would need for the coming year, provision and tools, and dry-goods—*rouenneries,* they called such goods after the French city with the wooly lamb in its crest, where they had been woven. Then nothing, the barrenness of the outpost returned.

But La Nouvelle France had been launched from this crude, tough beginning into the century of its greatest career. La Salle, the last seeker for the Great River, left his mark by founding Fort Frontenac, the first permanent French military installation on Lake Ontario, as an armed response to the ceaseless, draining war between the Wendat and the Long House League for control of the fur trade. There, in 1679, he constructed the *Griffin,* the first ship built in the European manner on the Great Lakes. Later, he claimed for Louis XIV, in April 1682, all lands drained by the Mississippi River—from the far-northern head-waters of the river to the Gulf of Mexico, east to the Appalachians and west to the Rockies; this he called Louisiana, in honour of his monarch.

In 1699, the vast arc of the French imperium reached its southern extent when Pierre Le Moyne d'Iberville arrived at Pointe du Mardi Gras, at the mouth of the Mississippi River, and claimed all the terri-tory north of it for France. In 1718, they founded New Orleans, as a trading station for furs descending from the great outlet at Cahokia, near what is now called St. Louis. In contrast to the English, who believed peaceable settlement of families and institutions to be the best way to build a new world, the French depended on the followers of Brûlé to put their stamp on the land. Though sharply different in dress, education and attitude, the Jesuits who came to Ontario were nevertheless men of the same age, and of a similar cast of mind.

The Jesuit priest Jean de Brébeuf was born in Normandy in 1593, which makes him almost exactly the same age as Brûlé. Though Brûlé wrote nothing, and we know him only by way of Champlain's hostile-to-cool descriptions, he seems near and knowable. Brébeuf and the other Jesuit missionaries who came out from France and died in Ontario or went home to tell tales of their adventures wrote abun-dantly about everything they did and saw. They were modern Europeans to the core and never identified with the ancient cultures they found abounding in this new world. But what really makes them foreign to us is their cultural radicalism and fervent belief that ideas (specifically, their own) could change the world. Brébeuf was more like a Red Guard during Mao's great cultural revolution than any Evangelical Christian today, and perhaps a bit fearsome to us for that reason alone. Like Brûlé, Brébeuf and his companions could have only been what they were outside Europe, being new people of the sort the openness of this new world was making possible.

Everything could have all turned out differently. King Henri IV wanted the new-found lands into which the St. Lawrence and Ottawa Rivers were leading the French settled by any means possible, and by anyone available. The first arrivals in Ontario, instead of fastidious and sophisticated Jesuits, could have been bands of outlaws, gangsters and predators. Champlain made all the difference, by deciding that the indigenous inhabitants of New France should be Catholic and well-behaved, as he understood good behaviour. That mean *French*. If he was to have his way, the mysterious lands west of Montréal, from his headquarters at Ville-Marie to the most westerly bounds of New France, would be French in matters of culture, Catholic in religion, modern—centralized, urban, monarchist—and in all points political. Champlain was an improver, not an exploiter. To many people nowadays, blessed with the clarity of hindsight, an improver is an exploiter by another name. But for the moment, let us give Champlain the benefit of the doubt and see what he wrought, or tried to bring about, in Ontario.

Champlain had wanted to penetrate the inner regions of New France with missionaries in hope of the "greater advantages in the interior, where the peoples are civilized, and where it is easier to plant the Christian faith and establish such order as is necessary for the preservation of a country." This led him to found Québec City as a centre of the evangelization and the establishment of classical civilization. His intention was always that the indigenous folk be "instructed in the law of God and good manners."

In his mind, his ideal accomplishment would be a City of God on American soil, an Arcadian republic of an ancient kind—perhaps he was a man, like other enlightened contemporaries, who believed in the virtues of the old Roman Republic, before the grand, corrupt Empire. He loved the wilds, as opposed to the over-civilized centres of culture—not as Brûlé did, as a zone of freedom to ramble, but as a blank place in which to build a new French civilization that would be *truly* French. Along with the merchants he sought to entice to come over or open markets for American goods in France, the missionaries became crucial elements in the plan.

He disliked Protestants intensely, and could not bear even to hear them singing. As it happened, more than half the fur traders in the official Company of New France were Protestants, and though prohibited from practising their religion in Canada they did so on their ships. There, they sang; and Champlain fled when they did.

To such a man, the Jesuits were the perfect instruments for the kind of evangelization he envisioned; and Brébeuf was the perfect Jesuit. He was not particularly learned, but he was completely a man of the Baroque age: emotional, dramatic, with a taste for theatre in which he would play a starring role. In the spring of 1625, he arrived in Québec with the Franciscan friar Joseph de la Roche Dallion, whom we have already met. Almost at once, Brébeuf set off up the Ottawa River by canoe to Georgian Bay, where he found a place called Ihonatiria and, with his companions, set up the first outpost of the Jesuits among the Wendat. As for the latter, they were unimpressed by these Europeans. Before long, with nothing to show for his labour, Brébeuf returned to Québec, and shortly thereafter to France.

He might have ended his days there, had it not been for a seething compound of business, politics and religion. In 1627, the princely Cardinal Richelieu—the de facto ruler and manager of both Old France and New—organized the Company of New France, headed by himself, and with Champlain as an investor. The organization was given complete domination over the fur trade, in return for the commitment to put permanent settlers in New France. Catholic ones only, however. Huguenots, though officially tolerated in Old France, were to have no place in the construction of the New.

Then, in 1632, Cardinal Richelieu decided to take away the Christianizing of Ontario from the Franciscans and give it wholly to the Society of Jesus. Nobody incarnated the principles of the Council of Trent and the Counter-Reformation like the Jesuits. And this was the particular, peculiar legacy of the Tridentine council: the austerity and remorseless brilliance of thought that could produce a René Descartes, the belief in civilization typified by Champlain.

In 1633, Brébeuf again set out for Canada. Quickly, the Jesuits began to establish themselves in the heartland of the Wendat. By 1639, Father Jérôme Lalement had created a mission headquarters on the south shore of Georgian Bay, near the site of Midland. It was to be a French town built in the North American interior, with arable fields on the outskirts, ditch drainage, a chapel, infirmary and a palisaded enclosure for Wendat converts.

Had the Wendat been willing to modernize themselves quickly and move into towns along French lines, they might have spared themselves the worst of a terrible consequence of contact with Europeans. The traditional longhouses in which the Wendat had always lived and slept and worked were hothouses for the diseases inadvertently brought by the Europeans. The epidemics that ensued slashed the Wendat population of around 25,000 in half. The French were accused by the shamans of the unconverted Wendat of magic and bringing death upon them—which, of course, they had unwittingly done. But conversions continued, as *les sauvages* decided they could not blame others for impersonal forces.

Brébeuf worked among them for sixteen years, dying horribly and famously at the hands of League warriors—sworn enemies of the Wendat—with very little to show for his presence.

What kept these men going? I believe that, like the desire behind Brûlé's career, it was the opportunity to be what they could not be in Europe. The Council of Trent had led to a revived humanism of the Counter-Reformation and sought to take the Church back to its Hellenistic and Roman roots, to the very idea of Civilization itself as defined in antiquity. The Council tried to revive the best of Renaissance thinking: reasonable, scientific, questioning. This was the keen scientific era that produced Isaac Newton and Samuel de Champlain and René Descartes, all apostles of a renewed mission of Civilization. It also was the culture that produced Galileo and Johannes Kepler.

But most people, as usual, paid little attention to the seismic intellectual changes shaking the last, feeble struts of medievalism into ruins.
The marvellously optimistic conviction of Brébeuf and his companions
about what had to be done seemed to find its potential fulfillment in
the Wendat, who had been kept largely distant from contamination by
corrupt metropolitan France. The Wendat were to be educated as
fully human, fully reasonable creatures, no less and no more so than
any European. They were "not so barbarous," reported one Jesuit, "that
they cannot be made children of God . . . Education and instruction
alone are lacking." In 1647, the Jesuit Paul Ragueneau concluded a report
to Paris with the generous sentiment, typical of his time and station:

> One must be very careful before condemning a thousand things
> among their customs, which greatly offend minds brought up in
> another world. It is easy to call irreligion what is merely stupid-
> ity, and to take for diabolical working something that is nothing
> more than human; and then, one thinks he is obliged to forbid
> as impious certain things that are done in all innocence, or, at
> most are silly but not criminal customs.

The word "silly" is, by the way, a peculiarly modern way to
dismiss beliefs thought to be insufficiently or ineffectively modern.
Ragueneau was continually reporting back to Paris on the silliness of
Wendat beliefs about the world. Not much to do with religion,
mind you. The Wendat were coming along slowly but satisfactorily
in that direction. But they were having a particularly hard time
(according to Ragueneau and Brébeuf and others) becoming urban,
unsilly and sophisticated.

The Jesuits of Ste-Marie-Among-the-Hurons, as their Georgian Bay
compound was called, were quite out of step with the larger developments of the day. They were minded to build a model Christian city,
on the south shore of Georgian Bay. But the Jesuit officialdom in Paris
decided, in 1640, to go along with the prevailing belief by the French
fur traders that the Wendat and Algonkian and other people were best

left in the forest, un-urbanized, so they could trap and fish in the old ways they knew well.

By mid-century, the Jesuits were caught in a bind. On one hand, they were still strongly driven by the need to establish pure Christian modernity in the wilderness; at the same time, they realized this could only be done by turning the old nations into French people. And it was increasingly hard to keep the Wendat and others free of the very influences the Jesuits had come to Ontario to escape and avoid. "The evil life of some of the French is a noxious example," wrote Father Gabriel Sagard, "and in all these districts the natives, although savages, reproach us with it, saying that [the missionaries] teach them things the reverse of what are practiced by the French."

The political authorities disagreed. The Indians were to become good Europeans and intermarry with the French to create a truly new people. Not the theologically pure people the Jesuits intended, but ones who would work better for France, so that, in the words of the new governor Frontenac, "in the course of time, having but one law and one master, they might likewise constitute one race and one people."

None of these developments were being conducted in a vacuum. The war for Ontario and the fabulous riches in pelts never ceased between the League of the Great Peace and its enemies. By 1647 the League had concluded a truce with the French, but they kept up their war against the Wendat. In the spring of 1649, a strong force of League warriors overran the settlements where Brébeuf and his companions had their headquarters, dragged them away, then put them to death after the usual cruelties doled out by the League to the unsubmissive. Other Jesuits died in similar ways in following years. To prevent more deaths of the suddenly vulnerable Wendat, the Jesuits torched their divine city in Huronia, and with their Christian Wendat comrades sought refuge on Christian Island in Georgian Bay. Thousands of Wendat refugees joined them, only to perish by the hundreds in the vicious winter of 1649–50. Only three hundred reached Montréal and Québec the following year. Having driven the Wendat from their lands, the League then went on to attack anyone else who stood in their way—Neutral, Attiwandiron and Nipissing—leaving southern Ontario virtually empty of people. So ended the ascendancy of the Wendat nation in Ontario, and also the Jesuit mission, in a debacle of disease, war, flight and misery.

Silence fell over the Ontario forests, as deep as that which had come with the great Ice Age. The strife of empires was not over. But a terrible pause had come to Ontario.

IN 1930, THE JESUIT DEAD were officially proclaimed by the Catholic Church to be men who had given their lives not for being in the wrong place at the wrong time but for their unswerving witness to God. There is a sense in which both things are true. These Jesuits were standard-bearers for a passing ideal: the sunset of an ancient notion rather than the dawn of a new one—the idea of a Christian civilization. Even for thoughtful Christians in modern culture, it is hard to imagine such a civilization as anything other than a kind of dictatorial theocracy, run by clerics who might be kind or might be cruel, but who would be unquestionably in control. The more stringent Islamic republics of the twentieth century, especially, have provided (at least for the time being) the definitive model for what such a civilization would look like.

The important point is that Ontario's Jesuits did not believe in coercion to make a Christian heaven on earth. They were appalled by the reluctance of the Wendat to become modern, but while complaining about it a lot they did not call in the troops to impose technological modernity or Christianity or anything else. There is no reason to believe they would have done so, even had they had the chance. After all, the new men and women they hoped to nurse into maturity were to know freedom, not enslavement. Despite the horror of the plagues, the Jesuit establishment in Huronia was a remarkable and historic accomplishment, not only because it brought civilization to the

Wendat but it introduced also an idea of theocratic democracy with the most progressive notions of society and education in the Baroque period.

It was an experiment that would have many descendants in utopian communities such as Mother Ann Lee's Shakers and in the community of visionaries who gathered in the wonderful temple at Sharon, Ontario (and of whom we shall hear more later). But neither Brûlé nor Brébeuf was horrible. These men and their companions in untimely death were either very stupid (which I do not believe), or they were simply people made indifferent to misery and death by love (in the case of Brébeuf) or adventure (in the case of Brûlé). Stupidity has always been a popular way to explain why people occasionally decide to die rather than stop doing what they like. The lives and deaths of Brûlé and Brébeuf serve as reminders of how hard it is to forsake an exciting new life once one has tasted it.

11
AGAIN, THE BEAUTIFUL RIVER

So far, my stories of la nouvelle france west of Montréal have been set largely in the districts along the Ottawa River, hence in the more northerly parts of the place that will (soon, but not quite yet) be called Ontario.

There is good reason for it. Until the military catastrophe that engulfed the Wendat, their European business partners and the Jesuit radicals around 1650, the French trappers and traders had been fortunate in the north, getting along amicably with the nations that preceded them along the fur-rich river. But the mid-century victories of the Long House People over most rivals in the Great Lakes region ended with the victors in control of the fur harvest throughout vast, deeply ravined and swampy forests triangulated between the Shield, Lake Ontario and the eastern shoreline of the upper Great Lakes.

And not only there. By 1680, at its greatest extent since the arrival of the Europeans, the zone controlled by the League and its client nations covered a vast area north as far as the lower end of Lake Michigan south to Chesapeake Bay and all of southern Ontario.

At this moment, the League and its allies—indigenous and Dutch, for the most part—were probably strong enough to have confined French influence strictly downriver along the St. Lawrence and kept the English newcomers on their farms and little towns clustered along the Atlantic seaboard. Had Dekanawida's Great Peace been more effectively honoured, and the in-fighting of League members stopped, the combined force could have halted the westward advance of the Europeans, at least for the time being, and confronted any interlopers with a powerful, rich commonwealth of fur-trading people, using the coastal English and French settlements as outlets for the European market. For a while—perhaps even until the dawn of the nineteenth century, had they not become embroiled in Europe's internal wars and revolutions—the League's interface with Europe along the Atlantic coast might have resembled Japan during the anti-Western shogunate: an absolutely closed boundary with trade zones on the edges.

In the struggles to control the riches of North America, Europeans were always ready to exploit the disunity of the League members, and the draconian provisions of the Great Peace for nations disinclined to accept the wisdom of League membership or protection. Yet the seventeenth-century reach by the French into what is now Ontario was not, or not only, motivated by greed. Like the Jesuits in Huronia—those impatient, frustrated modernizers—the three men who came to Ontario and left the stories to be retold in this chapter were driven by serious cultural values that had taken up firm residence in their hearts, wills and minds.

But I'm getting ahead of myself. To understand these very different men—the faintly old-fashioned adventurer René-Robert Cavelier, Sieur de La Salle; the flamboyant spendthrift and founder of Kingston, Louis de Buade, Comte de Frontenac; and the wily Belgian monk Louis Hennepin—it is necessary to stop by the gloomy Parisian home of a lonely little boy who never came to Canada, and very early in life found the world of all big ladies and gentlemen coarse, cold, indifferent and quite full of people quick to grovel but slow to give affection. So the little boy decided never to grow up.

Every privileged teenager tends to believe "l'État"—along with everything else that's important—"c'est moi," or ought to be. Then the child becomes a man—and, with any luck, negotiates a more workable settlement with the complex world as he finds it. The trouble with Louis XIV, the king of France—who pronounced the only memorable words of his fabulously long reign in 1655—is that he had the clout and wealth to make them come true. He was the State, or could become it. To the thousands of courtiers he gathered around him at Versailles, he was the Sun and centre of the universe. Louis never had to get any older than a child, so he didn't, and remained a gradually aging brat, eager and capricious, until his death in 1715.

Like other men who never transcend the normal teenager's greed for power and sensuous grandiosity, Louis was notable for his extravagance and triviality. The snob and diarist the Duc de Saint-Simon—who, by the way, did admire the King, warts and all—observed candidly that

> there was nothing he liked so much as flattery, or, to put it more plainly, adulation; the coarser and clumsier it was, the more he relished it. That was the only way to approach him; if he ever took a liking to a man it was invariably due to some lucky stroke of flattery in the first instance, and to indefatigable perseverance in the same line afterwards.

Even the generals in France's grandly successful wars learned early that the King was inclined to take "to himself the credit of their successes with admirable complacency," so they let him do so, the better to fortify their own bailiwicks of prestige.

To Saint-Simon, the job of manipulating Louis was made all the easier by the fact that the King's attention was occupied with small things rather than with great, and he delighted in all sorts of petty details, such as the dress and drill of his soldiers; and it was just the same with regard to his building operations, his household, and even his cookery . . . He imagined that all this showed his indefatigable industry; in reality, it was a great waste of time, and his Ministers turned it to good account for their own purposes. As soon as they had learnt the art of managing him; they kept his attention engaged with a mass of details, while they contrived to get their own way in more important matters.

There are two reasons for musing a bit about Louis XIV in a book of Ontario stories. One has to do with his role as trend-setter for the political and social life of his age. Every European ruler wanted to build his own version of the brilliant palace at Versailles, and strut through elaborate rituals costumed opulently, dispensing infallible, or at least unarguable, commands to courtiers largely taken up (as Saint-Simon tells us) with the useless ceremonial fussing he dismisses as "burning incense." The ideal of life enacted at Versailles was sweet, exquisite, extravagant. The term *nouveau riche* was coined, it appears, of the early nineteenth century, but we have a French phrase for it because it so nicely sums up all that comes to mind when we think of the new millionaires created by the fickle patronage of Louis XIV.

My more urgent reason for talking about Louis has to do with how his style fed variations, reactions, even an emerging avant-gardism. While providing a handy epitome of what passed for high culture in the minds of Frenchmen, the prodigal style and hauteur of Versailles was also a quirky caricature of far more compelling realities.

From the start of the seventeenth century, the Baroque in art and civilization had been about the infinite and the intricate, about intense curiosity and surpassing limits. The standards were activity, passion, devotion. Brébeuf was a perfect representative of the Baroque. Everybody, everywhere, was affected by this profound shift of attention, Europe's first steps into the industrializing, mercantile Modern Age.

The reality of the Modern, of course, can be traced to European mechanization, and many people have written about that, repeatedly and exhaustively. I want only to explain how French modernity established itself west of Montréal, after Champlain's fitful, unsuccessful initiatives. To do so, the best place to look is in the lives of three men who came to La Nouvelle France to be what they wanted to be, and couldn't be, in old Europe. We cannot imagine how they would have turned out had they stayed in France. And indeed they all three died in obscurity, having acted out the imperatives and energies of their era, played their role, then vanished.

René-Robert Cavelier, whom we know better by his aristocratic title Sieur de La Salle, was born in the cathedral city of Rouen in 1643. La Salle belonged to a wealthy family in a town made rich when Elizabeth, queen of England, nodded off during a patent hearing and declined to give the English clergyman William Lee a licence for his newly discovered knitting machine. The wonderful mechanism was snapped up by the cloth merchants of Rouen, La Salle's relations among them, whom it made very rich.

Young Robert, attending a Jesuit school vivid with new ideas and new learning, soon revealed a quick mind for mathematics and a delight in the natural sciences. But you might expect math and science to be stylishly enchanting in a school which had graduated, not long before, Blaise Pascal. Pascal was famous for inventing a mechanical calculator at age nineteen and, in La Salle's school days, his writings on the vacuum were winning him new glory everywhere. But even as hard science was dazzling young, bright people across Europe—Isaac Newton was born a year before La Salle—curiosity about the New World was being encouraged by the great Jesuit *Relations,* which were coming off the presses in Paris when La Salle was a teenager. The physical universe was being made to reveal its long-kept secrets; the cultural marvels of the New World were becoming known through the labours of those earnest Jesuit reporters.

By every account, La Salle was temperamentally inclined to an ascetic life, either in a scientific laboratory or a monastery. He apparently gave careful consideration to becoming a Jesuit and may have gone some way along the path toward that way of life. But the siren call of a business career in the New World had captured his heart, and at age twenty-three he left his schooling in Rouen behind and struck out for the larger university of the ocean and the continents beyond.

In 1666, La Salle was given a feudal grant of land at La Chine, on the St. Lawrence River, by the Sulpicians, who administered Montréal. He spent the first couple of years on his small holding in New France, it appears, peaceably studying the languages of the peoples round about. He had long dreamed of going to those places described in the *Relations,* and beyond. But it was in his second year in New France that he heard of wonders that peculiarly stirred his heart.

His sources were a group of Seneca, down from their strongholds inland for the annual trade fair at Montréal. They perhaps camped on or near La Salle's land. Speaking in the language of the Long House, he questioned the Seneca about their homeland, lying in hostile south-westerly territory, hence still shrouded from European eyes by mystery. The vision given him portrayed "a country so abundant in roebucks and wild cattle that they were as thick as the woods and so great a number of tribes that there could not possibly be more."

But yet more enticing to the young adventurer was the oft-told story of what lay beyond the western bounds of the realm controlled by the League. It had to do with what the Seneca called the Beautiful River, that "had its course to the West and at the end of which, after seven or eight months' traveling . . . the land was 'cut,' that is to say, according to their manner of speaking, the river fell into the sea."

The movements of La Salle for the next few years will probably remain cloaked in mystery forever. He was not at La Chine, nor did he return to France. Inspired by his Seneca friends, perhaps even invited by them, he may have made the journey upriver to Lake Ontario and into dangerous League-controlled territory. During his two-year absence, La Salle had time to reach, by lake, portage and overland, the upper reaches of the Mississippi River. We simply do not know. When he came back, he brought with him no surviving map or diary to suggest where his questing mind had taken him.

But when he returned to his estate at Ville-Marie, the studious and disciplined La Salle at last found the treasure of a kindred spirit, who was to become a mentor and sponsor of singular importance in the westward expansion of New France.

La Salle's new friend, a newcomer to these parts, bore the flourishing name of Louis de Buade, Comte de Frontenac.

Born near Paris in 1620 into an aristocratic Protestant family, Frontenac adored the extravagant luxuries of Versailles, where (like other noble spongers) he lived when not sallying forth in Louis XIV's battles of empire. But he tended to forget the little matter of paying bills, which continually dragged him into inconvenient trouble with creditors. He needed a place to get away from them. Frontenac was a vain flatterer much to the King's taste; and it was almost certainly exuberant flattery, not any sign of native ability, that kept landing him jobs at a safe distance from home. In 1669, he went off with Venetian forces defending Crete against the Turks, only to get himself thrown out of the army for conspiring against his superiors. Back in France, and once again seeking refuge from creditors, he was finally awarded, in 1672, a job that would take him, possibly forever, away from the bill collectors hounding him: the governorship of New France.

On the face of it, the appointment of Frontenac to so important a post seems absurd, and doomed to disaster. When his ship cast off from La Rochelle in June, 1672, he probably had very little idea where he was going. One can only imagine the dismay of such a fop upon arriving in Québec with an impressive royal commission in hand and walking into his dirty little headquarters in a frontier fur-trading town about as far from *grand* as a veteran of Versailles could imagine.

Sudden adversity preceded by high hopes can be devastating. In the case of the Comte de Frontenac, surprisingly, it turned out to be sobering, even tonic. His arrival in a remote backwater summoned forth a strength of mind and character that had been hitherto hidden behind frills and flattery. By the time of his death at Québec, twenty-five years later, he had justly earned honour as the most effective, active ruler of New France since Champlain and creator of a grand strategy for French expansion into the heart of the American continent that would frustrate the expansionist dreams of both the British arriving and multiplying in New England and the more powerful forces of the Long House People.

Like La Salle, he had heard the bewitching call of the Beautiful River. He believed the old stories that had been circulating since the time of Cartier: how the headwaters of the transcontinental river lay far to the southwest of Ville-Marie, and how a boat set loose upon those waters would be borne by the current to the Western Ocean, and the gates of China, Japan and Tartary. With good sense that might have surprised his old friends at the court of Louis XIV, the Comte de Frontenac hit on a two-step approach. First, he dispatched Louis Joliet, a Canadian-born explorer, and the Jesuit missionary Jacques Marquette to travel down the Great Lakes and chart the way to the upper tributaries of what they believed to be the Beautiful River. This, they accomplished in June, 1673.

But instead of leaving Ville-Marie as the usual western departure point for the continental interior, Frontenac decided to move the very boundaries of La Nouvelle France southwest, up the St. Lawrence to Lake Ontario. This was his second, and more original, approach, and one that was to bring permanent European settlement at last to the shores of the Great Lakes.

By this time, Frontenac had taken La Salle into his entourage as a kind of right-hand man for this adventure. Of course, La Salle knew the languages of the Long House People. And his travels of the late 1660s, wherever they took him, had left him with an air of authority about what lay in the continental interior. So it was, in 1673, that Frontenac ordered La Salle to strike out on the first, diplomatic part of the mission. He was to go to Onondaga, stronghold of the grand council of the League (and today in New York State), to herald the governor's visit.

Despite the thaw in French-League relations since Champlain's calamitous misalliances, La Salle's mission was still dangerous. The People of the Long House were skeptical. But then Frontenac showed both his flair and his courage. According to La Salle's biographer Frances Gaither, the 120 canoes of the governor came into Cataraqui Bay—the site of present-day Kingston—"mounted with cannon and brightly painted to impress the savages. Presumably, too, La Salle was at hand when Frontenac next day gave audience to his two hundred most ancient and influential Iroquois seated on sailcloth before the gubernatorial tent."

The meeting was a triumph for the French. During all the courtly carrying-on, Frontenac kept firmly focused on the real reason he was there: to gain undisturbed access to the waters of Lake Ontario, between the western frontiers of New France and the mysterious, vast southwest, where the French (apart from the odd straggler like Étienne Brûlé, and perhaps La Salle) had not dared go before. As the biographer tells us:

> Louis de Buade, Comte de Frontenac, might appear in the bright contemporary annals of Paris a man to whom had been given a colonial government to deliver him from his wife's imperious temper and, since he was completely ruined, to keep him from starving to death. But here in the Canadian woods he presented a dazzling figure: fifty-two years old, sophisticated, warm in his loves and his hates, a man of the courts equally at ease in the wilderness; an aristocrat with a sure instinct for governing savages . . .
>
> While the count charmed the Iroquois elders with his oratory, fondled the children and fed them prunes and raisins and made

gifts to the women when they danced for him, his engineers traced out the outlines of the fort; the work of clearing was speedily got under way; and during the last days of July [1673] log palisades were firmly planted.

The first great, westward political step of Old Europe into the northern reaches of the New World had been taken. Nothing would ever be the same in Ontario again.

Over the first decade of the place that was to become Kingston, La Salle demolished and replaced the thrown-up earthworks and wooden palisade with light grey local limestone. Nearby, as usual, a civilian village was springing up, for trade and worship. But if it got off to a good start, the western outpost of New France was to have a rocky future. The economy was always uncertain, due to the shifting relations between the League and the French, then the entry of the British into the fray over furs. In 1688, the whole experiment almost collapsed under League attack, but by 1695 that protracted season of cold and hot war was over, and Frontenac fortified and restored the fort, then invited a new wave of settlers to go there.

By that time, La Salle had already gone off into the interior, which was the count's real target. He had got on well with the League folk he knew at Fort Cataraqui, who turned out to be not as vicious and vile as he had been led to believe by the thrilling Jesuit *Relations* he had read as a boy. His greater tension was with the Jesuits working south of Lake Ontario.

They had no doubts concerning the education of Indians in the French manner. La Salle wanted to found in the North American wilderness—perhaps in that very river valley that he tenaciously, if still secretly, claimed for his own—"a new Paraguay" after the model that their Portuguese brethren had set up in the South American pampas and forests, a realm where, with the vices of white men proscribed, the natives could be recruited as perfect Christians.

But La Salle was soon to be beyond the compounds of the Jesuits and all else familiar. In 1681, he set sail from Fort Frontenac with

Gabriel Ribourde, Zenobe Membre and the Franciscan priest Louis Hennepin in a little ship that thus became the first of the Great Lakes ships. (Hennepin's narrative of the expedition was the inspiration for James Fenimore Cooper's tale *The Pathfinder.*)

La Salle had a little of the old adventurer in him, but he was more clearly a child of the Modern Age than any of the inland travellers who had preceded him. Louis Hennepin, later La Salle's Boswell and nemesis, was, in contrast, a relic from an earlier age of adventure—closer in spirit and rough style to Brûlé, whom, one imagines, he would have liked.

Father Hennepin loved to portray himself as a fearless adventurer for Christ and an explorer quite as daring as La Salle in the inward voyage along Lake Erie, and far west and south. After La Salle's murder in Texas, he even claimed to have discovered the mouth of the Mississippi years before the expedition's leader. He did not; but he could have.

The priest had been born in Belgium in 1626 to a modestly well-off family. As a lad of seventeen, he joined the Franciscans and began his itinerant religious training, which took him through several European countries, ending up with a sojourn at Calais. "My greatest passion," he wrote, "was to hear the stories ships' captains told of their long voyages . . . I would have spent entire days and nights without sleeping, listening to them, because I always learned something new." Following his curious nose, as he was to do throughout his career, Father Hennepin arrived in Québec in 1675, and shortly thereafter, at Ville-Marie, encountered La Salle, who was returning from France with patents of nobility, a deed from the King to the fort and rights to the seigneurie of Cataraqui.

Exactly how Father Hennepin continued his association with La Salle and was taken into his confidence—one imagines La Salle would have known better than to hang around with such vaultingly ambitious riff-raff—is not known. The only thing certain is that Father Hennepin made his way to La Salle's fortress at Cataraqui, or Fort Frontenac, very soon after his arrival in New France. He worked there among the traders and trappers from the League nations, until the autumn of 1678, when he got what he had long awaited: an invitation from La Salle to come aboard the ship that was to take them all into the interior. In a book published some years later, Father Hennepin left us this description of his sighting of Niagara Falls, the first ever by a European:

> Betwixt the Lake Ontario and Erie, there is a vast and prodigious Cadence of Water which falls down after a surprising and astonishing manner, insomuch that the Universe does not afford its parallel. Tis true, Italy and Suedland boast some such Things; but we may well say they are but sorry Patterns, when compar'd to this of which we now speak. At the foot of this horrible Precipice, we meet with the River Niagara, which is not above a quarter of a League broad, but is wonderfully deep in some places. It is so rapid above this Descent, that it violently hurries down the wild Beasts while endeavouring to pass it to feed on the other side, they not being able to withstand the force of its Current, which inevitably casts them above Six hundred foot high. . . .

The crew then built a ship called the *Griffin*, much larger than the boat that had taken them across Lake Ontario, and set off on the long voyage up the Great Lakes and down to the Gulf of Mexico. But La Salle's adventures or his dismal death in Texas at the hands of his disillusioned men need no detailed description here. By the time he died, La Salle had established the claims of the king of France to all lands drained by the Mississippi

River, inspired by the hope of laying the foundations for a French empire on American soil.

The explorers and creators of New France died one of the two deaths that most explorers do: by violent hands or in obscurity. The first of these fates came to La Salle; the second was reserved for Father Hennepin. After publishing his second infamous travelogue, in 1697, in which he claimed also to have explored the Mississippi Valley to the Gulf of Mexico, he disappeared into the bustle of Baroque Rome and was never heard of again.

But by that time, La Nouvelle France had attained the fullest extent of its existence, or near-existence. It was fragile, ephemeral. It could have lasted, but it did not. Ontario could have been part of the common-wealth, but it was not. But that story belongs in the next chapter.

12
THE LOST WORLD

Throughout the year 1999, big cities and little towns across the state of Louisiana threw gumbo cookouts and zydeco concerts, hosted family reunions of people named Landry, Boudreaux and Leger, presented exhibitions and generally made merry. The celebration was to mark the 300th anniversary of the day—Mardi Gras, 1699—when French civilization came to this southernmost place in the immense valley of the Mississippi River. It was on that Tuesday before Ash Wednesday, and the start of Christendom's solemn fast, when the Montréal-born adventurer Pierre Le Moyne d'Iberville and his crew from the northernmost reaches of La Nouvelle France paddled their longboat up the river against heavy winds until the grassy, brackish swamp bounding it congealed into a sturdy mud bank solid enough to stand on, where he then claimed all the lands drained by the river for the king of France. It was a repeat performance of La Salle's gesture on another, more northern part of the great river, when, in April, 1682, he, too, planted the fleur-de-lis.

The terrain where Iberville landed, near the Mississippi's mouth, was then, as now, so much mud, willows, scrub oaks, populated by egrets and alligators and venomous snakes—hardly an inviting place to start building an empire, at least by modern lights. But Iberville had been chosen by the king of France precisely because he was a frontiersman who knew nothing of Paris apart from rumour, and everything about the wild new land; and he would not turn finicky at the sight of the vast bleakness that others had found along the Gulf coast.

The explorer christened his landing place Pointe du Mardi Gras—a name that has clung a long time to a certain mudlump on the eastern bank of the Mississippi, even though the shifting course of the river long ago obscured the precise site of Iberville's landing. According to Louisiana legend, mass was celebrated by a Franciscan missionary in the company, the ancient, majestic hymn *Te Deum* chanted and a monumental cross raised. All we know for sure is what Iberville relates in his diary. Snakes, wind and mud notwithstanding, the hardened explorer wrote: "Lying on those reeds, we felt sheltered from the bad weather, [and] the pleasure of seeing ourselves protected from an evident peril."

Louisiana's harsh welcome to the first Frenchmen to set foot on its southernmost tip soon softened, and within only a few years French colonists were spreading along the tropical waterways sprawling over the territory, bringing their notions of law, economics and the arts of daily living. Around 1715, two cities were founded in this tropical zone of New France: Natchitoches, far up the Red River, a tributary of the Mississippi, and New Orleans. The old French influence in Louisiana was given fresh impetus, and a new complexion, in the 1750s with the arrival of the Acadians, deported from Maritime Canada by English settlers. For a moment a vision of North America, completely different from all that actually appeared, glowed on the continental map, and had the vision not passed as rapidly and decisively as it did I would be writing very different stories about Ontario, in French.

Iberville's mission of 1699 "was the start of an imperial design, meant to get control of the Mississippi's drainage basin for fur-trapping and trading," according to Louisiana archaeologist and historian

Dennis Jones. "Had things gone according to plan, the English would have only held on to lands between the Appalachians and the Atlantic, and Québec and New Orleans would have been two ends of a once-possible empire."

Had that empire matured and endured, Ontario would have been a part of it. The Great Lakes cities of Toronto and Kingston, Niagara-on-the-Lake and Sarnia and Windsor would still exist, though French-speaking and with different names, and with a very much smaller role to play in the political scheme of things. As we have seen, the French had ideas about colonization that differed from those of the English. In a francophone Ontario that was merely a place in a continental French commonwealth, Toronto would almost surely have remained a terminal for the inland beaver and lumber industries, gathering the interior riches of the continent and shipping them downriver to the huge metropolis of Montréal.

By the end of the eighteenth century, the old, monarchical name of La Nouvelle France would likely have been displaced by Québec as the territory grew and prospered, and (like the English colonies before

1776) gradually become increasingly remote from the old order of Europe, and attentive to the voices of Enlightenment. Then, with the Revolution of 1789 in France and the final breakaway of the European nation's New World colonies from the metropolitan centre, *La République du Québec* (as it might have been styled) would today have comprehended a tremendous territory arcing across *Amérique du Nord* from the Bay of Fundy to New Orleans.

On Mardi Gras, 1699, this future was possible. It was perhaps even probable, given the weakness of Britain's North American colonies.

The vision of a vast francophone realm in North America continued to stay alight in the colonial imagination for a couple of generations after Iberville, until snuffed out forever by France's defeat on the Plains of Abraham, the transfer of the Mississippi Valley from France to Spain in 1763 and the sale of the whole territory south of Canada to the United States in 1803. But it was a vision that had already left an indelible trace on the soil and imagination of Louisiana, where the old French presence lives on in speech and architecture, in the durable Mediterranean exoticism of New Orleans, in the memories that linger even today among knowledgeable visitors to the muddy spot called Pointe du Mardi Gras.

The reason things did not turn out as imagined by Iberville, or his superiors in Québec, or his king, lay in London and Paris and in their centuries-old enmity, not in the New World. Even before Britain became a serious contender for rule over the Atlantic seaways, France and Britain were at each other's throats, engaged in fabulously intricate squabbles about who got to rule what in Europe. The details of these conflicts are of no consequence to the story of Ontario and, anyway, I don't really understand the Pragmatic Sanction of 1713, though it seems to have gotten both France and England very hot and bothered. Two things about all this count in our story.

One is that this endless quarrelling in Europe heralded the beginning of the end of La Nouvelle France, as it could have become and remained.

The other is that Ontario was too far west and inland for many of these squabbles to matter, at least during the first half of the eighteenth century. Montréal was in busy commerce with the rest of the world, up to date on all the news of warfare and threats and alarms in Europe, as the great powers fought it out. But Ontario remained, for the most part, a vast woodland from which the beaver and muskrat were harvested and skinned by native French or Canadian-born adventurers and voyageurs and their comrades among the old Ontario nations. These untethered wilderness folk shipped the pelts down the Ottawa River each year, got their pay, spent a few weeks in wild revelry, then vanished into the wilderness that was their true and only home. They were wild folk, after their fashion. And their aristocratic French governors, it seems, took almost no interest in what they did.

The records we have from these times paint a rather charming picture of Parisians in the wilderness, where both the French and the Indian nations had been transformed by the beaver trade into rough, tolerant people. None followed the rules too carefully; all traded more or less with whom they liked—with the French settled downriver at Montréal and Québec, for the most part, but also with the English frontiersmen setting up trading posts at Oswego and other points in historic League territory along the south shores of the St. Lawrence River and Lake Ontario.

Before the end of New France had come into view, this apparent lack of loyalty by the voyageurs—French or aboriginal, but mostly mixed, and French-speaking—did occasionally discomfit the French governors sent out from Paris to oversee the colonies. In 1741, the Governor General came before the leadership of the Ottawa nation, gathered at Mackinac, to report on his recent trip to Paris and to express His Majesty's concern over the feckless ways of his forest subjects. What follows is a shortened version of his long, quaintly ignorant speech.

. . . The point in question at present, my Children, is to settle you in a place where you may find good land capable of yielding profitable crops, in order to enable you to procure subsistence for your families and retain your hunting grounds . . . Choose, my

Children, that one of all the places that suits you, and reflect well upon the matter. Remember the advantages you have enjoyed in being near the French, who buy your canoes, your gum, your Indian corn, your fats, and all that your industry produces; this enables you to live more comfortably with your families, and you would not enjoy those advantages if you were far away from them. . . .

I have learned, my Children, that you went to [the British garrison at] Oswego to get bad milk. There is good milk here. Why do you not come and get it since you like it so much? You have never been refused any and my Breasts are full. I will make them flow with pleasure when their milk does not spoil the minds of my Children, and I will give you tokens of my friendship for you and your villages.

The unravelling began in earnest in 1740, when the kings of England and France went to war in yet another dispute over who would rule what. But while earlier European wars had prompted outbreaks of strife between New World British and French forces, this war quickly became a broader and more intense conflict for empire. By the autumn of 1748, when the great powers decided to come to terms with each other and call off the dogs of war, the contentions of the peace treaty had less to do with who got to rule what than who owned New France's Atlantic outposts of Louisbourg, Cape Breton and Île St-Jean, all seized by the British.

The treaty was a saw-off. Louisbourg went back to France, and the British got Acadia, which comprised the present-day provinces of New Brunswick, Nova Scotia and Prince Edward Island. As for Ontario, it was too far west, inland and underpopulated to matter, at least so far. But soon enough, the conflict came here. The settlers in the British colonies south of La Nouvelle France were land-hungry. After a century of being peopled and farmed by new waves of immigrants from England and Scotland, land along the seaboard was running out, and the great westward push of the British North Americans was on.

In 1749, the British granted sixty thousand acres of land in the Ohio Valley to their American colonists, though it was already under official French reign. The Marquis de la Galissonière, governor of La Nouvelle France, sent his military aide Céloron de Blainville into the Ohio Valley to reassert the rights of France to the territory and warn off the British from trafficking in French land. It was already too late.

Yet the French hung on. The following year, with catastrophe closing in, Galissonière wrote that

> motives of honour, glory and religion forbid the abandonment of an established Colony; the surrender to themselves, or rather to a nation inimical by taste, education and religious principle, of the French who have emigrated thither at the persuasion of the Government with the expectation of its protection, and who eminently deserve it on account of their fidelity and attachment; in fine, the giving up of so salutary a work as that of the conversion of the heathen who inhabit that vast Continent.

The French had never tried to settle the land with farmfolk, earnestly and thickly, as the British had done along the Atlantic seaboard. Their concept of colonization was to create a few metropolitan centres, from which the exploitation of natural resources would be directed systematically and decorously by French aristocrats. But given the encroachment of the British and uncertainties about the Canadians, the Governor General declares himself ready to rush settlers into Louisiana, as the region drained by the Mississippi was called, with promises of "fertile lands, forests of mulberry trees, mines already discovered, etc." At the same time, the marquis recommends to his masters in Paris that Canada be regarded as "a barren frontier, such as the Alps are to Piedmont, as Luxembourg would be to France, and as it, perhaps, is to the Queen of Hungary . . ." Poor Canada! But even though it is a troublesome rump of empire, the region must be kept. As Galissonière declared:

It cannot be denied that this Colony has been always a burthen to France, and it is probable that such will be the case for a long while; but it constitutes, at the same time, the strongest barrier that can be opposed to the ambition of the English.

To strengthen this barricade, French officers sailed by a dismal, foggy stretch of the long, impenetrably forested northern shoreline of Lake Ontario in 1750, in search of a redoubt against English incursion from the south. Its main attractions were a deep harbour enclosed by a low circle of sand and fresh water at the mouth of this lagoon. The place was christened Fort Rouillé.

There was actually little to fear. Even at this late date, British power extended only a short way inland from the Atlantic seaboard. It is faintly surprising to find that Fort William Henry, established just north of present-day Schenectady, was Britain's most northerly inland outpost on the North American continent a decade before the Revolution. (Speaking of the fort: As every American schoolchild knows—if American schoolchildren read history books any longer— William Henry was the setting for James Fenimore Cooper's *Last of the Mohicans,* and also the site of some of the most horrible massacres of the American Revolution.)

This lack of danger on the Great Lakes helps explain the character of Fort Rouillé. In popular imagination, a *fort* still suggests a large defensible edifice, grandly planted beside some river or ocean to keep out invaders. The fort built by the French in the twilight of their rule over Ontario was nothing more than a military trading post manned by about ten soldiers and a few straggling traders who lived in the vicinity of the camp and carried on the fur trade. Nevertheless, the French militia were the first Europeans to set up any sort of official outpost on the site of Toronto.

From that time until the end of French rule came, a few years later, Toronto was never more than a tributary of the far more significant emplacements at Fort Frontenac (present-day Kingston) and at Fort Niagara. Even during the so-called Seven Years' War, which had actually been simmering and flickering for decades between France and Britain for the ownership of North America, the little fort was unimportant; and in 1759, when France lost the Battle of the Plains of Abraham, and the hope of a great future for France in North America was finally extinguished, the fifteen troops stationed at Fort Rouillé torched the fort, and retreated east to Montréal.

The burnt-out ruins of what local folk called "the old French fort" were still visible in the late nineteenth century, on what is now the grounds of the Canadian National Exhibition. Today, they are gone, along with the smoky haze from the fires that consumed the fort and ended the French world that could have been.

IN 1867, A FOURTEEN-YEAR-OLD LAD named Edward Lee, helping his father clear trees not far from the Ottawa River, found an astrolabe buried in the earth. A scoundrel named Captain Cowley offered Lee ten dollars for the navigational instrument. The boy saw neither the money nor the astrolabe ever again. After many changes of hands, the astrolabe ended up in the collection of the New-York Historical Society, where it remained until its acquisition by the Canadian Museum of Civilization in 1989.

There are many reasons to believe the astrolabe found by young Edward was lost in May, 1613, by Samuel de Champlain during a particularly rough portage in the district where it was found. It certainly dates from the early seventeenth century, and is French.

Never mind about the technicalities of how astrolabes work. It is a device used to discover where one is. Its discovery reminds us of where Champlain was, at that moment, near the village of Cobden, Ontario, when the astrolabe went missing.

It did not happen in Ontario at all, nor in Canada, as we understand it now. It happened in New France—a place without the violent, tormented and venerable history of Old France, without its disgraces and ossified institutions, without its magnificence. New France—the very words speak to us of a reality, immense and beautiful, long past— tenuous even at its height, in the years after Champlain; never densely populated, never tightly held under military control, only dotted here and there along its glorious waterways with fairgrounds for trading furs and with forts. But New France was, for those who dreamed it and created it and settled it, a reality destined to shine brightly, like the world's new creation. The astrolabe is a souvenir from that dream, and from that lost world.

III
THE WORLD UPSIDE DOWN

13
MISS MOLLY'S WAR

Molly Brant, whom everyone called Miss Molly, was forty and comfortably established on the Mohawk River near Albany, New York, in 1776, when the shot heard not much farther than the outskirts of tiny Concord, Massachusetts, was fired and the dismantling of her world began.

Like all other British subjects in the North American colonies, whatever their loyalties, she had known this day might come. The discontent with British rule had been gathering momentum rapidly in her neighbourhood since the spring of 1775, when an anti-British militia assembled along the Mohawk. By early summer of that year, citizens began to desert the valley, which seemed destined to come under fire if revolutionary war broke out. Others, including Molly Brant, decided to stay put. The valley of the Mohawk was her home and she was determined to remain there, as loyal to the Crown as ever.

Many Englishwomen, finding themselves caught between loyalties in the colony of New York, stuck as firmly as Miss Molly to their royalist beliefs—though none with more ferocity than Molly Brant.

She had been born to Christian Mohawk parents in 1736 and raised in the important village of Canajoharie, some sixty kilometres up the Mohawk River from Albany. It was her good fortune to be born female in a culture where being a woman brought instant advantage. As Dekanawida had decreed centuries before, the stability of the Great Peace rested with the women of the League. To them belonged the power to install and depose the male standard-bearers, to parcel out farmland and veto the decisions of warriors. Born to be political, Miss Molly began her apprenticeship in leadership when she was only eighteen, as a member of a delegation sent to Philadelphia to nego-tiate land matters on behalf of the League with the British colonial administration.

But in the middle years of the eighteenth century, disputes between the English and the member nations of the Great Peace were uncommon. The hostility of the Long House People toward the French had served the British well, during imperial military campaigns and skirmishes, and in lulls between. While the might of the League had been much diminished by Miss Molly's day, the relationships between the League and the British were cordial—and more than that. Nickus Brant, her Mohawk stepfather, had been European in manner, dress and language. His bright, ambitious daughter had grown up in colonial New York surrounded by important English friends of the family. Though she spoke the Mohawk language all her life, her natural culture was English for most, though not all, her days.

As Miss Molly was coming of age in genial surroundings, a distin-guished gentleman named William Johnson was doing quite well for himself a few kilometres downriver. Like so many well-connected men, from Maine to the Carolinas, he was snapping up huge land grants and doing a brisk trade in property and household goods with his neigh-bours, both British and aboriginal. He had spun an interesting social and political network around himself during his tenure as New York's royal representative in dealings with the aboriginal nations. Sir William's high standing among all the peoples who lived along the river was based, at least in part, on his courage on the battlefield. His knighthood had come as a reward for active military service to the Crown during the war that, in 1763, brought the reverie of New France to an end.

Sir William's wife had died young, and, for some time, writes a euphemizing Victorian biographer, "he illustrated in his own life the injury to morals which war, especially when successful, usually causes." In simpler language: he had mistresses. By the lights and standards of his day, Sir William was a decent enough man and a competent administrator, and he was no greedier for intimate companionship than most people. After begetting children on housekeepers, parlourmaids and such, he honourably admitted his paternity to all his offspring and assumed responsibility for their upkeep.

In the course of his duties as Indian administrator, he came to know and then befriended an outstanding Mohawk of Canajoharie named Joseph Brant. It was not long after the forging of this friendship that Sir William met Joseph's sister, Molly.

According to a twice-told tale, he fell in love with her at a military muster. For fun, the girl found an officer who would let her ride behind him. "To his surprise," continues an account, "she leaped like a wild-cat upon the space behind the saddle, holding on tightly, with hair flying and garments flapping, while the excited horse dashed over the parade ground. The crowd enjoyed the sight; but the most interested spectator was Sir William, who, admiring her spirit, resolved to make her his paramour."

In 1759, Molly gave birth to their first child. The father, at forty-four almost twice his young mistress's age, willingly turned over to her the running of his ample, dignified Georgian seat outside Fort Johnson, the toting up of the domestic accounts, the oversight of his house and field slaves and even the running of the Indian Affairs department when he was away on business. She bore him eight children before his death in 1774.

A contemporary witness has left us an account of the convivially hectic goings-on at Johnson Hall in Miss Molly's heyday—and, incidentally, an attractive vignette of an English colonial backwater before the American Revolution. The place, he tells us, was "a kind of open house" for all comers—aboriginal, European, anybody.

The gentlemen and ladies breakfasted in their respective rooms, and, at their option, had either tea, coffee, or chocolate, or if an old rugged veteran wanted a beef-steak, a mug of ale, a glass of brandy, or some grog, he called for it, and it always was at his service. The freer people made, the more happy was Sir William. After breakfast, while Sir William was about his business, his guests entertained themselves as they pleased. Some rode out, some went out with guns, some with fishing-tackle, some saun- tered about the town, some played cards, some backgammon, some billiards, some pennies, and some even at nine-pins. Thus was each day spent until the hour of four, when the bell punctu- ally rang for dinner, and all assembled. He had besides his own family, seldom less than ten, sometimes thirty. All were welcome. All sat down together. All was good cheer, mirth, and festivity. Sometimes seven, eight, or ten, of the Indian Sachems [chief men] joined the festive board. His dinners were plentiful. They consisted, however, of the produce of his estate, or what was procured from the woods and rivers, such as venison, bear, and fish of every kind, with wild turkeys, partridges, grouse, and quails in abundance. No jellies, creams, ragouts, or syllabubs graced his table. His liquors were Madeira, ale, strong beer, cider, and punch. Each guest chose what he liked, and drank as he pleased. The company, or at least a part of them, seldom broke up before three in the morning. Every one, however, Sir William included, retired when he pleased. There was no restraint.

Though we would like it to be, this is not a wholly accurate picture of Molly Brant's place in the world. Love has never been strong enough to conquer the stubborn reality—the urgency, the pandemic pres- ence—of racism in the heritage of English-speaking people. Writing many years after Sir William's death, an observer, obviously devoted to drawing a favourable picture of this lady, has left on his easel a typically mixed portrait of Sir William's beloved and charming companion.

> Mary [*sic*] Brant, though not only an Indian, but a Mohawk Indian in spirit, was to her dying day, in the old English and Hebrew sense of the word, a virtuous woman. She had the virile qualities of worth, excellence, and abilities, and not only managed her household to the satisfaction of her lord, but kept herself well informed and interested in the two worlds in which lived the people of the Long House and those of Christendom. More than one English lady visiting at the Hall was surprised to find this Iroquois woman so cultivated, refined, and alert, not only with womanly intuition, but equipped with information as to the life and thoughts in which they and their husbands moved.

This same writer goes on to say the "brown Lady Johnson" was "virtuous" not *because* she was Mohawk but *despite* her heritage. There is no acknowledgement that Miss Molly, unlike the "surprised" English ladies who dropped by Johnson Hall, had been reared from birth to be a leader. Sir William, as well, gave her only civil regard in public; nothing more. Though the couple apparently enjoyed a tender private relationship throughout their years together, and Miss Molly had assimilated European ways as much as anyone else who lived under the roof of Johnson Hall, Sir William never married her.

In his will, he left Molly and their eight children financially secure. But Miss Molly, still in her thirties, was hardly a woman to sit still and enjoy the stature of a popular widow. When the house she had lovingly tended passed by inheritance to Sir William's legitimate son John, Molly and her children moved the short distance back to her home town of Canajoharie, where she promptly set up a trading post to serve the local Mohawk community.

We can only imagine how her life might have unfolded from that time on, had life gone on as before in the Crown colony of New York. But it's not hard to predict. Molly Brant had a head for business and a

definite sense of her own worth—vital ingredients that would prob-ably have quickly turned her local emporium into a mercantile empire along the Mohawk River, and perhaps far beyond. Had that good fortune come her way, she would have stayed in New York all her days, being the English lady and shrewd businesswoman she was. She would never have come to Ontario to live, and so would not be in this book. The American Revolution changed everything for Molly Brant, as it did for myriad subjects, loyal and rebel, throughout Britain's American colonies. But even so drastic a challenge to her loyalties and sense of duty need not have catapulted her into the midst of revolutionary politics. She could have stayed out of the struggle for power and perhaps lived on at Canajoharie forever.

Many other members of the League of the Great Peace were inclined to do so. As revolutionary violence began to break out across the colonies south of Canada, the male leaders of the League hit on a position of neutrality, apparently because they sensibly regarded the conflict as a family quarrel, British against British, hence none of their concern.

At least two members of the League—Molly Brant and her brother Joseph—considered the Revolution very much the concern of the Indian nations. Molly chose sides without a moment's hesitation, and decided to let the leader of the rebellion know what was on her mind. In a letter written in 1776, the secretary of George Washington noted:

> This morning we were honored with a visit from the favorite of the late Sir William Johnson . . . She saluted us with an air of ease and politeness . . . The Indians pay her great respect and I am afraid her influence will give us some trouble . . .

Miss Molly made as much trouble for George Washington as she could. Together with her brother Joseph, she urged the League to revoke the treaty of neutrality with the Americans signed in 1777, and join the British struggle to retain the colonies, which they did.

The price exacted from the nations of the League for following the heroic urging of the Brants was blood, as fierce retaliation spread throughout the ancient League territories in upstate New York. At first, Molly did what she could in her home town, harbouring loyalist refugees and running guns to soldiers on the king's side. And there was to be no let-up for the mistress of Johnson Hall.

Late in 1777, she and her children, and a few slaves and servants, joined the widening river of League refugees being pushed north by advancing revolutionaries, over the border into the loyal colony of Ontario. It was in that disastrous year that she and her family arrived at Fort Niagara. But Molly Brant did not step into another version of the English world she had left. Something had happened. Deep inside this assimilated aboriginal woman, comfortable in English ways and language, and among English institutions, the Mohawk re-emerged. From society hostess and administrator for Sir William Johnson, she turned into the clan matron—one of those women whose ancient constitutional tasks included assuring the continuity and coherence of the Great Peace. Two years later, Daniel Claus, son-in-law to Sir William, who also fled to Niagara-on-the-Lake, dispatched an account of her plight and urgent activities to the British general Haldimand. Before leaving the valley, Molly was

> insulted and robbed of everything she had in the World by the Rebels and their Indians, which they said she deserved for giving us Intelligence of their Motions which occasioned their being surprised and defeated . . . [W]hen she was obliged to leave her home and flee for her and children's safety to the Five Nations . . . she was happily assisted by her brother Joseph & askd to stay but Cayuga being more centrical and having some distant Relations there, she fixed herself & family at the principal Chiefs home.
>
> Upon the news of General Burgoyne's disaster [the defeat and surrender of the British military leader at Saratoga, New York, in the summer of 1777], she found the five Nations very wavering and unstable and even the head Man of the Senecas Cayengwraghton, with whom she had a pointed conversation in Publick Council at Canadasegey, reminding him of the former great Friendship & attachment which subsisted between him and the late Wm Johnson, whose memory she never mentions but with Tears in her Eyes, which affects Indians greatly, and to whom, continued she, he so often declared and promised to live and die a firm Friend and Ally to the King of England . . .
>
> In the end, Miss Molly's "striking Arguments and reasonings," had so great an impact on the chief that he and his fellow leaders promised her faithfully to stick up strictly to the Engagements of her late worthy Friend, and for his sake and her sake espouse the Kings Cause vigorously, and steadily avenge her Wrongs & Injuries, for she is in every respect considered & esteemed by them as Sr Wms Relict [widow] and one word from her is more

taken Notice of by the Five Nations than a thousand from any White Man without Exception.

Throughout the years of war, Miss Molly shuttled between the encampments of displaced and often destitute League warriors and refugees at Niagara-on-the-Lake and Montréal, encouraging and inspiring loyalty among these thousands. Her brother Joseph had provided what political leadership he could. But Miss Molly reminded the League of its great past and integrity, the dignity of its people, the worthiness of their recent alliances with honourable Englishmen such as her late companion. Observing a sizeable Six Nations force assembled at Carleton Island, the fort commander recognized that "their uncommon good behaviour [was] in great measure to be ascribed to Miss Molly Brant's influence over them, which [was] far superior to that of all their Chiefs put together."

In 1783 the Treaty of Paris acknowledged the independence of Britain's former American colonies and set the legal bounds between the new Republic and the old Empire. In the end, however, the League was left to work out the future of its people wherever they found themselves at the war's end. Both Joseph and Molly Brant campaigned to assure land for the Nations of the League. At the conclusion of these negotiations, the Mohawk who had fled to Montréal were settled on the Bay of Quinte, while those who had taken refuge at Fort Niagara accompanied Joseph Brant to the Grand River, where their descendants live to this day. Later, the colonial administration in Canada also set aside land on the site of old Fort Cataraqui, established by Frontenac and La Salle a century before, when all the world was different.

Molly Brant decided to end her days not among the League members settled on secure Ontario reserves but in Kingston. With her war work as Mohawk clan mother done, she retired back into the life of an English gentlewoman that she had lived from childhood, and that had been interrupted only briefly by her sense of loyalty and duty. On her military pension of £100 a year—a substantial amount in post-revolutionary America—Molly settled at Cataraqui. By late 1783, no house had yet been built for this distinguished patriot—a matter of some embarrassment for the fort commander, when it got out that Miss Molly was still living in barracks. It was completed the next year.

Ensconced there, her spirited presence remains clearly in historical sight. Back in Schenectady in 1785 on legal business, she was offered the opportunity to return to the United States, and money to do so—a proposition to which she replied, according to a witness, "with the utmost contempt." From the end of the Revolution until the end of her life, she persisted in the life she was born to. In the summer of 1793, following a ball at York, the primitive capital of the recently created province of Upper Canada, a certain General Lincoln noted in his diary:

> They danced from 7 o'clock until 11, when supper was announced, and served in very pretty style. The music and dancing were good; everything conducted with propriety. What excited the best feelings of the heart was the ease and affection with which the ladies met each other, although there were a number present whose mothers sprang from the aborigines of the country. They appeared as well dressed as the company in general and intermixed with them in a manner which evinced at once the dignity of their own minds and the good sense of others. These ladies possessed great ingenuity and industry, and have great merit, for the education they have received is owing principally to their own industry, as their father, Sir William Johnson, was dead. Their mother was the noted Mohawk Princess, Molly Brant . . .

She worshipped at St. George's Anglican Church in Kingston for the remainder of her life, which ended in 1796. A visitor to the church noted seeing "an Indian woman, who sat in an honorable place among the English. She appeared very devout during Divine Service and very attentive to the Sermon . . ." The woman was, as the traveller well knew, the famous Molly Brant—patriot, lady, warrior and as worthy a heroine as one can find in the long story of Ontario.

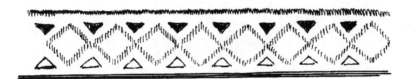

14
MUDDY YORK

THE JOURNEY OF ELIZABETH POSTHUMA GWILLIM to Toronto*
began in late September, 1791, when George III, King of England and
Elector of Hannover, received Elizabeth and her husband, John Graves
Simcoe, at Weymouth, in Dorset.

Elizabeth noted in her diary that His Majesty asked how she would
like being at sea—her reply is not recorded—and whether the children
were to be left in England for schooling. Domestic arrangements,
keeping a settled order to things—such matters interested this king,
who had never understood that the world was shaking under his feet.

That evening Mrs. Simcoe dined on corn-crake, a bird of the grain
fields. Upon finding in one of them "a sea shell as large as a nut," she
marvelled that some creatures could live merely by suction. The next
day, a storm blew up over the Channel. Watching it from her window,

---

* The Lake Ontario shoreline between the mouths of the Humber and Don Rivers
was called Toronto from ancient times through the French period. Lieutenant-
Governor Simcoe gave the town laid out upon the site the name of York. At its
incorporation in 1834, the city reverted to its ancient name, Toronto, by which it
has been known ever since.

Elizabeth found it "grand," but agreed with Queen Charlotte that it was "mixed with too much horror to be pleasing." At age twenty-five in 1791, and the daughter of great wealth, she belonged to a generation too young to be Romantics, but old enough to understand that one agreed with a queen's opinions about the marine weather.

The ship carrying the Simcoes to the New World departed Weymouth in heavy seas, which left Elizabeth prostrate with seasickness before England had disappeared behind her, and made the sailors "quite wet" after a window was blown in by the gale. She observed porpoises on October 7. Upon arriving at Niagara-on-the-Lake,* the

---

* Niagara-on-the-Lake, used throughout this book, designates the town established by Loyalists in the 1780s where the Niagara River empties into Lake Ontario. The capital of Upper Canada when Simcoe arrived, but abandoned once the construction of York had begun, the place has been known as Newark, Niagara and, most recently (and most unconfusingly), Niagara-on-the-Lake.

headquarters of Upper Canada and a glance away from the American Republic, she paid a visit to the Falls. She was nipped there by a mosquito, and did not see rattlesnakes. Her eyes were not greedily curious, like those of Father Louis Hennepin. She is a diarist who is observant, clear, specific, unoriginal—curious, but not astonished; engaged, but never losing a sense of herself in the wilderness, which God created not to amuse her or leave her wonder-struck, but to be organized.

Elizabeth was born to be an army wife, even as her husband was born to be a soldier of an empire. Colonel John Simcoe also knew where he was going, for he had been there before. He was a veteran of the botched war with the rebellious colonists south of Canada, a former captive allowed to return to England on parole. It had now become the job of John Graves Simcoe to govern a new place called Upper Canada, carved, earlier in 1791, from the western portions of Québec. There were not many Europeans who needed governing along the Great Lakes upstream from Montréal and Kingston. By his reckoning, the stretch of lakeshore between the Bay of Quinte, on the east, where Lake Ontario narrows until its waters empty into the St. Lawrence, and Burlington Bay—gleaming nowadays in the red flares of Hamilton's great steel mills—sheltered some fifteen families. There were also a few hunters and fishers of the Mississauga nation and the last of the old-time French fur traders.

But there was land lying back to the lake to be cleared and made productive and made attractive to colonists. But merely parcelling out land was only part of Simcoe's job, as he saw it. There was work to be done for empire and King and God in Upper Canada, by keeping the land quarantined from the democracy always threatening to boil over into what was left of His Majesty's American dominions.

Despite their energy and ambition, I almost left John and Elizabeth out of this book. John Simcoe is, to most Ontarians, I suspect, just somebody after whom Ontario towns, lakes and one public holiday are named. If there is any popular image of him, it is as the epitome of the stuffy Englishry that makes Ontario different from the United States, and presumably uninteresting. After all, he merely did his job. His

American contemporary Patrick Henry, on the other hand, was an interesting fanatic who gave firebrand speeches about liberty and death. Benjamin Franklin investigated lightning and invented things, while Elizabeth Simcoe played cards and attended little dances held at Niagara-on-the-Lake and Kingston and Toronto, unless her fingers got cold or bad news arrived, such as Marie Antoinette's meeting with the guillotine. Thomas Jefferson did architectural experiments, building and incessantly working on a philosophical temple called Monticello, until he went bankrupt. John Simcoe built muddy roads. Jefferson fantasized about reviving the ancient Roman republic on American soil, but Colonel Simcoe harboured no fantasies about anything, as far as we know. He was not remotely as exotic as Étienne Brûlé had been, or the strange, ascetic Champlain, or the Jesuits at Ste-Marie-Among-the-Hurons. His idea of success was finding a deep harbour and a trustworthy civil engineer. Though Ontario is not dull, and John Simcoe couldn't be blamed if it were, he and his entourage get the blame anyway.

Like many people in this book, John and Elizabeth are interesting because they were survivors of a lost world, or one disappearing quickly or gradually. They created Ontario more or less as it exists today: surely not La Nouvelle France, but just as definitely not the United States. John had been on this side of the Atlantic, Elizabeth never; but for this young couple America was a place on the far edge of the world, a destination at

Mrs Simcoe receives news of Marie Antoinette's execution. . . .

the end of a transoceanic passage still long and fearful. The war for the Thirteen Colonies was over, but the republic being cobbled together during ferocious debates among intellectuals and rich merchants to the south of Upper Canada was, if not really new, unlike anything anybody alive in Europe in 1791 had ever seen. The whole world was becoming utterly strange for people like the Simcoes.

True, a king still reigned in France, glumly rubber-stamping the edicts put before him by bureaucrats already plotting his death. When the Simcoes took up their post at Niagara-on-the-Lake (or Newark as it was known at the time), the Terror was about to sweep France, leaving all the old monarchies of Europe aghast and afraid. But every European who could read already knew the grim prophecies of Edmund Burke in his meditation *On the Revolution in France,* published the same year Upper Canada was created; and they all knew the Old World was finished, and that nothing would be the same again.

IF NIAGARA-ON-THE-LAKE HAD SEEMED, in 1763, to be a likely spot to plant the capital of Canada's western province—readily accessible by water from both Montréal and New York—the British side of the sublime river became the worst, least defensible place after the Revolution. So Lieutenant-Governor Simcoe began to look for a place that could be held in the likely event that rebels decided to go to war against their northern cousins.

Simcoe's first choice of a seat of government was in the southwest, at the forks of the Thames River, in an area that had only recently been ceded to the Crown by its owners. After the governor had returned from a sleigh ride to Detroit via London in 1792 with that remarkable Mohawk leader, Joseph Brant, Mrs. Simcoe noted in her diary that her husband was "confirmed in his opinion that the forks of the Thames is the most proper cite [*sic*] for the capital of the country, to be called New London on a fine dry plain without underwood but abounding in good oak trees."

But while London was defensible, it was also inaccessible from the fastest and most important technology of the British empire: the navy. Thus Simcoe's superior, Guy Carleton, Lord Dorchester, governor of what remained of Britain's former colonies on the Atlantic side of North America, vetoed the decision to go to London and, in the early spring of 1793, dispatched his Upper Canadian lieutenant to the site of Toronto, accompanied by seven officers.

The Lieutenant-Governor's plans for York became abruptly more urgent that summer, when Simcoe discovered his king and country at war with the republicans in France. He began to fear an attack by the two young republics, the French and the American, and so he decided to move his administration to Toronto at once.

In her diary for July 29, 1793, Elizabeth Simcoe tells of the move from Newark's little enclave of Englishry into the real wilderness with her usual attention to ceremony and pacing.

We were to sail for Toronto this morning, but the wind changed suddenly. We dined with the Chief Justice and were recalled from a walk at nine o'clock this evening as the wind had become fair. We embarked on board the "Mississaga," the band playing in the ship. It was dark, so I went to bed and slept until eight o'clock the next morning, when I found myself in the harbour of Toronto. We had gone under an easy sail all night, for as no person on board had been at Toronto, Mr. Bouchette was afraid to enter the harbour till day light, when St. John Rousseau, an Indian trader who lives near, came in a boat to pilot us.

This Jean-Baptiste Rousseau had long lived at the mouth of the Humber River, where, you may recall, Brûlé became the first European to see Lake Ontario. Rousseau was, for Mrs. Simcoe anyway, a pilot. Yet he hovers on the edges of the story of early Toronto like a slightly unreal phantom from the past, a remainder and reminder of the continental empire that never came to be. He traded with the Mississauga. In 1763, these Algonkian people, survivors of the League's wars for

Ontario, had lived along the north shore of Lake Ontario for several years and occupied by right of possession the harbour where Simcoe wished to erect his headquarters. The British wanted to be sure the spot was taken legally.

To that end, Lord Dorchester—who obviously already had the idea that the banks around the Humber might have some military useful-ness some day—had sent a deputation of loyal Seneca to Toronto harbour in the summer of 1788. It was met by Rousseau, who brokered the deal with the Mississauga. The agreed-on price was a little cash and a valuable heap of trading goods: two thousand gun flints, twenty-four brass kettles, ten dozen mirrors, two dozen laced hats, a bale of flowered flannel and ninety-six gallons of rum. British survey-ors did some preliminary plans for a town. Then the Seneca left, leaving Rousseau and his Mississauga clients unvisited for the next few years, until John and Elizabeth Simcoe came sailing into the harbour to establish a political presence—but also to cast a certain spell, having to do with Englishry and a mix of upper-class grace and philistinism that has not completely vanished to this day.

Lieutenant-Governor and Mrs. Simcoe, and their three children, made landfall at Toronto harbour on July 30, 1793.

For a few nights, they slept on ship; then the Queen's Rangers, dispatched by Simcoe, set about pitching camp.

Tues. 30th. The Queen's Rangers are encamped opposite to the ship. After dinner we went on shore to fix on a spot whereon to place the canvas houses and we chose a rising ground, divided by a creek from the camp, which is ordered to be cleared immediately. The soldiers have cut down a great deal of wood to enable them to pitch their tents. We went in a boat two miles to the bottom of the bay and walked thro' a grove of oaks, where the town is intended to be built. A low spit of land, covered with wood, forms the bay and breaks the horizon of the lake, which greatly improves the view, which indeed is very pleasing. The water in the bay is beautifully clear and transparent.

The place they chose was very near the site of old Fort Rouillé. After the French burned the fort and retreated to Montréal, the lakeside vegetation quickly retook possession of the land at the mouth of the Humber River, shrouding the ruins of the conflagration. The land around then became almost empty of human life, other than a few trappers like Rousseau and his Algonkian clients. It was far more wild than Mrs. Simcoe appears to have thought. According to a contemporary witness, the area was "not only a wilderness itself, but surrounded by forty miles of pathless, uninhabited forests."

As for Lieutenant-Governor Simcoe's projected "metropolis," it was to lie some three kilometres east of the fort along the inner shoreline of the harbour, then and now defined by the curving loop of sand-spits known as the Toronto Islands. Looked at on a map, the site makes perfect sense. It is protected and undented or rumpled by creeks and ravines. And it impressed an early surveyor, Joseph Bouchette, who recalled warmly the wild place to which he'd been sent to design a modern city.

"I still distinctly recollect the untamed aspect which the country exhibited when I first entered the beautiful basin," wrote Bouchette.

Dense and trackless forests lined the margin of the lake and reflected their inverted image in its glassy surface. The wandering savage had constructed his ephemeral habitation beneath their luxuriant foliage—the group then consisting of two families of Mississaga—and the bay and neighbouring marshes were the hitherto uninvaded haunts of immense coveys of wild fowl. Indeed, they were so abundant as in some measure to annoy us during the night.

The early views of the shoreline site of Toronto, recorded in words or pencil or watercolour, are like that. There is no fear, no trepidation—but usually appreciation of the natural beauty which has not wholly vanished from the place. The only thing it lacked was what Elizabeth Simcoe would call *civilization*. In contemporary usage, she would mean by it *civility* (which Dr. Johnson preferred, presumably believing its denotations of *manners* clearer). Needed were dances and visiting, the society of others, books and music and religion. As her stay that autumn progressed, along with her sketching and diarizing, Elizabeth came to adore the lagoon and the wooded sandbanks that ringed it and the outer eastern shoreline that becomes sharper and higher east of the town site.

Sun. Aug. 4th—We rode on the peninsula opposite Toronto, so I called the spit of land, for it is united to the mainland by a very narrow neck of ground. We crossed the bay opposite the camp, and rode by the lake side to the end of the peninsula.

We met with some good natural meadows and several ponds. The trees are mostly of the poplar kind, covered with wild vines, and there are some fir. On the ground were everlasting peas creeping in abundance, of a purple colour . . . We then walked some distance till we met with Mr. Grant's (the surveyor's) boat. It was not much larger than a canoe, but we ventured into it and after rowing a mile we came within sight of what is named, in the map, the highlands of Toronto. The shore is extremely bold, and has the appearance of chalk cliffs, but I believe they are only white sand. They appeared so well that we talked of building a summer residence there and calling it Scarborough.

The area is called Scarborough today and the dramatically sculpted embankment, the Scarborough Bluffs. Winter residences, summer house in the country: Mrs. Simcoe was already laying claim to the ancient wilderness of Ontario, as newcomers usually do, by turning it into a reminiscence of where they came from, and by naming it after places they know and have found pleasure or comfort in. If anywhere was to become the capital of Upper Canada it must be London, or Kingston or Newark (as its original settlers called Niagara-on-the-Lake). Renaming is always a regularizing process, of claiming that the new place is really an outpost of the old. Simcoe thought the traditional name Toronto "outlandish," so decided to rename it after the brother of the King, another warrior. Elizabeth jotted down the event in her diary on August 24.

The Governor has received an official account of the Duke of York having distinguished himself in an action at Famars in Flanders by which the French were dislodged and driven out of Holland. The Governor ordered a royal salute to be fired in commemoration of this event, and took the same opportunity of naming this station York. There are a few twelve and eighteen pounders which were brought here from Oswegatchie [Ogdensburg] or from Carleton Island. The "Mississaga" and "Onondaga" fired also, and the regiment . . .

There was a party of Ojibwa Indians here, who appeared much pleased with the firing. One of them, named "Great Sail," took Francis in his arms and was much pleased to find the child not afraid, but delighted with the sound.

But the more immediate problem was where they were to spend the night, if not on board ship. They slept in a tent—one unmatched in historic interest, as it happened. For Simcoe brought ashore at Toronto the very tent Captain James Cook had used during the explorations of the southern Pacific that had left all Europe reeling with fascination. Simcoe had bought it at a sale of Cook's effects in London before leaving for Upper Canada. The tent thus became the first work of English architecture erected in Toronto, and one, unfortunately, of which not a trace remains.

It was in this tent that the proper founding of York took place, on September 2, 1793, when the first executive council meeting was held. The garrison was established at Fort York, while at nearby York the town proper slowly began to take shape. By the time the English traveller Anna Jameson wrote her account of the town, in 1837, it had reverted to its ancient name, though made little progress toward its great future. Anna wrote:

> Toronto!—such is now the sonorous name of this our sublime capital, was, thirty years ago, a wilderness, the haunt of the bear and deer, and with a little, ugly, inefficient fort, which, however, could not be more inefficient than the present one. Ten years ago Toronto was a village, with one brick house and four or five hundred inhabitants; five years ago it became a city, containing about five thousand inhabitants, and then bore the name of Little York; now it is Toronto, with an increasing trade, and a population of ten thousand people . . . When the engineer, Bouchette, was sent by General [*sic*] Simcoe to survey the site, (in 1793), it was a mere swamp, a tangled wilderness; the birch, the hemlock and the tamarac-trees were growing down to the water's edge, and even in to the lake . . . Colonel Bouchette says, that at this time the only vestige of humanity for a hundred miles on every side was one solitary wigwam on the shore, the dwelling of a few Mississauga Indians. Three years afterwards when the Duc de Rochefoucauld was here, the infant metropolis consisted of a fort and twelve miserable log huts, the inhabitants of which, as the duke tells us, bore no good reputation.

The Simcoes departed this sorry place for England when John's commission expired in 1796, but not without regrets. In that year, Elizabeth made a note about her trip between Canterbury and her estate in Dorset that speaks clearly of her love for what she left behind across the seas. "The weather is damp, raw and unpleasant," she writes about one of every diarist's favourite topics.

I could not but observe, as we passed many good houses, that those mansions appeared very comfortable habitations, in which people might live very happily, but it could not be supposed they could ever be induced to go out of them in such a damp climate, for the fields looked so cold, so damp, so cheerless, so uncomfortable from the want of our bright Canadian sun.

15
HANDSOME LAKE

BY 1794, THE WAR OF AMERICAN INDEPENDENCE WAS OVER, and British rule over its rebel colonies was drawing to an end in a twilight of surveys and pacts and gradual, sporadic withdrawals of militia and loyal civilians from remote wilderness forts. It was during the last decade of that fateful century that the victorious Americans cast westward a Seneca nobleman named Handsome Lake, along with hundreds of his people, to the Alleghenies from his Genesee River homeland, south of Lake Ontario. Devastated by defeat, disease and drunkenness, the elderly man gradually declined into an illness that, after four years, left him a helpless cripple, wholly dependent on a married daughter.

Crown and Republic were defining and consolidating their strongholds on the American continent all around the sickbed of Handsome Lake, leaving the once-mighty League of the Great Peace in tatters, its people scattered and powerless. The final erasure of the dream of Dekanawida—that all humankind would someday gather and unite under the mighty limbs of the Tree of Peace—was begun in earnest in 1783 by the Treaty of Paris. A few villages remained in the old homeland of the League, along the south shore of Lake

Ontario. The Upper Canadian settlements of loyal League warriors, on the Grand River and at Akwesasne and Deseronto, held all that was left of the Loyalist members of the League. But by late in the eighteenth century, these people laboured under dire poverty, disease and the heartbreak of broken promises. The final, fatal results of the League's disastrous political miscalculations and misalliances and disease were upon them, and the great pre-Columbian political power was in imminent danger of disappearing forever.

In any of the makeshift, disease-riddled settlements where the remnants of the League had been put, few would have known or cared when a man unnaturally aged by drink tottered out of the hut where he had lain paralyzed for four years and collapsed in the arms of his daughter. The year was 1799. Perhaps seven thousand members of the once-huge League remained alive. To all appearances, Handsome Lake was dead. But once his relatives and friends had assembled for the rites of farewell, some began to notice a certain warmth in the body. Then the warmth spread, and Handsome Lake's inert limbs began to quicken, his silenced voice to speak. All who witnessed this astonishing revival knew that something wondrous and powerful had brought Handsome Lake back to them. As the strength he had lost long ago rapidly returned, he told his guests all that had happened during his sleep, deep as death.

In a long narrative still solemnly recited by the spiritual leaders of the Long House religion that Handsome Lake revised and revived, he recalled the anguish he endured during the last days of his passage toward miserable death—enslaved by liquor and by vices practised over a lifetime. Then he thought of the sunshine, and gave thanks to the Creator for it. When night came, he looked up the chimney of his wretched hut and saw stars, and for these, too, he raised his heart in thanksgiving. "Now he hears the birds singing," the story continues, "and he thanks the Great Ruler for their music. So then he thinks that a thankful heart will help him."

Then profound sleep engulfed him. And Handsome

Lake heard a beautiful voice, summoning him to rise from his bed and come into the open. "I thought that in my sickness I myself was speaking," he said, "but I thought again and found out it was not my voice." When he emerged, he found that the beautiful voice belonged to one of the resplendent beings who appeared in the form of men, their faces freshly painted, carrying arrows and huckleberries.

Now they said, "We shall continually reveal things unto you. We, the servants of him who made us, say that as he employed us to come unto you to reveal his will, so you must carry it to your people. Now we are they whom he created when he made the world and our duty is to watch over and care for mankind. . . .

Then began the delivery to Handsome Lake of what the Long House People call *Gai'wii'*, or The Great Message.

Four words tell a great story of wrong and the Creator is sad because of the trouble they bring, so go and tell your people.

The first word is *drink*. It seems that you never have known that this word stands for a great and monstrous evil and has reared a high mound of bones. . . . So now all must now say, "I will use it nevermore. As long as I live, as long as the number of my days is I will never use it again. I now stop. . . ."

We now speak of the second word that makes the Creator angry. The word is *witchery*. Witches are people without their right minds. They make disease and spread sickness to make the living die. . . . When you have told this message and the witches hear it, they will confess before all the people and will say, "I am doing this evil thing but now I cease it forever, as long as I live."

This is the third word. It is a sad one and the Creator is very sad because of this third word. It seems that you have never known that a great pile of human bodies lies dead because of this word, *charms.* Now the Creator who made us commands that they who do this evil, when they hear this message, must stop it immediately and do it nevermore while they live upon this earth-world.

Now another word. It is sad. It is the fourth word. It is *abortion.* . . . The Creator created life to live and he wishes such evils to cease. He wishes those who employ such potions to cease such practices forevermore. Now they must stop when they hear this message. Go and tell your people.

Handsome Lake was also commanded to condemn the desertion and abuse of wives by their husbands, and of children and the elderly. To this intensely sad catalogue of the afflictions and self-afflictions of the League, the Beings add stinginess, adultery and anxiety. The warnings always end with the same refrain: "Tell your people that these things must cease. Tell them to repent and cease." But these solemn admonitions always end in a promise, which, because of Handsome Lake's willingness to obey the Creator, has been fulfilled.

"You have the constant fear that the white race would exterminate you," they tell him. "The Creator will care for his *Oñgwe'o"we* [Real People]."

ARMED WITH THIS MESSAGE, the revived Handsome Lake began to go through the devastated villages of the League, preaching and teaching. To people living in the ruins of their beliefs and dreams, he recalled the central tenets of the traditions, especially the importance of women as bearers of wisdom and sources of political order. Too, he was a dreamer from a people who had not lost the profound belief in dreams as gates to higher worlds, brought eons before from the shamanistic faith of the far north.

The Seneca prophet's mission to the League came to the attention of President Thomas Jefferson only two years after its commencement. In 1802, Jefferson wrote to "Brother Handsome Lake," praising him especially for preaching against "the ruinous effects which the abuse of spirituous liquors" had wreaked on the League. The President goes on to condemn the merchants from "all the nations of white people who have supplied [the League's] calls for the article. But these nations have done to you only what they do among themselves." His letter includes a key exhortation that Handsome Lake would not only succeed in delivering but that would be key to the revival.

> Persuade our red brethren to be sober and to cultivate their lands, and their women to spin and weave for their families. You will soon see your women and children well fed and clothed, your men living happily in peace and plenty, and your numbers increasing from year to year. It will be a great glory to you to have been the instrument of so happy a change and your children's children, from generation to generation, will repeat your name with love and gratitude for ever. In all the enterprises for the good of your people, you may count with confidence on the aid and protection of the United States, and on the sincerity and zeal with which I am myself animated in the furthering of this humane work. You are our brethren of the same land: we wish to see your prosperity as brethren should do.

But Handsome Lake was under attack. A formidable power in the League named Red Jacket sought to expose him as an impostor. Handsome Lake was ridiculed, physically abused, chased from the villages where he sought to plant his celestial gospel. The reasons for this harsh treatment can only partly be written down to hardness of heart. Red Jacket and others must surely have seen as clearly as Handsome Lake what alcohol, the habitual abuse of women and other habits were doing to the integrity of the ancient nations. But Handsome Lake was not calling for a simple return to the ancient principles of the League. His message, rather, was a mixed gospel of conservative renewal and radical cultural thrust in the direction of the modern.

Arthur C. Parker, who wrote down the text recited by the followers of *Gai'wii'*, observed that it "revolutionized" the religious life of the League, first in its most ancient homeland, south of Lake Ontario, then in the loyalist League settlements in Ontario.

> Handsome Lake sought to destroy the ancient folk-ways of the people and substitute a new system, built of course upon the framework of the old. Finding that he made little headway in his teachings, he sought to destroy the societies and orders that conserved the older religious rites, by proclaiming a revelation from the Creator. The divine decree was a command that all the animal societies hold a final meeting at a certain time, throw tobacco in the ceremonial fires, and dissolve.

His last years were darkened by discouragement and ferocious opposition to his message both from Christians and from adherents of the old ways. The effect on him was to plunge him into profound depression. It was while in semi-retreat at Tonawanda that he received an invitation to visit Onondaga, the ancient capital of the League, and decided he would accept—while telling those around him that the visions commanding him to go also foretold that there he would "sing his third song" and die. Handsome Lake set out with some disciples on the walk to Onondaga, with more and more people joining the throng. He arrived, and went to a small cabin where he became very ill and despondent. A game of lacrosse, a sport symbolic of healing and redemption, was played to cheer him. Then he said:

> I will soon go to my new home. Soon I will step into the New World for there is a plain pathway before me leading there. Whoever follows my teaching will follow in my footsteps and I

will look back upon him with outstretched arms, inviting him into the new world of our Creator. Alas, I fear that a pall of smoke will obscure the eyes of many from the truth of *Gai'wii'* but I pray that when I am gone that all may do what I have taught.

Perhaps, in those final hours, he recalled the final messages of the Four Beings, who told him of the Road he must walk—the Milky Way, each star the footprint of a soul who has gone before. "Now it is the time for our departure," they told him.

We shall now go on a journey and then you shall see the coming of the fourth messenger, the journey of our friends and the works of the living of earth. More, you will see the house of the punisher and the lands of our Creator . . . Suddenly, as they looked, a road slowly descended from the south sky and came to where they were standing. Now thereon he saw the four tracks of the human race going in one direction. The footprints were of different sizes from small to great. Now moreover a more brilliant light than the light of earth appeared . . .

Handsome Lake died on August 10, 1815. In the years following his death, the recitations of the Great Message began to change. Concerned that the words would eventually be lost, Chief Cornplanter began, in 1903, to write the *Gai'wii'* in an old minute-book of the Seneca Lacrosse Club. The English translation used by Arthur C. Parker was done by William Bluesky, a Baptist lay preacher. In this way it was preserved. No matter how discouraged he became, no matter how great the opposition to his preaching, Handsome Lake continued to believe the revelations given him would endure, to the good of his people, for all time. And so they have.

Once a beautiful girl had come to him and said: "When you leave this earth for the New World above, it is our wish to follow you." He replied:

I looked for the damsel, but saw only the long leaves of corn twining around my shoulders. And then I understood that it was the spirit of the corn who had spoken—she, the sustainer of life.

So I replied, "O spirit of the corn, do not follow me, but abide still upon the earth, be strong, be faithful to your purpose. Ever endure and do not fail the children of women. It is not time for you to follow, for *Gai'wii'* is only in its beginning."

16
SERINETTE

ON JUNE 21, 1812, DAVID WILLSON, Quaker, of the Yonge Street Meeting, and farmer in East Gwillimbury Township, north of Toronto, fell into an enchanted sleep and dreamed.

In his vision, he beheld a stunningly beautiful woman naked from the waist up, arising like the dawn from the east. "He then beheld her shining face and red mantle which was stained by the blood of Christian martyrs and fastened around her waist by a belt of pure gold, her pure faith in God." (She came from the East, which was "the traditional home of knowledge and enlightenment.")

A voice instructed him to put the woman upon the sea, where she would be safe from the wild animals bent on destroying her children. Next Willson saw a naked toddler coming toward him, its little feet in a stream flowing from the east. "And as it was from the east it is an expression of ancient wisdom being restored to the world, and the naked infant walking therein implies walking back to ancient simplicity—when the heart of man had a communication with God."

A few days later he had another dream, also featuring a naked child, this one "wrapped in a stream of water." He was told to "dress the child and keep it clean." The child kept walking, and Willson followed it to a peaceful sea, where it turned into a glorious maiden. "Her hair was the color of pure gold; her face was fair as the eastern sun; her breasts were bare, and she was without shame." The miraculous being promised her human companion, he recalled, that "as I had guarded her in her infancy, so she would guard me in my old age, and when I had done all things below I should return to her and partake of all her glory."

In his final dream, Willson saw a youth covered only with a "scarlet robe stained by the blood of Christ." The boy stripped himself, threw the blood-stained cloak on Willson's shoulders. Then, "naked and beautiful," the boy vanished—only to reappear the next morning, this time draped in a robe "colored as the skies, ornamented with the lights of heaven wholly, and sparkling with unusual lustre, with a border of gold encompassing the mantle round about." He put this second, celestial mantle on Willson, who "received an assurance that I had part both in present and ancient order, but that I must first ornament the Christian Church with all the glory of Israel."

To Willson's self-taught, eccentrically learned mind, this meant music, ceremonial and glorious spectacle, all strictly forbidden by the Society of Friends. This insistence on adding forbidden "glory" to the worship of the Friends led to his expulsion. The Quakers lost a member, but Ontarians gained the most marvellous work of visionary architecture ever built in the province, and one of the most astonishing to be constructed anywhere in North America.

On land cleared in 1801, Willson assembled his flock—only six souls by the end of the year of the visions, but 280 by 1834—and in 1825 set the master craftsman Ebenezer Doan to work on the seven-year task of raising the temple. In 1829, a separate one-room study for the prophet was added. All stands today.

According to Willson, the scheme for the temple at Sharon was that laid down by God in the First Book of Kings and in the twenty-first chapter of the Revelation. As in the construction of the Jerusalem temple, so in East Gwillimbury "there was neither hammer nor axe nor any tool of iron heard in the house while it was in building."

The result is an external four-square facade that rises in three graduated tiers meant to represent the Holy and Undivided Trinity. The twelve interior pillars supporting the four-square framework, said Willson, signified the "twelve foundations" of the New Jerusalem described in the New Testament book of The Revelation of St. John. Similarly, the equivalent number of windows on each side, together comprising 2,952 panes of glass, symbolizes the light of Christ, falling without prejudice on all, from every direction. The golden globe that crowns the temple has been described by a modern commentator as a symbol of "the world at peace." If the temple strikes a modern visitor as delightfully childlike in its simplicity and gentle theological fancy, David Willson would doubtless be pleased, for he loved children dearly, and held no fewer than fifteen festivals each year for them.

In May, 1831, shortly before Doan completed the temple and it was opened for worship, Willson addressed his flock as follows:

I freely give this house, its orders and the ground on which its pillars stand, my brethren. It was not materially mine; but committed to my trust from Israel's God, and he will give me more, because I have been faithful in this small matter, continuing to the end. Ye must not make it a habitation of priests though they would say they came from heaven. It is the Lord's dwelling; he hath shut me out of it, my feet shall never enter there. It is your great salvation to keep it this way, it is a bright polish'd sword against priestcraft in the earth.

DAVID WILLSON'S ORIGINS WERE STURDY and humble, and little different from those of other early Loyalist settlers of Ontario. He was born to a linen merchant from Ireland who, in 1770, had settled in Dutchess County, on the Hudson River, the homeland of many American Quaker newcomers to the Bay of Quinte after the Revolution. The Willsons were "poor, but pious," wrote David Willson, and they were Presbyterians. Exactly when and why he became a Quaker is not known, though from the deeds of his later life one gathers he was a man drawn less to external law and the inexorable fate of Calvinist predestination than to the democratic light shining in each person's heart.

He probably came to Canada for the usual reasons most of the early inhabitants came: land, a belief in farming, an ability to do it. By his own description we learn that, lacking formal education, he became a carpenter, being "inclined to mechanical business in joining timber, one part unto another." He moved to East Gwillimbury with his wife, Phebe, and their sons John David and Israel, in 1801. A third son came in 1802. In his memoir, Willson says he "passed seven years in retired life, beginning in the year 1801; often seeking lonely places wherein to retire and worship the spirit that had received my soul in trust." By 1806, he was a member of the Yonge Street Meeting of the Quakers, and listed as "recorder of certificates."

We have a good idea of what led him into terminal conflict with the orthodox Quakers in 1812. One was music; another was a reliance on the inner radiance of Christ even more radical than the Quakers were prepared to put up with. "My soul was not only separated from all flesh as to my inward feelings," he wrote, "but from all religious records, even to the bible, and I was constrained to live by my own knowledge of the word of God, operating upon my mind." He quickly drew unto him the defectors who formed the first congregation of the Children of Peace. "His doctrine was unto us very singular who were bred up strict sectarians," recalled one who knew Willson and followed him. "He is a man of scarcely any education; but hath been able to teach us doctrines we never knew."

He found himself "unbound from all parts of the world, since the day my brethren pronounced me unworthy of communion. The storm arose, and I fled before excommunication. The cause of censure was, erroneous doctrine; but I aimed at the truth and could not retract what I had delivered . . . I was not disposed to stand the contest, but bowed my shoulders, received my burden and walked away."

Even before Willson and the Children of Peace had begun the construction of the Temple, the congregation was singing. By 1820, there was a brass band and a wind-operated instrument called a "serinette," quite possibly the first organ to arrive in Ontario.

This remarkable instrument stood at the centre of worship at the Temple. Invented in the eighteenth century, it appears to have been (like the player piano) an imaginative transfer to musical machinery of the operating system of jacquard looms, which were controlled by cards perforated with holes in various patterns. The earliest versions took the form of small wooden cabinets with an external crank, a bellows and an internal mechanism controlling the air supply to a dozen tiny organ pipes. The fashionable Parisian painter Jean Baptiste Siméon Chardin sold a print called *La Serinette (The Bird-Organ)* to Louis XV.

In this work, a lady turning the handle of the instrument is teaching a canary how to sing. The destiny of the serinette, after David Willson's day, was to become a feature of mass culture. It is a true ancestor of programmed theatre organs, and indeed all recorded music: hence a true child of the Industrial Revolution and the Enlightenment.

David Willson himself was an offspring of the Enlightenment's revolutionary thinking, and incomprehensible outside it. For him, the mind and the cosmos are moments on a single physical continuum that bears along a connecting electricity between the individual and the universe. He reported in his autobiographical *Impressions of the Mind* that: "The mind is an atmosphere in itself, containing wonders to us unknown. The atmosphere changeth by an over-ruling providence, and there appeareth to be life and motion, in the whole moving system, and this to me is the distant and uncomprehended life of God."

His self-portraits in words always show us a yeoman farmer, the basic Enlightenment icon of industrious labour and stalwart champion of the home, hearth and morality.

Like Simcoe and the other early inhabitants and rulers of Ontario, though more rigorously than they, Willson believed that Britannia was

BRITANNIA

the guardian goddess of the farmer. Two years before the republican rebellion that briefly shook Ontario in 1837—of which, more presently—Willson set out his apocalyptic beliefs in *Impressions of the Mind,* his fullest attempt to declare himself. The age of revolution, which had left North America divided between monarchy and republicanism, similarly divided the prophets of the day. In England, William Blake could see the French Revolution as liberty and joy. Willson, in Ontario, is an uncompromising believer in the apocalyptic message of the British empire as sacrament and salvation.

Britain is the star of nations; the sun will rise and shine upon her
as morning rays on the western hills. Britain will become a
saviour to the world; as the mother of nations, she will receive of
God, and crown her offspring with peace . . . Britain is restoring
the poor to their right, and pleading for a free circulation of just
principles, and the preaching of the Gospel on the principles it
began in Israel and in Judah.

Whatever we make of God's message to Willson, the divisions in
Ontario's vision of its future were laid bare by the conflict of 1837. In
his view, Willson was leading disciples from the desert of worldliness
to the Promised Land, which would be an amalgam of Britain, monarchy and the rule of Christ on earth. Many farmers in East Gwillimbury
Township dissented, and took their marching orders from the republican rebel William Lyon Mackenzie. During the rebellion against the
Tory ascendancy at York, twelve prominent members of the Children
of Peace and two of Willson's sons took up arms against the Lord and
His Anointed King.

Willson never recovered from this defection from the great hope he
had laid before the Children. He had not seen that, in the years following Lieutenant-Governor Simcoe's initiatives, the Upper Canadian
wilderness was becoming peopled and thick with towns. Mills were
beginning to dot the banks of the many rivers flowing south toward
Lake Ontario, establishing prosperity that had not existed when
Willson made his way from Dutchess County to East Gwillimbury.
The primitive isolation of Ontario from the world was ending. So was
the simplicity required to sustain the joyful communal values of the
Children of Peace. David Willson died in 1866, and in 1889 the final
meeting of the Children took place in their marvellous Temple.

IT IS SURELY APPROPRIATE that the Temple should remain alive in
Ontario in an opera. *Serinette,* a collaboration between the poet James

Reaney and composer Harry Somers, premiered in Toronto in 1990. It all began, Reaney has said, when he was working on a farm camp in the Holland Marsh, north of Toronto, during the Second World War.

> I had to walk to Newmarket to cash a money order. I stumbled across the temple by accident and I was stunned by its beauty. When the opera was commissioned, it was obvious that it should relate to David Willson. Willson was too "noisy" for the Quakers because he placed more emphasis on the Holy Spirit speaking in tongues through people than most Quakers wanted to see. They had toned down these mystical "inner voices" erupting at meetings. He was also a Quaker reformer because he loved music in a religion that had no tradition in the arts. In the commune Willson set up, everyone had to be an artist as well as a craftsman.

For the poet, the pacific world of visionary artist–craftsfolk in Sharon is put to work as propaganda. In a review of *Serinette,* the Toronto critic Tamara Bernstein wrote in the *Globe and Mail* that

> the drama hinges on the conflict of the pacifist, communal ideals of the Children of Peace (represented primarily by the fictional "good" son, Colin Jarvis, and the historical David Willson), and the violent, exploitative world of the upper Canadian ruling class (embodied by the rest of the Jarvis clan).
>
> Symbolism, too, stays simple and direct: the play moves from what Reaney terms the "pagan darkness" of St. James Cathedral in York to the moving illumination of the Sharon Temple in the finale; and the musical creativity of the Children of Peace counterpoints the image of the caged bird who is forced to learn Rossini arias for the entertainment of Upper Canadians with aristocratic pretensions.
>
> But in the end, the strongest presence in the show was perhaps the Temple itself, which architecturally embodies David Willson's

ideals of equality, openness and communality. *Serinette*'s magic works not through the transformation of a neutral theatre into the playwright's world, but through a script and score that, as they tell the story of the Children of Peace, bring the extraordinary building to life.

The scholar Ernest R. Sandeen has commented that "America in the early nineteenth century was drunk on the millennium. Whether in support of optimism or pessimism, radicalism or conservatism, Americans seemed unable to avoid—seemed bound to utilize—the vocabulary of Christian eschatology." The remarkable thing about David Willson, the prophet of East Gwillimbury, is that he not only used this vocabulary but he sought to invent an architectural embodiment of it, an expression of the Kingdom of Heaven that was also the coming of the Kingdom itself. This is architecture with an apocalyptic message, but also an eschatological agenda: to pinpoint a place where heaven had touched the earth and left it blessed by a monument of goodness, openness, civility, democracy without parallel in Canadian sacred building.

17
JOHN TORONTO

MORE OFTEN THAN NOT, early visitors to little York admired the townsite from afar and hated it up close. Today, all that is left of it is an indefinite downtown swatch of pleasant condominiums, warehouses converted into office lofts, car washes and such, and the odd late-Victorian building. Landfill along the waterfront has erased the old docks and left Lieutenant-Governor Simcoe's townsite inland, and a wall of buildings and expanse of expressway and railway tracks has further rendered its former proximity to Lake Ontario illegible. Nor does it have any focus to remind us where it was, because, as the architectural historian Eric Arthur has written, the "practical but indescribably mean and unimaginative" plan of York never had a focus to begin with. "Had there been provision for a school, a church, or, more particularly, a village green, the plan of Toronto today would have been different. It also lacked direction, so that when expansion was inevitable, the town grew merely by adding more squares."

The plan Arthur so disliked was the brainchild of one Alexander Aitken, a military engineer who drew it off on a topographical map for John Graves Simcoe in 1793. Aitken ignored the beaver ponds, dense forests, creeks and ravines on the site, so bewitched was he by the Platonic perfection of the rectangular grid and the military plans fashionable in the day. York was to be, after all, a military town. Thus did Toronto get a street plan of mindlessly multiplied squares "with which we have had to cope," wrote Arthur, "for almost two hundred years and with which posterity will have to deal till the end of time."

Arthur's complaint is grounded in the assumption that things would have turned out better, had Alexander Aitken come up with a more picturesque layout for York. I doubt it. Cities grow as they will. Many of the tangled European cities beloved by tourists began as Roman military grids identical to young York. But the criticism is a good reminder of what York was supposed to be: neither a resort nor a charming English village, but a serious little centre of imperial administration and headquarters for a colonial élite.

This élite was dubbed the Family Compact by its early enemies. The name has stuck. Organized by Lieutenant-Governor Simcoe and sustained by his followers in office, this tight-knit collection of lawyers, financiers, clergymen and educators determined the conservative, Tory, loyalist and anti-American tone of modern Ontario's first half-century and shaped economic and political arrangements, and a certain cultural attitude, that have persisted to this day. The Compact itself, however, did not endure as long as its spiritual legacy. By the 1830s, power was slipping from its hands. Though handily put down by Loyalist troops, the farmers' revolt of 1837 sufficiently upset the established order of things to allow a genuinely multi-party ruling class to emerge in Ontario.

Though I did not grow up in Ontario, or because I didn't, I did not learn about the Family Compact until it was too late to despise them. The demonizing of these men and women, I discovered, is part of every Ontarian's upbringing. It is now assumed by some Canadians in Ontario that the early years of our province were shrouded in reactionary gloom and ruled by self-serving tyrants. Of these despotical fiends, none played his part as Prince of Darkness more assiduously than the Anglican minister and first bishop of Toronto, John Strachan—or, as he signed his name: John Toronto.

His early life hardly prepared him for such high and mightiness. Bishop Strachan was born in 1778, the son of a poor Scottish stonemason, but contrived to get advanced education anyway, at King's College in Aberdeen. Despite his later reputation for grandeur, he was a labourer's son, with a working-man's drive and energy—teaching the adult sons of farmers in Scotland by age sixteen, and continuing to do the same for a while until 1799, when he got a job tutoring the children of a family in the relatively civilized Upper Canadian town of Kingston.

John combined common sense and a shrewd sense of when to seize the main chance. There was no place for Calvinists in Simcoe's Upper Canada, so John abandoned the Kirk and become a Church of England clergyman. After moving to Canada, he fell in love with a young woman named Ann Wood, but could not marry her, being himself penniless. So when she got a marriage proposal from a rich, elderly Montréal bachelor named Andrew McGill, Strachan remarked: "Tak' him. I can afford to wait." It was a good investment of patience. Andrew quickly and conveniently died, leaving Ann rich and free to marry the man she had loved from the start. After

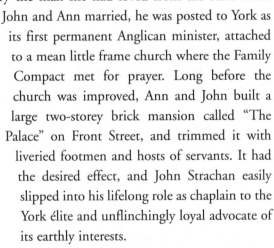

John and Ann married, he was posted to York as its first permanent Anglican minister, attached to a mean little frame church where the Family Compact met for prayer. Long before the church was improved, Ann and John built a large two-storey brick mansion called "The Palace" on Front Street, and trimmed it with liveried footmen and hosts of servants. It had the desired effect, and John Strachan easily slipped into his lifelong role as chaplain to the York élite and unflinchingly loyal advocate of its earthly interests.

As evidence of the flamboyant Toryism that modern critics love to hate about John Strachan, I here enter into the record a sermon

he preached about King George III in 1809, before his remove from
Kingston to York.

> Were we to model our lives by the conduct of our sovereign,
> corruption and venality would hide their heads, and all would be
> cheerfully obedient to the laws. Instead of pride, cruelty, and
> oppression, Christian charity would reign, each would embrace
> his fellow subject as a brother deserving of his confidence and
> friendship. As no vicious character ever had access to the King,
> such would be hunted from society and the irreligious, spurned
> as corrupters of the public happiness . . . Animated by that pure
> patriotic flame which is the noblest passion that can enter the
> breast, he is forever seeking his people's good, and always teach-
> ing them, by his illustrious example, how to procure it. Though
> far distant, we are no less the objects of his paternal care.

Then, with a jab at the Enlightenment thinkers who inspired the
revolutions in both France and America, he declares that

> the unwritten British constitution partakes of all the advances
> which an experience of several centuries has accumulated. It is
> not, therefore, the work of a day; it rests upon old and tried foun-
> dations, the more durable, because visionary empirics have not
> been allowed to touch them. No fine-spun theories of meta-
> physicians, which promise much and end in misery, have shared
> in its formation; such men may destroy, but they can never build.

He calls upon his listeners to witness

> comfort, health, and grandeur flowing in upon us, and our
> liberty giving our country the most solid charms, notwithstand-
> ing its freezing sky and procrastinated snows. . . . Other countries
> may enjoy a warmer climate, and may produce more delicious
> fruits, but are these an equivalent for anarchy, for despotism and

oppression? And, my children, living under a King so generous, so benevolent and just, a King whose greatest joy is to see his subjects happy and free, what do we wish for that we do not possess?

As John Strachan lived to see, Upper Canada was liberally sprinkled with people who wished for several things they did not possess, including a republican form of government, freedom from Compact paternalism and good riddance to the likes of John Strachan. If these rebels failed to overthrow Ontario's imperial government in 1837, one reason may be a lingering popular memory of the day when Mr. Strachan's loyalties suffered their severest test, and emerged shining.

It all began in 1812, during ferocious controversies in the United States over the need for a second War of Independence, to rid North America of British rule and establish the mastery of trade. Like the colonies' first war, the impending second one was prompted less by consensus than the urging of a radical élite. In an "Address to the People of the Eastern States," the editors of the New York *Post* argued that the

war-hounds that are howling for war through the continent are not to be the men who are to force entrenchments, and scale ramparts against the bayonet and the cannon's mouth; to perish in sickly camps, or in long marches through sultry heats or wastes of snow.

According to the *Post,* Thomas Jefferson was the arch-warmonger—a "gowned warrior," "lodged safe at Monticello or some other secure retreat," and altogether too eager to send the Republic's youth to war. And what, in the end, was to be gained by such a conflagration?

"Citizens," cries the *Post,* "if pecuniary redress is your object in going to war with England, the measure is perfect madness . . . Will you spend thousands of millions in conquering a province which, were it made a present to us, would not be worth accepting?" The editorial rings with a flaming imperative: "Canada, if annexed to the United States, will furnish offices to a set of hungry villains, grown quite too numerous for our present wide limits; and that is all the benefit we ever shall derive from it."

The editorial writers were, of course, quite wrong about the economic benefit of annexing Canada. It would have been immense. And they were ignorant, it appears, of the formidable morale of the Compact that had kept Canada free from U.S. domination since the Revolution. On June 28, 1812, President James Madison sided with the warmongers and declared war on Britain. In the same week, John Strachan became missionary minister at York.

He was soon beset with tragedy in his family, when his daughter died and he was tormented with worry about the future of his flock. In the early autumn of the war's first year, he wrote a letter to a Montréal friend, in which the two concerns are linked: grief over losing a child and sorrow over the fumbling military pursuit of the war against America.

You and Mrs. Richardson will sympathize with us in the loss of our little girl who died last week of a severe worm fever. It was a sweet infant two and a half years old, exceedingly interesting. Mrs. Strachan finds relief in tears. We are not much pleased with the languid manner in which the war [is being] carried on; forbearance will never answer with our present enemy; it is founded upon a most fallacious idea of the American character, and the situation of parities in that country, and it will, should the war continue, be highly detrimental to this province and perhaps prove its ruin. An active prosecution of the war along our line . . . would produce many solid advantages, but acting merely on the defensive is exceedingly pernicious . . .

He laboured under no illusion as to what the ends of the American aggression actually were. The capture of Upper Canada, he wrote to James McGill, was determined upon by the United States. Nor can it be concealed that the importance of this country to them is incalculable—the possession of it would give them the complete command of the Indians who must either submit or starve within two years, and thus leave all the western frontier clear and unmolested. The Americans are systematically employed in exterminating the savages, but they can never succeed while we keep possession of this country. . . .

President Madison's war came to York early on the morning of April 27, 1813. Strachan notes in his diary:

Got up at four. The enemy in sight. Mount my horse and ride up to the garrison. The ships, fourteen in number, approach the shore, about two miles above the garrison—proceed towards them, discover them anchoring—return to the garrison—look through a glass, find the vessels thickly governed with troops—from which I infer that they are come prepared to land in great force.

By dawn, the U.S. troops had done exactly what Strachan feared.

Went again to the upper batter, nothing doing, return to the hospital and while there heard a violent shock. I go to town to look after the ladies, and soon after I reach town a tremendous explosion takes place. I consider all over as it must be the grand magazine. On going home find that Mrs. Strachan has been terrified by the explosion and run with the children to one of the neighbours. Send her to a friend's a little out of town. Go up toward the garrison, which we had by this time abandoned, find the General and his troops in a ravine, the militia scattering. The General determines to retreat to Kingston with the regulars and desires to make the best condition they could with the enemy for the town—Offer my services to assist them.

The British regulars accepted Mr. Strachan's offer, which was surely made as much from exasperation with the swiftly retreating British troops as Christian charity. The republican forces had come ashore without any counter-force marshalled against them and quickly overcome the gaggle of 119 soldiers and a few loyal Indians. The first thundering explosion that alarmed Ann Strachan was the accidental explosion at the fort, when a gunner blew up everything and a number of loyal soldiers. The second explosion heard by John Strachan was the sound of the main powder magazine at the fort deliberately set afire by British regulars as they withdrew eastward toward York. This second manoeuvre killed General Zebulon Pike, the leader of the attack on York, but did nothing to stop the Americans. The Stars and Stripes of the American Republic were flying over Fort York by day's end, and the tatters of the British legionary force had burned the warship *Brock* and were withdrawing to Kingston.

The town now lay undefended and unguarded against whatever the American occupiers might do. The Americans were not in a good

mood, having captured Muddy York but having lost the *Brock,* which was their main reason for coming. As Strachan and his adversaries sat down to talk about the terms of occupation, Strachan angrily notes:

> Difficulty arose from a ship and naval store having been set on fire during our negotiation, this considered very dishonourable. At length a capitulation is agreed upon, subject to the ratification of their commanding officer—broken—Major Allan, tho' under the protection of a flag of truce is made prisoner and deprived of his sword—I accompany him to town in the middle of the enemy's column . . .

The curious thing about this scenario is that a minister rather than a militiaman should be engaged in the negotiations at all. But neither the military nor civilian leaders of the town were prepared to confront General Henry Dearborn (who had taken command of the Americans after Pike was killed) over the possible burning and looting of the town.

On Wednesday, April 28, Strachan was in serious talks with Dearborn, of whom he writes: "Treats me with great harshness, tells me that we had given a false return of officers, and told me to keep off—not to follow him as he had business of much more importance to tend to—"

The dogged rector of York did not keep off, however, but continued to pester Dearborn, who was foot-dragging on the terms of capitulation. For Strachan,

> the delay was a deception calculated to give the riflemen time to plunder, and after the town had been robbed they would then perhaps sign the capitulation and tell us they respected private property; but we were determined that this should not be the case . . . Soon after General Dearborn came to the room where his deputation were sitting and having been told what I had said settled the whole amicably. The officers and men were released on their parole and we began to move the sick and wounded.

Put to the test, however, Dearborn's assurances proved to be unenforceable, or perhaps only unenforced. While helping move the sick and wounded out of harm's way on the Friday following the occupation, Strachan notes the ruin being visited on York.

> The govt. buildings on fire, contrary to the articles of capitulation. The church robbed. Call a meeting of the judges and magistrates. I ran up a short note stating our grievances, wait upon General Dearborn with it. He is greatly embarrassed, promises everything—Visit the hospital—Get a poor soldier buried.

By May 1, Strachan was still at it, helping a neighbour, Mrs. Givins, whose home had been plundered, only to find himself "in great danger of being shot by the rascal who was pillaging. Accompany Mrs. Givins to Gen'l Dearborn, state the insults and injuries she had received. He confesses that he is not able to protect any family connected with the Indians. Embark towards evening." On the next day the Americans were done with the prostrate town, and ready to depart, "except some stragglers, who are taken up by one of their officers sent on shore on purpose."

The spiritual healing of the town was to go on long after the Americans had taken leave of the harbour. "After this departure," writes Strachan, "we had some difficulty with our own disaffected of which we have too many . . ." And little wonder: York had been scantily defended, the civil leaders had proven ineffectual in protecting the tiny population, and only one man had been able to restrain the Americans in their pillage of York: John Strachan.

In relating Strachan's readiness to take control of a civic situation, his compassion and quickness to serve the interests of King and citizenry, I do not wish to romanticize him. He was a testy, humourless man, who could take quite unholy pleasure in the disgrace of his enemies. He found especially sweet the revenge for York visited by the British who, in the summer of 1814, pushed up the Potomac and captured Washington, the hotbed of all he detested, putting James and Dolly Madison to flight from the White House. The torching of Washington followed, with the Capitol, the White House and the offices of the War and Treasury departments destroyed by flame.

The only thing the Americans got out of the War of 1812 was "The Star-Spangled Banner," composed by Francis Scott Key while he was held aboard a British warship in Baltimore harbour. They did not destroy the British presence in North America. They did leave a trace of bitterness in the soul of John Strachan.

In a letter posted in 1815 to "Thomas Jefferson, Esquire, of Monticello, Ex-president of the United States of America," John Strachan attacks Jefferson at a particularly sensitive moment, when the former president's great library was being dissolved because of its owner's crushing indebtedness. There is a rush of sarcasm in the mocking graciousness of his tone.

> Permit me, Sir, to remark, that the destruction of the public buildings at Washington entitled the British to your gratitude and praise, by affording you a noble opportunity of proving your devotion to your country. In former times, when you spoke of the magnitude of your services, and the fervor of your patriotism, your political enemies were apt to mention your elevated situation, and the greatness of your salary. But, by presenting your library as a free-will offering to the nation, at this moment of uncommon pressure, when the Treasury is empty, every help to the acquisition of knowledge is so very necessary to keep the government from sinking, you would have astonished the world with one solitary action in your political life worthy of commendation . . .

It is hard to be sympathetic with John Strachan's nastiness. At that moment, Thomas Jefferson was being forced to give away one of the finest libraries in America—"an opportunity . . . given you of disposing of a library at your own price, which, if sold volume by volume, would have fetched nothing," writes Strachan, driving in the knife.

"You have, no doubt, seen that old libraries do not sell well after the death of the proprietors; and, with a lively attention to your own interests, you take advantage of the times."

The letter is signed "John Strachan, D.D., Treasurer of the Loyal and Patriotic Society of Upper Canada, York, 30th January, 1815."

It is easy to see why he became the public personality most earnestly disliked by those opposed to the Family Compact after 1812, and especially in the Rebellion of 1837. He served on the Executive Council of Upper Canada, and in 1820 he was appointed to the Legislative Council, thus officially and institutionally joining the Tory élite governing Upper Canada's public affairs. In 1839 he became first bishop of the diocese of Toronto, while continuing his work of education—founding the University of Toronto, for example—and remaining a political power until nearly 1850, when political changes at last brought an end to the Compact's control over Ontario's affairs and launched Canada on its way toward nationhood.

John Strachan had come to York when it was muddy indeed, little more than a patch of dwellings bordered by a small lagoon and tilted down toward a fever swamp. He died in 1867, the year of Confederation, when Toronto was strong and large, with a population far exceeding anything he had seen in 1813. He was by that time a relic of a bygone age, skipped by Canadians on their way to the North American mercantile future. But he must not be forgotten, if only because of the role small heroisms in remote places played in the creation of modern Canada.

Inside the enclosure of Fort York today, one finds a scatter of buildings—a fine bomb-proof gunpowder magazine, a couple of log blockhouses and some long, one-storey barracks—mostly built between 1813 and 1815. In those days, the fort occupied a hilltop, and Garrison Creek ran alongside the earthworks into Lake Ontario, which lapped its foundations. Today, the creek runs through sewers underground, invisibly. Landfill has pushed the shoreline a kilometre away, and the little fortification itself is dwarfed by the immense concrete colonnade bearing the Gardiner Expressway and by smokestacks and tall, flashing billboards meant to catch the eye of commuters. The stone wall running round the site is a make-work project of Depression-era vintage.

This unprepossessing place was once part—if only a minor part—of a network of defences intended to disappoint the nineteenth-century Americans on those occasions when they decided to seize what was left of British North America. Had the architectural repulses later constructed at York been already in place in 1813, the Americans might not have found York so easy to take, loot and terrorize. By 1814 the fortifications were imposing enough to make an American naval unit on the lake think twice about attacking, and eventually back off. Although Fort York is advertised as a relic of the War of 1812, it was used for military purposes, most of them peaceable (housing, training and such), until the 1930s. Some were not peaceable. The fort's troops went briefly into action against the Upper Canadian rebels in 1837, and in 1906 were sent in to stop violence during a strike by Hamilton streetcar operators. It never again saw hostile military action after the War of 1812.

But as recently as the 1860s, defence planners considered using it to help save this country should the huge armies of the American North and South decide to stop fighting each other and join forces against Canada. And in the 1890s, and again in the 1920s, Canadian military strategists seriously weighed the fort's prowess in the event of American invasion. In the present-day era of continental harmony—or absolute American hegemony—Old Fort York is obsolete, quite useless apart from the one important service it will always provide: to remind us of the will to defend the liberty of John Simcoe's new British Empire and the stubborn resistance of John Toronto to the republican impulses he believed to be devastating the earth.

18
VOYAGEURS

For JOHN GRAVES SIMCOE, the ten thousand or so farmers and soldiers who came over to Ontario from the Thirteen Colonies during the age of revolutions were all King's men, loyal and true. It seems not to have occurred to him that the motives of these settlers, on whose shoulders the future of his royalist Ontario rested, might be various. Perhaps his urgency about peopling Ontario with British subjects kept him conveniently blinkered.

In any case, historians nowadays are all too eager to show how wrong he was. By this account, the so-called Upper Canadian loyalists were a motley and unseemly crew, motivated only rarely by love of Crown and Motherland, and much more commonly by greed for land.

The truth is best served, it seems to me, by a more nuanced, practical view. There can be no doubt that many of the Americans who arrived here in the 1780s left their homes in New York and New England to escape terror and expropriation. Others, such as the Quakers who populated the Bay of Quinte, abandoned the United States because their faith forbade them to take up arms. The great majority of these immigrants were farmers, so the availability of land in Ontario played an important part in their decision. As usual in human affairs, the motives were mixed. So be it. Ontario may have gotten some half-hearted monarchists in the bargain and more than a few covert republicans. The province's first great wave of immigration nevertheless brought thousands of skilled men and women to new homes here and created a golden age of peace and general prosperity that persisted from the time of John Simcoe to the War of 1812.

But if evidence of unimpeachable loyalty is still wanted, the north shore of Lake Ontario is probably not the best place to look, nor is the 1780s the best time. The place where it's to be found lies far to the north of Captain James Cook's tent, where Mrs. Simcoe perfected her game of whist and John Graves Simcoe dreamed of empires in the wilderness. So far north, in fact, that Lieutenant-Governor Simcoe probably gave it little thought. After all, upon his arrival in 1791, Ontario's British population, which was the kind that principally interested him, was concentrated at Kingston and Niagara-on-the-Lake, with a sprinkling of new towns and farming communities near the Bay of Quinte. In the rocky wilderness beyond the fertile hill country of the lower Great Lakes basin lay only a handful of towns—if one can call a huddle of cabins a town. As recently as the 1860s, the outposts of Sault Ste. Marie, Fort William, Fort Frances and Rat Portage—as Kenora was known then—were among the very few settlements in that northern vastness.

But this is certainly not to say that those endless tracts of swamp, lake and thicket were innocent of human life. The aboriginal people knew and loved this country. So did the spiritual offspring of Étienne Brûlé, those trappers and hunters who had once been French but had long since melted into the forests and become a race of folk more Christian than pagan. Too distant from the institutions of French Christian civilization to think much about them, most nevertheless kept the names of their French ancestors—Chevrette, Boyer, Côté, Cadieux, Desaulniers, Lacourse, Lepine, Lacroix, LaPlante—who had been coming up from Montréal along the Ottawa River in their long, shallow-draft boats to Lake Huron since 1608, when Champlain dispatched Brûlé to make the first, crucial contact with the western Wendat. The voyageurs brought from the western edges of European civilization the trade goods valued by the ancient nations dwelling inland: guns, buckshot, bullets and gunpowder above all, but also copper *chaudières,* iron tools, wire. They also hauled in daintier things, much treasured by the inland peoples: the porcelain beads known as *rasade,* mirrors and bells, combs and earrings. They hauled over the portages, then downriver to Ville-Marie the precious pelts that shaped the economy of New France.

These adventurers had founded a new culture grounded in two domains. One was the forest, into which the trappers scattered to hunt and skin the precious beavers. The other was the trading post, where the furs were brought in an annual festival that became notorious for its wild licence and abandon. In the usual way of lonely men, the voyageurs who came from France or Ville-Marie found mates, and produced a new people.

Young Ezekiel Solomon, for example, arrived in the summer of 1761 at Mackinac Island, at the narrows between Lakes Michigan and Huron, to do business with the Indians. According to family memories kept by his grandson Louie—an offspring of Ezekiel and his Indian wife—he had come from Berlin. In 1964, an historical plaque was erected at Mackinaw hailing Ezekiel Solomon as "Michigan's First Jewish Settler." Peace be unto Michigan!—But it did not exist when Ezekiel came to the island and became a successful fur trader, sometimes captive in the wars between British and French, but always a good King's man.

Believing himself far removed from Europe and Europe's wars, Ezekiel watched the world and its great events closing in on his busy trading post at Michilimackinac. He had inadvertently settled on what was becoming, and was long to remain, a pressure crack between empires. On June 4, 1763, during a horrible massacre at Mackinac, Ezekiel was snatched from his post by the militia and taken into custody. Rescued by daring friends among the Ottawa Indians, later ransomed at Montréal, he might have stayed among the civilized folk in the south. But by the relatively peaceable 1790s—just as permanent log houses were finally going up at the makeshift Lake Ontario outpost of York and the British were strengthening the frail lakeshore fortifications that were to fail in 1812—trader Ezekiel was back in the north, and now settled on Drummond Island. The relatively peaceable last decade of the eighteenth century was a good time to create a family, so he did, fathering the first Jewish-aboriginal children born in those high latitudes of Ontario.

Ezekiel lived on to about 1808, rearing his children on the beaver frontier. He also was forced to shepherd his young family through the changes that involved the invisible lines of surveyors, commissioned and approved by faraway powers. For more than a decade after Britain conceded defeat, and even as Elizabeth and John Simcoe were packing their belongings for the treacherous voyage back to England, the boundaries between the United States and Upper Canada's far northwest region were still fluid. They would remain so for decades. In 1796, the British military post at Michilimackinac was transferred to the United States by treaty. Preferring to live and work under the Union Jack, Ezekiel Solomon and his family, the soldiers and other civilians retired the short distance to St. Joseph Island, at the Sault, establishing a fort and blockhouse to mark the edge of empire. Then came the Second War of American Independence, and in 1812 the British regiments recaptured Mackinaw, only to lose it again in 1815.

Once again, the Solomon boys, soldiers, old voyageurs and all others doggedly loyal to the Crown pulled up stakes and moved, this time to Drummond Island, not far across the water from the old post of St. Joseph. Then came the final blow to those migrants along the shifting northwest borders of empire: yet another British-U.S. treaty survey, which made a loop in the line between territories and abruptly put Drummond Island and its inhabitants back inside United States territory.

It was then that Ezekiel's children and grandchildren, and dozens of other children of the wilderness, decided at last to move so far into the Ontario interior that no more twists in the international boundary would land them on the wrong side. Here were Loyalists who probably would never have called themselves that, but whose loyalty prompted one of the most fascinating journeys in the story of Ontario.

Because most of the travellers could neither read nor write, their exodus would probably be forgotten by now—had it not been for the prescience of A. C. Osborne, a local historian in the community of Penetanguishene, on Georgian Bay. At some point late in the Old Queen's reign—perhaps in 1895—Mr. Osborne wrote down the reminiscences of several elderly Drummond Island émigrés, "almost," he tells us, "or as nearly as possible, in their own words." What he produced may not be accurate reports of what happened—Osborne complains of "a little disregard for the correct sequence of events, and a tendency to get occurrences mixed." But from within his narratives, real people emerge, each trying his best to tell the stories he had lived with for decades, and that nobody before had bothered to ask him about.

The interviews were published in 1901, then, as far as I can tell, forgotten. As the editor of that publication tells us,

> the story of the transfer of the British garrison from Drummond Island to Penetanguishene in 1828 and the migration of voyageurs connected with the post has never been told in print. In the following notes Mr. Osborne has endeavored to gather this story from the lips of the few survivors who migrated at that time. Descendants of French-Canadians largely predominated in this movement, but we also get glimpses of what a strange and heterogeneous people once gathered around Mackinaw and Drummond Island . . . The migrant voyageurs settled principally near Penetanguishene, in the township of Tiny, Simcoe County. Offshoots of the band settled at Old Fort Ste. Marie, at Desertion and Coldwater, and another south of Lake Simcoe, near Pefferlaw, York County . . .

The story that Osborne heard began in the far northwest as the winter of 1828 started to close in on the scattered islands at the very top of Lake Huron. A certain Sergeant Rawson was given the solemn task of hauling down the British flag for the last time from its mast on Drummond Island. A British officer handed over the keys to the fort to United States officers as the soldiers and civilians loyal to the King made ready to leave forever their island home.

The first of the seventy-five families of voyageurs followed the military to Penetang that winter, where they settled on the land grants routinely doled out to those prepared to settle in Upper Canada. The others came later, by bateau, making their way down the shoreline of Georgian Bay. When they reached Penetang, they found only a few huts made of poles covered with cedar bark. One of Osborne's informants, a boy at the time, recalled that "there were only three houses there: a block-house, the quarters of Capt. Woodin, the post-commander; a log-house covered with cedar bark for the sailors near the shore; and a log-house on the hill, called the 'Masonic Arms,' a place of entertainment kept by Mrs. Johnson." The civilian townsite, that summer of 1829, "was mostly a cedar swamp, with a few Indian wigwams and fishing shanties."

But the men and women who came from Drummond Island did not expect luxury or the subtle virtues and graces of a new British Empire being cultivated along the north shore of Lake Ontario. They were citizens of the wilds, and knew how to make do. The blacksmith father of Michael Labatte, one of Mr. Osborne's informants, had come up from Lower Canada with the British Army and witnessed the capture of Mackinaw in 1812. Michael's mother, who was Chippewa, taught her son to speak her language. Michael recalled late in life that "nothing but French and Indian was spoken at Drummond Island," and he learned English only after arriving at Penetanguishene, the first place he'd ever heard it spoken. Whatever their mix of ancestries, all the voyageurs shared the French language, ignorance of the world outside the wilderness of Lieutenant-Governor Simcoe's Upper Canada and immense knowledge of their land. And they shared the spirit of Étienne Brûlé, who, like them, had been born with a restless, wandering heart. As the dominion over all North America east of the Rocky

Mountains passed from Versailles to London, then to the capital of the United States, Old France lived on in two places.

One was in the speech, customs and the angle of rooflines of the houses of families settled along the shadowy bayous and sluggish rivers of south Louisiana. The other was in the green stronghold of the beaver kingdom, where even after 1763 and the cession of France's holdings in North America to Spain and England, the voyageurs and coureurs de bois continued to work as they had for more than a century.

Unlike the Quinte Loyalists, the voyagers who came down from Drummond had little to gain, and perhaps something to lose. They could easily have chosen to live under the Stars and Stripes. Some of their kindred and comrades did so, and the traffic between Penetang and Drummond Island never stopped during the century when Osborne was conducting his interviews. But they were patriots of a kind easily overlooked, because their patriotism was without fanfare or fireworks. Going to Penetang made sense to them, once they had decided to remain loyal to their King.

A Scottish trader named Gordon had come down from Drummond Island in 1825 and set up what he called the "Place of Penetangoushene." It was hardly a grander or easier place to come to. The tales of the passage are ominous forecasts of the life they would live, at least in their first years in southern Ontario.

As the boy-voyager Solomon—"spelled L-e-w-i-s—though they call me Louie"—told Mr. Osborne:

When the military forces removed from Drummond Island to Penetanguishene, the Government authorities chartered the brig *Wellington* to carry the soldiers, military and naval supplies, and government stores; but the vessel was too small, and they were obliged to charter another vessel, and my father was instructed by the Government to charter the schooner *Alice* commanded by the owner, Capt. Hackett. On her were placed a detachment of soldiers, some military supplies, and the private property of my father, consisting of two span of horses, four cows, twelve sheep, eight hogs, harness and household furniture.

A French-Canadian named Lepine, his wife and child, a tavern-keeper named Fraser, with thirteen barrels of whiskey, also formed part of the cargo. The captain and his crew and many of the soldiers became intoxicated, and during the following night a storm arose, during which the vessel was driven on a rock known as "Horse Island" (Fitzwilliam) near the southernmost point of Manitoulin Island.

The passengers and crew, in a somewhat advanced stage of drunkenness, managed to reach the shore in safety; also one horse, some pork, and the thirteen barrels of whiskey . . . The whole company were too much intoxicated to entertain an intelligent idea of the operation, but were sufficiently conscious of what they were doing to secure the entire consignment of whiskey.

The woman and her infant were left on the wreck, as her husband, Pierre Lepine, was on shore drunk among the others, too oblivious to realize the gravity of the situation, or to render any assistance. Mrs. Lepine, in the darkness and fury of the storm, wrapped the babe in a blanket, and having tied it on her back, lashed herself securely to the mast, and there clung all night long through a furious storm of wind and drenching rain, from eleven o'clock till daylight, or about six o'clock in the morning, when the maudlin crew, having recovered in a measure from their drunken stupor, rescued her from her perilous position in a yawl boat.

Such an experience on the waters of Lake Huron, in the month of November, must have certainly bordered on the tragical. The vessel and the remainder of the cargo proved a total loss. The lurching of the schooner from side to side pitched the big cannon down the hatch way, going clear through the bottom, thus, together with pounding on the rocks, completing the wreck. The horse, a fine carriage roadster, remained on the island for several years. My father offered a good price to any one who would bring him away, but he never got him back, and he finally died on the island. This circumstance gave it the name of Horse Island. The infant lived to grow up and marry among the later settlers, but I do not remember to whom, neither do I know what became of her.

If the little girl so miraculously saved did live on in Penetang, her life there would have been rough, unsafe—as Louie Solomon made clear to Mr. Osborne.

Tom Landrigan kept a canteen, and bought goods and naval supplies stolen by soldiers from the old Red Store. He was found guilty with the others, and sentenced to be hung. It cost my father a large sum of money to get Tom clear. He was married to my sister.

One day I went up to the cricket ground and saw something round rolled in a handkerchief, which was lying in the snow, and which the foxes had been playing with. When I unrolled it, the ghastly features of a man looked up at me. It was such a horrible sight that I started home on the run and told my father. He went up to investigate, and found it was the head of a drunken soldier, who had cut his throat while in delirium tremens at Mundy's canteen, and had been buried near the cricket ground.

Dr. Nevison, surgeon of the 15th Regiment, had said in a joke, in the hearing of two soldiers; that he would like to have the soldier's head. They got it, presented it to him, when he refused it, horrified. They took it back and threw it on the ground, instead of burying it with the body, and it was kicked about in the way I mention for some time. One of the two soldiers afterwards went insane, and the other cut his thumb and died of blood-poisoning in Toronto. The names of the two soldiers were Tom Taylor and John Miller.

Michael Labatte's memories of Penetang are a list of such occurrences.

> . . . I carried the mail to the Sault in winter on snow-shoes. I
> made the trip from Penetanguishene to the Sault and back—
> three hundred miles—with a sleigh and two dogs in fifteen
> days—snow three feet deep.
>
> I once made the trip in fourteen days. Dig a hole in the snow
> with my snow-shoes, spread spruce boughs, eat piece of cold
> pork, smoke pipe and go to sleep. I often had *mal de racquette*. I
> would sharpen my flint, then split the flesh of the ankle above the
> instep in several places, and sometimes down the calf of the leg
> for a remedy.
>
> I was in the Shawanaga country for furs on two occasions
> when I could not get out, on account of floods. I was four days
> without food, which was cached at the mouth of the river. At
> another time I was five days without food, except moss off the
> rocks on account of floods and soft weather.
>
> . . . I knew about the Tom Landrigan scrape—getting into
> trouble about stolen Government military supplies. Mighty close
> shave for Tom—he was sentenced to be hanged. I saw Prisque
> soon after he fell and broke his neck in Penetanguishene. He
> looked as if he had a black handkerchief tied round his neck.
> He was sawing off a board lying across the beams, and sawed it
> too short and pitched down head first. I saw the drunken soldier,
> who cut his throat at Mundy's Canteen, and who was buried
> near the old cricket ground . . . I went with the volunteers to
> Chippewa and Navy Island to clear out the Mackenzie rebels.
> My father was married twice. I was the eldest of the first family,
> and worked for myself since I was fourteen years old. I have had
> a family of fifteen children.

Myriad forces, some darker than others, have conspired to keep the
loyal travellers from Drummond Island a secret and out of the grand

narrative of Ontario's founding and establishment. To the élite founded by John Graves Simcoe, they existed simply beyond the mental horizon. Ezekiel's descendants and their kin and friends were not pure British breeding stock, stalwarts of the Church of England, fit for peopling the new British Empire in America. They were something else—Catholics, if anything, and children of the wilderness, for whom work meant disappearance into the forests and for whom marriage was a matter of simple agreement and moving in together. (The irregularity of marriages among the northerners he inherited troubled Lieutenant-Governor Simcoe deeply.)

Never mind that these people lived only 130 kilometres north of Upper Canada's capital. They were foreigners or, at best, good guides. Most of the men interviewed by A. C. Osborne remembered guiding notables into the wilderness—members of the Ontario ascendancy, English aristocrats. Lewis Solomon remembered a "lordship" he took into Lake Huron, whose first call of the day was "'Louie, are you there? Bring me my cocktail.'—Soon to be followed by the same call from each of the other tents in rotation, and my first duty was always to prepare their morning bitters."

Despite their treatment as serfs and lackeys by the rulers of Ontario and by British tourists, the Drummond Island voyagers never drop a hint of disapproval or complaint. Many of those so high-handedly dismissed by the nobs they couriered up the Ontario waters on tame adventures bore wounds earned by defending the Crown during the War of American Independence, and again at Mackinaw, St. Joseph Island, Sault Ste. Marie and other places during the war of 1812–15. They relate with

pride their backing of the Crown against the "Mackenzie rebels" in 1837.

But there *is* something mysterious and different about these people and their ease in worlds no southern Ontario urbanite would ever recognize or understand. Among the stories Lewis Solomon told A. C. Osborne is one that comes from the realm of faery, the twice-told tale of the wilderness, where nothing is quite what it seems to be.

Once I took a Jesuit priest to Beausoleil Island to look for a Eucharist said to be buried there, with French and Spanish silver coins guns, axes, etc. The spot, he said, was marked by a stone two feet long with a Latin inscription on it. The priest had a map or drawing showing where the stone ought to be, and where to dig, but we found nothing.

I knew the hemlock tree and the spot where it was said Father Proulx found the pot of gold, and I saw the hole, but it was made by Indians following up a mink's burrow. Peter Byrnes, of the Bay View House, Penetanguishene, and a friend spent a day digging near an elm tree not far from the same spot, near the old Fort on the Wye. Sergeant James Maloney, of the militia, found two silver crosses on Vent's farm, near Hogg River.

Many pits have been dug on Beausoleil Island, Present Island, Flat Point and other places in search of hidden treasures. An Indian and myself once found a rock rich with gold near Moon River. We marked the spot, but I never could find it on going back.

IV
THE SETTLING

19
MRS. JAMESON'S WILDEST TOUR

IN HIS 1877 NOVEL *The American,* Henry James introduces us to Mr.
Babcock, a pale young Unitarian minister from Massachusetts, abroad
on the Grand Tour. Alas, poor Babcock! To have a soul in which the
aesthete and the moralist are always at war!

"European life seemed to him unscrupulous and impure," James
tells us.

> And yet he had an exquisite sense of beauty; and as beauty was
> often inextricably associated with the above displeasing condi-
> tions, as he wished, above all, to be just and dispassionate, and as
> he was, furthermore, extremely devoted to "culture," he could
> not bring himself to decide that Europe was utterly bad. But he
> thought it was very bad indeed.

> To keep himself morally alert, and free from swooning before paint-
> ings and beautiful churches, he "carried Mrs. Jameson's works about in
> his trunk; he delighted in aesthetic analysis, and received peculiar
> impressions from everything he saw."

While she adored Europe with a passion foreign to Mr. Babcock, Mrs. Jameson—the former Miss Anna Brownell Murphy, of Dublin— would have been an excellent travelling companion for any Victorian worried about tumbling headlong into embarrassing raptures. Her *Memoirs of Early Italian Painters* (1845), *Memoirs and Essays on Art, Literature and Social Morals* (1846) and especially *Sacred and Legendary Art* (1848)—almost certainly among Mrs. Jameson's works in Mr. Babcock's mobile library—were intended to aid the new, middle-class cultural tourist on a swing through European churches and museums, but in fact cushioned the blow of all that opulent Catholicism. These are quite modern books. Mrs. Jameson gives short shrift to "Taste," the "Sublime" and other preoccupations of eighteenth-century tourists, who thought travel was more about swooning than looking and less about thinking. For many gallery-goers nowadays, art's value as evidence about the textures of a certain historical moment is taken for granted. In Mrs. Jameson's day, it was still novel to be told that art appreciation was largely a matter of seeking "the true spirit and signifi-cance of works of Art, as connected with the history of Religion and Civilization." Mrs. Jameson's best Victorian readers—men and women more morally earnest and better schooled in history, on the whole, than their Georgian grandmothers—found the notion novel and quite interesting. It also made painting and sculpture easier to look at, by emphasizing the storytelling that is never really absent from any artwork.

If her books were intellectually *au courant,* so was Anna. She moved easily through Georgian London's literary and scientific circles after her launch by betrothal, in her mid-twenties, to Robert Jameson, a well-connected London attorney. Among her friends were the poet Hartley Coleridge, son of Samuel Taylor Coleridge, the essayist Charles Lamb and Elizabeth Jesser Reid, a Unitarian who had been active in the successful movement to abolish slavery throughout the British Empire.

Given the bright, serious men and women with whom she easily socialized, one can only wonder what kept brilliant Anna and plodding Robert on track together. At every point along the way, the engagement seemed ready to collapse and come to nothing. In June, 1821, she broke it off, and decamped for Italy to work as a governess. By 1825, however, she was back in London, married to Robert, and the author of her first notable work, *The Diary of an Ennuyée,* a fiction based on the travels in Italy she had undertaken to elude Robert four years before.

From the outset, Anna's husband seemed more keenly intent on escaping domestic bliss than enjoying it. In 1829, he sailed off to Dominica without her to become a judge. Not one for sitting idly by, waiting to be fetched over the ocean by a husband obviously disinclined to do so, Anna returned to the continent with her father, an accomplished painter of miniature portraits, and his patron, Sir Gerard Noel. Jameson quickly became bored with life in the British Caribbean—"a dismal, vulgar, sensual, utterly unintellectual place to spend the best years of one's life in," he complained in a letter to Anna. In 1832, he announced to Anna his impending arrival in England. Together for a few months thereafter, Robert and Anna parted again when he picked up a commission as magistrate in Upper Canada and sailed off without her.

But unfortunately, high and sociable intelligence did not translate quickly into cash; and Anna, long of the former, was notably short on the latter after Robert's departure for Canada, and all her life. Hence, she produced money-spinning books about notable women, written for serious middle-class readers eager (like Mr. Babcock) to see in culture the grand unfolding of moral themes, calamities and triumphs: *Memoirs of the Loves of the Poets* (1829), *Memoirs of Celebrated Female Sovereigns* (1831), *Memoirs of the Beauties of the Court of Charles II* (1831) and her durably, commercially successful study of Shakespearean heroines, *Characteristics of Women* (1832).

Separated from her husband a second time, Anna went back again to the continent, this time to Germany. There, as everywhere, she quickly fell into a circle of intellectually cultivated people. Among early literary acquaintances were the great literary critic August Wilhelm von Schlegel, and Ottilie von Goethe, daughter-in-law of Germany's most celebrated poet. Anna soon became a regular visitor at Ottilie's table in Weimar, and her lifelong friend.

Anna Jameson, toast of international literary coteries, was the sort of person one might have expected to turn up in Ontario at the dawn of Victoria's reign, just for curiosity's sake. Middle-class Britons had long been interested in their immense Empire, especially its exotic margins, and were interested in going there. But the attraction of Ontario for Anna Jameson was not the usual one. She sailed from England in October, 1836, bound for Toronto, on yet another doomed mission to reconcile Robert to life with her.

She arrived in Toronto, discovered Jameson in his lakeshore house between the town of York and Fort York—*The Globe and Mail* newspaper building now occupies the site, set back from the lakeshore behind a kilometre-wide apron of landfill—and moved in with him to begin her work of persuasion. Her success, as well as her sureness about where she stood, can be judged from a letter she wrote in April, 1837, to her father.

> . . . I hope to be with you about the end of summer . . . Mr. Jameson is just the same and I am just the same therefore we are just as much and as hopelessly separated as ever; he has done nothing to make the time tolerable to me, but this is not from absolute unkindness, but more absence of feeling . . .

The next month, she wrote to her friend Robert Noel (a cousin of Lady Byron), including a sour portrait of the place she had come to.

> Your wish that I might find here a sphere of happiness and usefulness is not realized. I am in a small community of fourth-rate, half-educated, or uneducated people, where local politics of the meanest kind engross the men, and petty gossip and household cares the women. As I think differently from Mr. Jameson on every subject which can occupy a thinking mind, I keep clear of any expression . . . of my opinions.

Another woman might have retreated from the field quietly and caught a ship home as soon as possible to nurse her battle wounds. But Anna being Anna, she decided that, if she could not regain a husband in the New World, she could at least get another book out of the attempt. The result was *Winter Studies and Summer Rambles in Canada* (1838)—a remarkable testament to the great natural beauty of Ontario in the early nineteenth century and a witness to the surprise many urbane European visitors felt upon first encountering the wilderness of the New World, dense, magnificent, seemingly limitless.

On her first trip to Niagara-on-the-Lake, in January, 1837, Anna wrote:

I think that but for this journey I never could have imagined the sublime desolation of a northern winter, and it has impressed me strongly. In the first place, the whole atmosphere appeared as if converted into snow, which fell in thick, tiny, starry flakes, till the buffalo robes and furs about us appeared like swansdown, and the harness on the horses of the same delicate material. The whole earth was a white waste: the road, on which the sleigh-track was only just perceptible, ran for miles in a straight line; on each side rose the dark, melancholy pine-forest, slumbering drearily in the hazy air. Between us and the edge of the forest were frequent spaces of cleared or half-cleared land, spotted over with the black charred stumps and blasted trunks of once magnificent trees, projecting from the snow-drift. These, which are perpetually recurring objects in a Canadian landscape, have a most melancholy appearance . . . A few rods from the land, the cold grey waters, and cold, grey, snow-encumbered atmosphere, were mingled with each other, and each seemed either.

Even a snippet as brief as this one is enough to prove *Winter Studies and Summer Rambles* to be the work of a superb travel writer. But Anna most fervently wanted to be remembered as an adventurer up Lake Huron and into the Superior wilderness. Of the canoe trip north, in the summer of 1837, she writes:

I cannot squeeze into one or even 20 sheets of paper all I was about to tell you; therefore for the present I will only say that I am just returned from the wildest and most extraordinary tour you can imagine, and am moreover the first Englishwoman—the first European female who ever accomplished this journey.

She did not, of course, reach this farthest point on her wildest tour without help from the people who knew the land best. Mrs. Jameson's accomplishment was remembered by those voyageurs with their usual bemusement at the doings of sophisticated European visitors. Here are some rambling remembrances about Anna by Lewis Solomon.

Neddy McDonald, the old mail-carrier, sometimes went with us . . . It is said that it fell to Neddy's lot, on the trip with Lady Jameson, to carry her on his back from the canoe to the shore occasionally when a good landing was not found. As Mrs. Jameson was of goodly proportions, it naturally became a source of irritation to Neddy, which he did not conceal from his fellow voyageurs.

Mrs. Jameson had joined the party of Colonel Jarvis at

the Manitoulin Island. She was a rich lady from England, well educated, and traveling for pleasure. She was an agreeable woman, considerate of others and extremely kind-hearted. I was a pretty fair singer in those days, and she often asked me to sing those beautiful songs of the French voyageurs which she seemed to think so nice and I often sang them for her. Mrs. Jameson ran the "Sault Rapids" in a birch-bark canoe, with two Chippewa Indian guides. They named her Was-sa-je-wun-e-qua, "Woman of the bright stream."

I was attendant on Mrs. Jameson, and was obliged to sleep in her tent, as a sort of protector, in a compartment separated by a hanging screen. I was obliged to wait till she retired, and then crawl in quietly without waking her. Mrs. Jameson gathered several human skulls at Head Island, above Nascoutiong, to take home with her. She kept them till I persuaded her to throw them out, as I did not fancy their company. When I parted with Mrs. Jameson and shook hands with her I found four five dollar gold pieces in my hand.

THE MOST CELEBRATED PAGES in *Winter Studies and Summer Rambles* have always been those describing her guided trip past the Sault and into Lake Superior. But to my mind, no episode related in her Ontario book is more riveting or revealing than her brief stay with the reclusive squire of Lake Erie, Colonel Thomas Talbot.

In Montréal, in 1793, the strikingly handsome young Irish officer Thomas Talbot, just twenty, caught the eye of Elizabeth Simcoe, and the more businesslike attention of the Governor, who made the young man his private secretary and aide de camp. Talbot persisted in these positions for a year before returning to England and military service in the Napoleonic wars. Though his high connections and friendly temperament made him perfect material for a long and illustrious career in the imperial service and pleasant retirement to a

British country house thereafter, Talbot abruptly resigned his commission in 1800 and announced his intention to return to the Upper Canadian wilderness, to establish an outpost of empire on the north shore of Lake Erie. Exactly why a young officer, not yet thirty, would renounce an easy career in London society for a hard life in Ontario may never be known. His biographers have hinted at failures in love and dislike of Regency frippery. "Being much at Court," writes one,

> he had become sated and disgusted with the artificiality, the frivolity, the vices, and dissipation of fashionable society; probably this had something to do with his decision . . . He was yet at an age, when young men dream dreams, and like other idealists he hoped to realize his Utopia in the New World.

Be all that as it may, Thomas Talbot made firm his decision to establish his colony by acquiring five thousand acres of lakeshore property south of London, Ontario. The timing was right. The depopulation of southwestern Ontario by the calamitous conflicts between the League of the Great Peace and the Wendat, between French and English, and finally between the British and the United States in the War of 1812—all this desolation was being ended by the influx of settlers from across the seas. From his refuge on the Lake Erie shore, Talbot invited yet more farmers, trading them land while building a reputation sharply at odds with his earlier portrait. The dashing officer had become known as an eccentric, baronial despot by the time Anna Jameson arrived in Ontario—exactly the kind of romantic relic to whet Anna Jameson's intellectual appetite.

While interested in dropping by Ontario's London, she had no intention of lingering.

> I was anxious to push on to the Talbot Settlement, or, as it is called here, the Talbot *Country*—a name not ill applied to a vast tract of land stretching east to west along the shore of Lake Erie,

and of which Colonel Talbot is the sovereign *de facto,* if not *de jure*—be it spoken without any derogation to the rights of our lord the king. This immense settlement, the circumstances to which it owned its existence, and the charter of the eccentric man who founded it on such principles as have insured its success and prosperity, altogether inspired me with the strongest interest and curiosity.

. . . That a man of noble birth, high in the army, young and handsome, and eminently qualified to shine in society, should voluntarily banish himself from all intercourse with the civilized world, and submit for long tedious years to the most horrible privations of every kind, appeared too incomprehensible to be attributed to any of the ordinary motives and feelings of a responsible human being.

She knew of his aristocratic disdain for "gentlemen settlers" and his preference for common working men, upon whose obedience and strong backs he could depend. She had caught intriguing tales of his annual appearance, like a mysterious high priest emerging from his shrine of the hidden god, at the village of St. Thomas (which had been named in his honour) to preside over the anniversary solemnities of his settlement.

With typical forthrightness, she hired a trap at a London inn and set out south in the direction of Col. Talbot's Lake Erie domain, without any firm assurance that "this hermit-lord of the forest" would receive her.

The reports I had heard of his singular manners, of his being a sort of woman-hater, who had not for thirty years allowed a female to appear in his sight, I had partly discredited, yet enough remained to make me feel a little nervous. However, my resolution was taken, and the colonel had been apprized of my intended visit, though of his gracious acquiescence I was yet to learn; so, putting my trust in Providence as heretofore, I prepared to meet the old buffalo in his lair.

What she found is surely best described in her own words.

We had traveled nearly the whole day through open well-cleared land . . . Suddenly we came upon a thick wood, through which the road ran due west, in a straight line. The shadows fell deeper and deeper from the depth of foliage on either side, and I could not see a yard around, but exactly before me the last gleams of twilight lingered where the moon was setting. Once or twice I was startled by seeing a deer bound across the path, his large antlers being for one instant defined, *penciled,* as it were, against the sky, then lost. The darkness fell deeper every moment, the silence more solemn. The whip-poor-will began his melancholy cry, and an owl set forth a prolonged shriek, which, if I had not heard it before, would have frightened me . . .

The road, mocking my impatience, took so many bends, and sweeps, and windings, up hill and down hill, that it was an eternity before we arrived. The Colonel piques himself exceedingly on this gracious and picturesque approach to his residence, and not without reason; but on the present occasion I could have preferred a line more direct to the line of beauty. The darkness, which concealed its charms, left me sensible only to its length. On ascending some high ground, a group of buildings was dimly descried; and after oversetting part of a snake-fence before we found an entrance, we drove up to the door. Lights were gleaming in the windows, and the Colonel sallied forth with prompt gallantry to receive me.

My welcome was not only cordial, but courtly. The Colonel, taking me under his arm, and ordering the boy and his horses to be well taken care of, handed me into the hall or vestibule, where sacks of wheat and piles of sheepskins lay heaped in primitive fashion; thence into a room, the walls of which were formed of naked logs. Here no *fauteuil,* spring-cushioned, extended its comfortable arms . . . Colonel Talbot held all such luxuries in sovereign contempt.

Though darkness had fallen by the time Anna's trap came rambling up to the door of Colonel Talbot's *château,* as she calls it, and the hour was late, the proprietor engaged her immediately in conversation.

I was pressed with a profusion of questions as well as hospitable attentions; but wearied, exhausted, aching in every nerve, the spirit with which I had at first met him in his own style was fast ebbing. I would neither speak nor eat, and was soon dismissed to repose.

Upon waking the next morning, she found herself in a wildly picturesque situation and Talbot in charge of his mansion "like the eagle his eyrie." Anyone who has visited the Canadian side of the smallest Great Lake will recognize the landscape Anna discovered—a wild, rough home site bounded by

a precipitous descent into a wild woody ravine, along the bottom of which winds a gentle stream, till it steals into the lake: this stream is in winter a raging torrent. The storms and the gradual action of the waves have detached large portions of the cliff in front of the house, and with them huge trees.

The master of this forest domain was an elder of sixty-five, "in rustic dress," with a "good-humoured, jovial, weather-beaten face." He eagerly told Anna the story of his passage from England with Lieutenant-Governor Simcoe in 1793 and his travels with Simcoe on his first expedition to study and map the western districts of

Upper Canada. He seems to have known nothing about the bloody, dismal conflicts and epidemics that in earlier centuries had emptied southwestern Ontario of its inhabitants. In the version he gave Anna, in any case, the district had been deep wilderness *ab origine,* with no European settlers and only a "few wandering tribes of Huron and Chippewas, and the Six Nations settled on Grand River."

It was during his western expeditions with John Simcoe in the early 1790s that the fashioning of a scrap of feudal Britain in Upper Canada "took possession of Colonel Talbot's mind, and became the ruling passion and sole interest of his future life." For the first sixteen years after taking possession of his land grant, he rapidly planted settlers on two-hundred-acre lots—the yeoman guard and guarantee of his private fiefdom—and got down to work with the same zeal he demanded of the newcomers. As he told Anna, he

> slept upon the bare earth, cooked three meals a day for twenty woodsmen, cleaned his own boots, washed his own linen, milked his cows, churned his butter, and made and baked his bread . . . To all these heterogeneous functions of sowing and reaping, felling and planting, frying, boiling, washing, wringing, brewing, and baking, he added another even more extraordinary;—for many years he solemnized all the marriages in his district!

By the time Anna arrived, Talbot reckoned his Ontario holdings at 650,000 acres, of which 98,700 had been cleared and put under cultivation. The inhabitants, including the population of the villages that dotted the Lake Erie shoreline between Long Point and Detroit, numbered about 50,000. "'You see,' said he gaily, 'I may boast, like the Irishman in the farce, of having peopled a whole country with my own hands.'"

Upper Canada's governors had come to suspect him of establishing an independent barony in their territory. This, in fact, the restless squire was doubtless trying to do. When Anna asked his motives for advocating a life so different from Britain's new, progressive civilization, he stormed against

the follies and falsehoods and restrictions of artificial life, in bitter and scornful terms; no ascetic monk or *radical* philosopher could have been more eloquently indignant.

But the soul of Anna Jameson, somewhat improbably, was enchanted by Thomas Talbot.

Family and aristocratic pride I found a prominent feature in the character of this remarkable man. A Talbot of Malahide, of a family representing the same barony from father to son for six hundred years, he set, not unreasonably, a high value on his noble and unstained lineage; and, in his lonely position, the simplicity of his life and manners lent to these lofty and not unreal pretensions a kind of poetical dignity.

But as much as Anna admired Talbot for his Stoic simplicity and virtue, she concluded that he had inflicted upon himself a life "worse than solitude." Because he would allow no social equal in his vicinity and dealt only with inferiors, "whose servility he despised, and whose resistance enraged him," he had become old before his time and deeply isolated from the world of affairs and events that so fascinated his visitor.

He has honour, power, obedience; but where are the love, the troops of friends, which also should accompany old age? He is alone—a lonely man . . . He suffers, I think; and not being given to general or philosophical reasoning, causes and effects are felt, not known . . .

Another thing . . . was the sort of indifference with which he regarded all the stirring events of the last thirty years. Dynasties rose and disappeared; kingdoms were passed from hand to hand

like wine decanters; battles were lost and won;—he neither knew,
nor heard, nor cared. No post, no newspaper brought to his
forest-hut the tidings of victory and defeat, of revolution of
empires, "or rumours of unsuccessful or successful war." When
he first took to the bush, Napoleon was consul; when he emerged
from his solitude, the tremendous game of ambition had been
played out, and Napoleon and his deeds and his dynasty were
numbered with the things o'erpast. With the stream of events
had flowed by equally progress of social improvement—the
changes in public opinion. Conceive what a gulf between us! But
though I could go to him, he could not come to me—my sympa-
thies had a wider range . . .

The principal foreign and domestic events of his *reign* are the
last American war, in which he narrow escaped being taken prisoner by a detachment of the enemy, who ransacked his house,
and drove off his horses and cattle; and a visit which he received
some years ago from three young Englishmen of rank and
fortune, Lord Stanley, Mr. Stuart Wortley, and Mr. Labouchere,
who spent some weeks with him. These events, and his voyages
to England, seem to be the epochs from which he dated. His last
trip to England was about three years ago. From these occasional
flights he returns like an old eagle to his perch on the cliff,
whence he looks down upon the world he has quitted with
supreme contempt and indifference, and around on what which
he has created, with much self-applause and self-gratulation.

What Anna had intended to be a visit lasting one day—if Talbot
would see her at all—turned into a week-long stay. They obviously
liked each other. They could have met, on one of Talbot's later excur-
sions to visit his old friend, the Duke of Wellington, and other army
friends from his youth. But Anna Jameson and Thomas Talbot never
met again.

Mrs. Jameson departed Ontario for England, via New York City, in
September, 1837, having made the necessary arrangements with

Robert for a final separation. For the remaining twenty-three years of her life, she was a busy woman of letters, travelling between England and Germany, making friends with the literati wherever she went. In 1846, she helped rescue Elizabeth Barrett from imprisonment by a tyrannical father and enabled her friend and the poet Robert Browning to elope to Italy. Less dramatically, she continued her notable labours in art history, writing the works on the iconography of painting that James's Mr. Babcock found indispensable.

If her meeting with Colonel Talbot has proven unimportant to her biographers, who barely take note of it, Anna's account is rich in information about the background of modern Ontario, which did not embrace modernity quite as quickly as the rest of the world. In Talbot, she found a man who had staked his life on *not* keeping the pace of rushing change, industrial and intellectual. Though herself a modern woman, Anna went out of her way to paint a kindly picture of her antique host. Talbot recalled that, in 1812, when Britain and the United States plunged into fresh war, he had looked on as Americans invaded his territory, destroying crops and driving farmers off their land. Yet he was unshakeable. Anna writes:

> Colonel Talbot, a true hero after another fashion, was encoun-
> tering, amid the forest solitude, uncheered by sympathy,
> unbribed by fame, enemies far more formidable, and earning a
> far purer as well as more real and lasting immortality.

Anna knew, of course, that his little kingdom in southwestern Ontario could not last for long. The tumultuous, mechanized, egalitarian world was destined to catch up with the Talbot settlers, if they didn't catch up with it first. They were remarkably unreliable royalists in the War of 1812, and prompt to adopt American-style republicanism in Ontario's Rebellion of 1837. Talbot died in 1853, unforgiven by his settlers for his high-handed autocracy; and he died without forgiving them for their ingratitude for his benevolent dictatorship. Anna did not know that, along with other founders of modern civilization in

Ontario, Thomas Talbot was destined to be lost to our collective memory; or, if remembered at all, recalled as a caricature. Yet he deserves at least the respect Anna Jameson paid him, along with admiration for his principled conservatism and the enthusiasm with which he crafted the heraldic romance of his life.

20

1837

DURING A STOPOVER IN THE VILLAGE of St. Thomas, Mrs. Jameson found two newspapers published there, "one violently Tory, the other as violently radical." With this comment, Anna made her nearest approach to thinking about Canadian politics, or to be more precise, to acknowledging that Canada had politics. She seemed unaware that a storm was brewing between factions in Ontario, and nowhere more menacingly than in the Lake Erie domains of her new friend, the odd Colonel Thomas Talbot. And, of course, she could not have known that the year of her wildest tour was destined to become a mythic date in Canadian imagination.

The myth-making has done little harm to Canada over the years, and it has provided a tale of heroic death and patriotic mayhem in a province that has long viewed its history as embarrassingly short on both. The names of its leaders in Upper and Lower Canada have been preserved in the name of a gaggle of Communist legionnaires, the Mackenzie-Papineau Brigade, who fought for Stalin in the Spanish Civil War, and its principal actors recalled in at least one interesting play, Rick Salutin's *1837: The Farmers' Revolt*. So far, however, it has not found a writer to do Swiftian justice to its absurdity.

In the piously leftist version of folk memory, the Rebellion pitted two factions against each other. One, very wicked indeed, was the Family Compact—which, as you know if you have been reading this book carefully, was not a powder-puff container for Georgian ladies but the platoon of British civilizers, rulers and satraps whom John Graves Simcoe had installed in his new capital at York forty years earlier. Viewed sympathetically (as I'm inclined to do), the Compact members were conservative royalists, guardians of British political traditions in a revolutionary world and attractively dull. (No sensible person wants flamboyance in a politician, banker or dentist.) They stayed put in their offices at York during the gradually swelling influx of immigrants into Ontario during the early nineteenth century and supervised the scattering of these newcomers to their rich, bountiful grants of land.

If the Compact had a besetting sin, it was to be ordinarily greedy. Having started with some advantages on the edge of a disadvantageous wilderness, they wanted more, and were not very careful about how they got it. A transplanted and artificially created class of folk, they accumulated wealth to themselves and dominated banking, education, the political process and the courts, the Anglican Church Established and practically everything else that mattered in the cultural or public life of the citizenry. Being, for the most part, military or civil-service nobodies who had become colonial somebodies, they predictably became snobs, putting on airs, marrying into each other's families just like proper English gentry, while remaining, on the whole, dowdy. Anna Jameson saw through them instantly. So did the shrewd, largely republican farmers rapidly peopling the province and envying the Compact.

But once everything mean is said about it, the Compact neverthe-less ensured the continuity of British institutions and ideals of justice in the place they had come to. They rebuilt the parts of British Ontario overrun by the Americans in the War of 1812. And the Compact numbered a few men who would have been outstanding wherever they landed. One was John Strachan, arch-priest of the Compact from the eighteenth century until 1867, when he died. Another was the highly capable lawyer and banker John Beverley Robinson, the Compact's civil leader, who was among the first members of the Ontario élite to have been born in Canada.

Interestingly enough, some men with Compact loyalties were leaders in the Rebellion. But in order not to confuse matters, or appear more tendentious than I am, I shall now pay tribute to the heroes and martyrs in the revolutionary opposition. Though forgotten today, the revered rebels in their own time were the two put to death for their treason against the Lord and His Anointed King: Samuel Lount, a native Pennsylvanian and Ontario blacksmith, and Peter Matthews, a rich farmer in the town Pickering, lying west of Toronto along the Lake Ontario shoreline.

The rebel whose name is today virtually synonymous with the 1837 revolt is one who fled to the United States to escape martyrdom. He was a journalist named William Lyon Mackenzie, born in Scotland in 1795.

Mackenzie arrived in Canada in 1820 and quickly became that most tragically comical of modern personalities: the journalist who blabbers long and loud enough to convince himself he's a politician. Within four years of his arrival, Mackenzie had founded a newspaper, the *Colonial Advocate,* in Queenston, dedicated to attacking those he considered jumped-up grandees in the Family Compact. Despite the presumably pervasive, crushing power of the Compact to suppress and exclude, this self-appointed spokesman for the voiceless was elected member of the provincial parliament in 1828 and several times thereafter. In 1834, little York was incorporated as Toronto, and Mackenzie was elected its first mayor, combining mayoralty with parliamentary busywork. In 1836, however, the Tory activists in York convinced the town that Mackenzie was exactly what he was—an actively disloyal republican—and he went down to defeat.

As fanatics tend to do, Mackenzie took his public defeat as a deep personal affront, giving him licence to cast aside civility and plot the violent overthrow of British rule, the Compact, the whole kit and caboodle. Mackenzie's inspiration was his American contemporary, Andrew Jackson, an activist who had ridden to the U.S. presidency in 1829 from the backwoods on a platform of overturning the Jeffersonian ideals of planter aristocracy. The attractiveness of Mackenzie's position, if it can be called that, was given impetus by an economic downturn in the fortunes of Ontario farmers that swelled his rabble-rousing sessions in Ontario's small towns and villages.

In December, 1837, Mackenzie made his move against the British colonial administration, with the intention of replacing it with a provisional republican government. In the vanguard of some eight hundred comrades armed with pitchforks and guns, the rebel ex-mayor marched down Toronto's Yonge Street and crashed into an overwhelming loyal force. The Battle of Toronto was over in fifteen minutes.

Mackenzie escaped, first, to Navy Island in the Niagara River—Canadian territory—where he attempted to muster a fresh force of rebels. Failing, he escaped at last to his ideal land, the United States, where he was swiftly clapped in jail. The official charge against him was a breach of neutrality laws—though anybody can spot a born trouble-maker. With characteristic (if incomprehensible) magnanimity, Canada allowed Mackenzie back in 1849, and let him rail and rabble-rouse until his death in 1861.

The Rebellion was a fiasco wherever it flared up. It need not have happened at all. Perhaps to the surprise of those who have believed the myth of 1837, the colonial office in London disliked the faux-nobility of York almost as much as Mackenzie did. When visiting Whitehall in 1832, the rebel leader had found a sympathetic ear among the bureaucrats and support for reform, if not revolution, in Upper Canada. Within months of the Yonge Street incident, London had begun to lob criticism at Toronto. In an anonymous letter dated March 27, 1838, written to Sir George Arthur, successor to the autocratic Lieutenant-Governor Sir Francis Bond Head, the process has begun, in words of prophetic admonition to the new governor. Of the York ascendancy, the writer warns with dramatically furrowed brow:

> The errors of your predecessors, and more particularly Sir Francis Bond Head, have all originated in holding to a certain party in this Province which has been its ruin . . . You will be surrounded by them, and their cunning devices to entrap you, Beware of them, they are unwise, and treacherous professors full of deceit. They are latent enemies of our enlightened ministry who have sent you here. The Chief Justice is at the head of what is called the Family Compact, which is as overbearing as it is wicked—
>
> You have unsafe Executive Councillors, Mr. Sullivan who is the first, is a man without character or influence, who has been amongst the Ranks of the worst of Radicals, elevated by Sir Francis Bond Head from the very dregs of Society, who should not have been any other than the trade of a Tallow Chandler, whose father

was in a very small way not many years ago. The Comfort, the prosperity of us depends on you, and if you avoid The Shoals of the Family Compact, you will find your situation a happy one— Beware of the Smooth and Silvery tongue of the Chief Justice, Keep your eye on Hagerman, Draper, Robinson's and Boulton's. Pause, and look well before you act on their opinions, for on every case, rest assured they have their own purposes to serve . . .

The story of 1837, resurrected as a hero-myth by Canadian nationalists of the early 1970s, has attained a kind of immortality, though as a kind of Punch and Judy show. Given such a portrayal, it is altogether too easy to disregard the whole affair and ignore the genuinely interesting people cast into high relief by the events of the day. One, whom we almost certainly would never have met had it not been for William Lyon Mackenzie was the sawmill operator and revolutionary Benjamin Wait.

An historian has dismissed him as "a boisterous and prevaricating Upper Canadian agitator." Be that as it may, he was a remarkable diarist, who has left us an unusual and telling record of tribulations. His notes on the Rebellion, on his arrest, condemnation to death and subsequent exile to Tasmania, and his eventual return to Upper Canada, were, according to his account, written at monthly intervals as dispatches from exile to one "Thaddeus Smith, Esq., of Canada West." The texts were published as *Letters from Van Dieman's* [*sic*] *Land,* in Buffalo, in 1843.

Wait was born in what became known, in 1841, as the Dominion of Canada. He was twenty-four in 1837, married, the father of a daughter, living and working on the Grand River, some sixty kilometres west of Niagara-on-the-Lake. Like many other settlers in the Lake Erie domains of Thomas Talbot, Wait was already a convinced republican before Mackenzie raised the alarm. "At the first intimation of the rising near Toronto," he writes, "I armed and left my home, at York on the Grand River, without a regret; all ardency to mingle in the strife for freedom; and proceeded towards a known point of concentration."

He reached London, with the purpose of taking up arms, after Mackenzie's defeat and escape and "just in time to witness the unhappy dispersion" of the would-be southwestern rebels. He escaped over the Niagara River to "the Land of Freedom"—the United States—where, as he writes, "I partook a cheerful Christmas dinner beneath the banner of the sister stars."

Like William Lyon Mackenzie, young Benjamin seems to have thought that the "sister stars" would lead him to liberty, only to find them less predictable guides. In flight through Ohio, he was captured on June 21, 1838, by a joint force of Upper Canadians and Americans and sent back to Niagara-on-the-Lake, and to jail. The charge:

High Treason, by having appeared "armed with swords, spears, muskets, bayonets, rifles, pistols and other offensive, against the peace of her Majesty, Victoria . . . with intent to do her some grievous harm."

In August, he and fifteen other men were condemned to death. The sentence was pronounced in dire words that Wait recalled during his Tasmanian exile.

"You, Benjamin Wait, shall be taken from the court to the place from which you last came, and there remain until the 25th. Of August, when, before the hours of 11 and 1, you shall be drawn on a hurdle to the place of execution, and there hanged by the neck, until you are dead, and your body shall be quartered. The Lord have mercy on your soul!!!"

Such was the horrid sentence passed upon me by Judge Jones, on the 11th August, 1838. It will be supposed that a doom of such ignominious import, must have made a deep impression upon my mind. But I firmly believe it created a greater, or at least, a more sensible effect upon the crowd of spectators, (for the house was literally crammed,) than within my own breast; for I was prepared for the event . . .

Upon his imprisonment at Niagara-on-the-Lake he had been told

by a gentleman high in government esteem, that I was a "man marked by an exasperated governor, as a fit subject to wreak his utmost vengeance upon . . ."

Perhaps the indifference with which I listened to the ominous sentence, induced the authorities to treat me with greater sever-ity than the others; for immediately after "guilty" was said by the foreman of the jury, I was hurried away to the iron bound stone cell, known in the jail as the "condemned cell"; and there locked up, consigned to the solitary musings of my own mind . . .

"My life I never valued," he continues, "and to sacrifice it in the cause of liberty, truth, and justice, was the end I most desired . . ." But thoughts of his young family and their fate inspired more dire imaginings. "The thoughts were bitter, and created an agony of mind that only give way to the pure and holy influence of religion, which can alone produce that proper resignation to the Divine will in the last trial of nature . . ."

As matters turned out, Wait was able to put off the "last trial of nature" for a while longer than he had thought. The death sentences dealt out at Niagara-on-the-Lake were swiftly commuted and reduced to imprisonment at Kingston, then exile abroad.

The mercy dealt out to most agents in the rebellions came from Quebec City. In this matter, the Earl of Durham, Governor General, and his fire-breathing lieutenants upriver in Ontario were sharply at odds. Wait's wife, Maria, was witness to the strife when she appeared before Lord Durham to plead successfully for her husband's life. "When Sir George [Arthur, Lieutenant-Governor of Upper Canada] heard of the Earl's reprieve in favour of 'transportation,' he burst into rage against the Earl, 'to listen to the appeals of a wife and daughter of two of the most aggravated Offenders, and interpose between them and the just execution of the law.'"

On the face of it, the punishment of Benjamin Wait may seem

clement. It certainly seemed so to Sir George Arthur and other furious Ontario Tories bent on revenge. But though he had his life, Wait had lost his liberty and had been plunged into a hell of unfreedom and fear barely more tolerable than death. A few days after his banishment to Van Diemen's Land—present-day Tasmania—

the clanking of chains announced an intended removal. When the execrable fetters were riveted on my limbs, the cauterizing iron entered my soul; and not till then did I feel, I was no longer free; *a manacled slave!* was a conception I never before rightly understood. . . .

I kissed and caressed that dear, dear child, you speak so tenderly of, and wrung the hand of her whose affectionate care I fancied I was no more to experience. A sense of desolation came over me that I could not shake off; and had it not been for the superior fortitude taught me by Mrs. Wait, I fear I should have shown a feminine spirit—a want of manhood.

By every account, Benjamin's destination was one of the most horrible places on earth, where one was not merely banished for a time, but forgotten until the end of time, wiped from the memory of humankind. It was the worst punishment, short of death itself, that the vengeful could mete out to their opponents.

But ghastly as the destination might be, the way to it was as dangerous and loathsome to a man accustomed to Ontario's open air. On the shoreline along his way up the St. Lawrence to Montréal, Wait witnessed "Canada, unhappy, poor, torn to pieces, burnt up . . ." He saw British regulars

fresh from the scenes of conflagration, carnage, and ruin. Thousands of the volunteers, men from the dregs of society; and the militia, loaded with the booty and plunder of Beauharnois followed in their wake. This scum of society, this offscouring of the Canadas, or, I might say, of the world, exhibited an inconceivably disgusting appearance. They went along . . . in one confused, tumultuous mass; cursing, swearing, singing, and loudly exulting in the destruction and misery they had caused. They had pressed hundreds of French horses and carts, to transport their plunder; and poor, dumb animals! They suffered severely the brutal passions of those hands of legal robbers—those enemies to order, law and right . . .

As his prison ship sailed up the ever-broadening St. Lawrence toward the ocean, Wait became lost in "speculations on the probable greatness of the Canadas," once they had "shaken off the tyrant's yoke, and paralysed the hand of oppression."

A shudder, a feeling akin to horror shot through my frame, as my eyes were first directed to the yet smoking ruins of a proscribed Canadian's homestead. Every building that might have afforded the slightest shelter to man or beast, was burnt to the ground. Every tree cut down, and every particle of food destroyed or carried away. We soon swept past this mark of a tyrant's displeasure . . .

There stood a mother and five children, vainly weeping over the ruins of their home, as if their tears could restore what they had lost; no doubt a husband, parent, brother, or friend were weltering in their own blood, or if living, groaning in irons, reserved in dungeons, as victims for the insatiable gallows, or exiled from their families, whose sufferings they could not know the extent of, and distracted in the knowledge that Sir John Colborne [the lieutenant-governor] was relentless in his furious revenge.

A different sense altogether pervades his reverie when the ship passes the place where France's New World ambitions came to an end and Britain's ascended.

The ride down this part of the St. Lawrence, was a glorious and a pleasant one, and I enjoyed the prospects with unsurpassed delight. About noon the heights bounding the plains of Abraham were visible, up whose rocky shelves the bold and adventurous Wolf[e] wended his way to glory and to death; and where the valorous and gallant Montcalm, poured out the red streams of life, in defence of the chivalry of France.

Every word I have read of this celebrated spot, animatingly recurred to my memory; and my bosom burned to view, more closely, the landscape of those plains, richer in soul-stirring incident to me, than would be the classic ground of Italy. I could have gazed, for hours, with veneration, upon the monument that bears, jointly, the names of those two heroes; and which not only perpetuates their memory, but also impressions of the former power, chivalry, and contests of two great nations. The magnanimity, on the part of one, however, I felt by a glance at my chains, was dwindled down to a low, revengeful despotism; and as a counterpoise to the lasting monument of *discoloured* fame, pillars that would hereafter be erected to the memory of the self-devoted Lount, Matthews, Morrow and many others, would stand as still more enduring monuments of her shame.

As the Gulf of St. Lawrence began gradually to open and the Canadian shoreline receded toward the horizon, the false front of British civility crumbled utterly before Wait's eyes, and the true nature of British justice manifested itself in the warders' cruelty, "as though the very sluice gales of demoniac pleasure were unlocked; for now they had occasion, however trifling, for punishing the very men they so greatly feared, and whom they anxiously sought to terrify." A new monarch was on the throne in Britain. As so often with men abused and crushed by underlings, Wait believed that when Her Majesty became acquainted with "our unhappy situation, and read our faithful representations, and listened to our appeals to her sense of equity, she *would* grant our petitions . . ."

But nothing was moderated. Once the rebels were put on board the transports headed south from Liverpool to Van Diemen's Land, Wait found himself in the hands of the "world's most degraded wretches," determined upon "immersing us into this present indistinguishable state of debasement." What followed was the voyage from Liverpool around the Cape of Good Hope to Australia—in Wait's description, a masque of degradation, in which sadistic guards flog boys who have been condemned to exile for crimes hardly more serious than prankery, or for stealing potatoes simply because they had nothing to eat. Even the ship's rats become actors in the general drama.

"Oh, my dear sir," he writes, "you cannot conceive the slightest approach to the torment we endured while subject to these ruthless invaders of human comfort—those *implements* of exclusively British torture." Wait's final vestige of hope in the honour of his jailors vanished as he saw the squalor of the British criminals among whom he had been placed. "Thus ended all our trust in British clemency; and thus, in eager, anxious destitution, we commenced our voyage of 16,000 miles, to the Antipodes of our homes, in connexion with a mass of corruption and crime to which the world could scarce find a parallel."

Though separated from his loved ones, and from his country, and tempted to despair by mistreatment, Wait found Van Diemen's Land a hell in paradise, surrounded by "magnificent scenery, and grandeur of prospect, if mountains on mountains, reared to the clouds with their concomitant, awful precipices, ravines, and forest can be called so." Wait first worked at quarrying, breaking and moving stone, but later became an accountant, looking after cattle. From this vantage, he was able to witness the coming and going of governors, making themselves wealthy from the slave labour of the prisoners. "One governor supplanted another, until the reigns fell into the tyrannical hands of our *ci-devant* Governor Arthur, who drew so *tautly*, that many of the prison population fled to the woods—choosing to seek a precarious existence by plunder and robbery, or an unmolified death, amid rocks and gum trees, rather than submit to his high handed control . . ." While cruelly oppressing anyone who opposed him, this Arthur gave his shepherds and stockmen free rein to express "their brutal, diabolical passions" on the harmless aborigines.

Wait made good his escape in 1842 by hailing a ship and catching a ride with "benevolent Americans who delivered me from the horrors of slavery . . ." Seven months after his escape he was reunited with his family at Niagara Falls. When his wife died, in the next year, Wait moved to Michigan, where he resumed his pre-revolutionary career in the timber business—and, with that removal, passes from the annals of Ontario history, having left behind only his remarkable testament.

For most Upper Canadians, the Rebellion had ended almost before it began. Catharine Parr Traill, a remarkable Englishwoman with Tory convictions and botanical fascination, whom we will meet again, was living near Peterborough in 1837. She heard of the events at Toronto on Thursday, December 7, and noted:

> This morning my brother Sam came over to communicate the startling intelligence that an armed force was on the march for Toronto . . . It seems we have been slumbering on a fearful volcano, which has burst and may overwhelm us . . . Surely ours is a holy warfare; the rebels fight in an unholy and unblessed cause.

Three days later, on December 10, she got word that the Rebellion had been crushed and the rebels scattered.

> It is a glorious thing to think how few traitors, and how many loyal hearts, the Province contains . . . God be praised who has confounded the malice of the enemies of our adopted country.

Did the Rebellion make any real difference in the future course of events in Ontario? There is no simple answer. For Benjamin Wait, writes an historian, "the fall of the radicals and their aristocratic opponents left Canada to the mercies of the 'corporations, monopolies, banks of issue,' to the men of 'mercenary character.' That was the ultimate tragedy of the failure of the rebellions of 1837." It neither transformed the governments of Ontario nor Canada into some version of the American republic, as Mackenzie had wanted, nor did it reconfirm the autocrats in their former position. It did, however, coincide with Ontario's turn from a chiefly agrarian society of mixed loyalists and republicans into the modern, urban and industrialized constitutional monarchy it is today.

And it also had one other interesting side effect in its aftermath: the amnesty and return from exile, in 1849, of William Lyon Mackenzie, who promptly climbed back into his political pulpit and again denounced the tottering aristocrats of Ontario, long after their greatest heyday was past.

21
KINDLY LANDINGS

CATHARINE PARR TRAILL MAINTAINED HER WATCH during the 1837 rebellion at her log cabin on Lake Katchewanook, one of the shining waters that dot the rumpled, rocky Kawartha region of eastern Ontario. She had come out to Upper Canada five years earlier with her husband, Thomas Traill, of the Royal Scotch Fusiliers. She was fortunate to have the companionship of her sister Susannah Moodie, the poet, who had come out to the sparsely populated homestead district around present-day Peterborough, with her officer husband, to protect North America's rump British Empire from its enemies.

Had Catharine met Mrs. Jameson, Anna's view of Ontario society might not have been so very dim. The Traills and Moodies were loyal British subjects without the airs and graces of the Family Compact, and with the education and general sense of civilization Anna found so conspicuously missing in Toronto. They were the sort of people Lieutenant-Governor Simcoe had wanted to rule his province, in order to set the loyalist tone despised by Mackenzie and other republicans.

They were also remarkable in their own right. Their home, Reydon Hall in Suffolk, was a sort of factory for quick, talented women.

Among the daughters of Thomas Strickland was an historian of Rome and, in Susannah, a fine poet. There was also a student of royal biography. As it happened, Thomas Wait passed the time when docked in Liverpool making paper cut-outs, which came to the notice of a certain "Miss Strickland, (Compiler of the Queen of Scots Letters) who kept a Bazar," and who prized them so warmly that she ordered up a batch of them, with "the maker's name and patriotic mottoes to be carefully imprinted upon them." In Catharine, the Stricklands brought forth a bright botanist and author of a delightful book of description and advice, called *The Backwoods of Canada*, for intended immigrants to the wilds of Upper Canada.

The circumstances of Catharine's arrival in Canada, narrated in her book, are among the reasons some people think the history of southern Ontario's British period is tiresome. It would make an uplifting but dull movie. Absent from the story are main-street shootouts in cow towns and bandits in the hills preying on wagon trains. There were no wagon trains pressing westward, or gold-crazed explorers, or Indian fighters. Catharine seems to have known nothing about the rambling loners like Étienne Brûlé and the voyageurs who spread across northern Ontario in his wake. The great American myth of its settlement celebrates individual bravery against a hostile wilderness, while the colonizing of Upper Canada is, more often than not, a story of orderly passage and kindly landings in the new world.

The traditional institutions that uphold civilized society were not reconstructed or invented anew in Canada, as happened on other, more isolated frontiers of expanding nineteenth-century empires. They were expected to be in place by upper-class arrivals such as the Traills and Moodies. And the establishment of banks, land agencies and other services were often orchestrated by benevolent societies in England, in order that refugees from British poverty could find peaceable familiarity in the wilds of this new land.

"In the late 1820's and early 1830's," writes historian Hugh Kenyon, living conditions for the great mass of country people, particularly in the counties south of the Thames, were of disaster proportions and far beyond the scope of parish welfare systems. Agriculture could no longer absorb the steep rise in population, nor could farm workers pay the very high price of wheat, which had trebled during the long Napoleonic war. Men were struggling to support a family on 6s. a week or less and there was a grinding destitution surpassing our comprehension today, for men in rags, anxious to work, were found dead in ditches, their stomachs full only of dandelion leaves.

In Sussex the misery attracted the sympathy of worldly powers and clerics, but it took a street demonstration on November 18, 1830, to propel the authorities into action. A thousand men had gathered in the town of Horsham and angrily demanded a living allowance from the local government, which replied by promptly clapping many of them in prison. After similar uprisings in Hampshire and Wiltshire, 250 rebellious men and boys were meted out the same penalty that came down on Thomas Wait: "transportation" into exile.

Then the workers confronted the ranking nobleman of the district, George Wyndham, the third Earl of Egremont, J. M. W. Turner's staunchest patron and a great art collector. The earl's response blended prudent regard for social stability, self-interest and apparently genuine compassion for local people, the hapless victims of the great cultural changes attendant upon industrialization. His solution

The earl of Egremont, J. m. W. Twrner's staunchest patron

took the form of the Petworth Emigration Committee. The project was active between 1832 and 1837—chartering ships, rounding up likely candidates from among both working poor and lower gentry, dispatching them to waiting land grants in Britain's New World dominion. If the words *colony* and *colonialism* today carry with them a distinctly bad odour, the Petworth scheme suggests that colonizing could be done with benefit to everyone concerned and damage to none. Given a choice between dole, workhouse or starvation at home and an adequate grant of farmland in a new place, some 1,800 people opted for Canada. If Thomas and Catharine Traill were not typical of these Petworth newcomers, neither were they unlike them entirely. The travellers included officers, as well as middle-class English families eager for new starts, new opportunities.

In a brochure issued in 1833 "to Persons desirous of emigrating from this Neighbourhood, to Upper Canada," the committee offers passage aboard "the ship *Lord Melville,* 425 Tons register, A. 1. coppered and copper fastened, and sheathed, with 7 feet height between decks, and extra ventilating scuttles, which is to be comfortably fitted up at Portsmouth . . ." Attending to the travellers will be "a superintendent (with his wife and family)," whose duty is to "conduct them direct to York, in Upper Canada, (in, or near, which city he intends to settle) paying every attention to their comforts on the route. A surgeon also sails in the ship, whose duty it will be to attend (gratis) to the health of the passengers."

Further on in their advertisement, the committee gives sound advice about the avoidance of certain troubles awaiting the unwary and untravelled—the sort of people, that is, most likely to take advantage of the offer.

Experience has proved, that the practice pursued on many former occasions, of landing emigrants at the first American port, and leaving them with a small sum of money in their pockets, has exposed them to every kind of fraud and imposition; they having been soon pillaged of what they had, or led to squander it idly away, and thus left penniless, and without employment in a strange land. To guard against this evil, the above plan has been adopted, of conveying the emigrants, AT ONCE, to where work can, with certainty, be found; and placing them under the charge of a superintendent, whose business it will be, in conjunction with the government agent, to attend to them till that object is obtained; little or no money is therefore required by labouring emigrants, on their arrival: still, any sum paid to the Petworth Committee, will be repaid at York, Upper Canada, into their hands, or to their account, as may be desired . . .

Along with "a warm great coat, a flushing jacket & trowsers, a duck frock and trowsers, a canvas frock and two pairs of trowsers, two Jersey frocks, four shirts, four pairs of stockings, three pairs of shoes, a bible and prayer book," each man and woman

should take with them a good character, (if they should have the happiness to possess one,) fairly written, and well attested; also, copies of marriage or baptismal registers, or any other certificates or papers likely to be useful; the whole to be enclosed in a small tin case.

The promise of a fair send-off for British immigrants in the early 1830s, and of civil and mindful reception in Upper Canada, appears, for the most part, to have been kept. We need not wonder why. While its interest in Canada waxed and waned over the decades, the British government was usually keen to empty its islands of the rural poor and potential troublemakers and make sure they were settled happily abroad.

To that end, another descriptive advertisement was issued on this side of the Atlantic, "To be obtained without fee or reward, with every other assistance and advice that can benefit the Emigrant proceeding to the Canadas, from James Buchanan, Esq. His Britannic Majesty's Consul, Nassau Street, New York."

The Wild lands may also be purchased from the Upper Canada Company [Canada Company], on very easy terms, and those persons wanting improved farms will find little difficulty in obtaining such from private proprietors. On no account enter into any final engagement for your lands or farms without personal examination, and be certain of the following qualifications:

A healthy situation.

Good land.

A pure spring, or running stream of water.

In the neighbourhood of a good moral and religious state of society, and schools for the education of your children.

As near good roads and water transport as possible, saw and grist mills.

A good title.

These advantages you can obtain in the Canadas with more ease to yourself and family, and with prospects of as good success and sure independence, as perhaps in any other portion of the American Continent; besides, you have the British Laws and Constitution to which you have been accustomed, with the full benefit of all your industry, and that in a country free to all denominations of Christians, and less burthened with taxes than any other on the face of the globe.

This description is followed by detailed directions and assurances that, at every step from New York to the homestead in uncleared bush, an agent of His Britannic Majesty will be there to help—if, indeed, the ambitious immigrant to Upper Canada needs help. For what that voyage from New York was actually like, we have the testimony of Anne Langton, who came to Canada with her parents in 1837 to join her brother near Peterborough, and like so many other ladies of her time wrote books about their travels. Miss Langton's book is entitled *A Gentlewoman in Upper Canada* and consists of her journals and those of her mother.

After a list of "hints in case you or any of yours cross the Atlantic"—
"Bring a small mattress with you, for the aching of the bones when
obliged to toss upon a hard, uneven surface for some days is no trifling
inconvenience," and so on—Miss Langton issues the usual admonitions about shipboard food.

I generally contrive to perform the great task of dressing myself
in time for breakfast, which meal appears about nine o'clock. The
transatlantic ladies eat cold and hot meat, fried or pickled fish, or
oysters, to this first meal, which seems with them a substantial
one. A cup of coffee and a cracker is generally mine. The eggs are
dubious, and your basket was a most wise and acceptable addition to our sea store on my father's account.

After arrival in New York, the Langton family went up the Hudson
and the Erie Canal, finally arriving at Lewiston, near Niagara-on-the-
Lake and its famous cataract, which made little impression. A couple
of days later, the family was in Toronto.

Dined there and embarked about 2; had a nice cool sail but
nothing interesting, the land so far away, scarcely visible till we
came in sight of the city, which appeared flat and agueish. Our
road to the Hotel, on a wooden foot-path, with unpaved street,
gave one at first a poor opinion of the Capital of Canada, and our
reception at the Hotel was most uncomfortable, as we were
shewn into a little, dirty, unbenched room, and the lodging
rooms offered us were up some stairs out of the yard. . . .

In late summer—as Anna Jameson was seeking to win back her
husband in another part of town—the family completed their trip to
Peterborough.

August 4. Though I was still weak we embarked about ten o'clock
in the evening in the steam packet for Port Hope. No sleep

during the whole night; at 6 o'clock we disembarked and went to a disagreeable damp old inn for breakfast, and found that we had some hours to wait for the stages which were to convey us for about nine miles to Rice Lake, but we had a most agreeable specimen of Canadian hospitality from Captain Kingsmill. . . .

The stage is a kind of wagon with two seats slung across, the back bound with buffalo-skin—and over good roads would not be an unpleasant carriage. Some part of the road was good, other parts very shaking and uneasy, but no corduroy . . . We had two hours to wait for the steamer, which we tried to make less tedious by botanizing a little. The day was beautiful, not too hot yet bright.

At last we saw a ponderous body slowly approaching us—it was certainly the most uncouth steam packet we had ever seen—it was the first on these lakes—its machinery of bad construction, and of slow motion. We dined on board, a comfortable clean dinner with few people. I was glad to get a sort of bed made up on a table with our pillows, bags, etc., for I began to be worn out . . . It was quite dark before reaching the place of disembarking, and we had then to be rowed up the river about a mile before reaching Peterborough . . .

Notwithstanding her complaints, Miss Langton came out to Canada at a golden moment of immigration, already headed toward twilight. Since the British conquest of the old French empire in America, settlement of the shorelines of the southern Great Lakes, between Windsor and Sarnia on the west and Kingston on the east, had been sporadic. There had been the sudden influx of land-hungry exiles from the United States and administrators from Britain in the decades on either side of 1800, then a lull. For most of the early nineteenth century, the population of Ontario was clustered in lakeshore farms and small towns stretching between the Bay of Quinte and Kingston, in the vast swath of thick forests and gloriously fertile soil between the Great Lakes and the ancient, worn-down crags of the

Canadian Shield. The land was good, and in the hands of people who knew how to make the most of it.

Catharine Parr Traill is the poet of this golden hour, and witness to its disappearance. In 1832, the year she came to the Kawarthas, Catherine began *Backwoods of Canada*

to afford every possible information to the wives and daughters of emigrants of the higher class who contemplate seeking a home amid the Canadian wilds. Truth has been conscientiously her object in the work, for it were cruel to write in flattering terms calculated to deceive emigrants into the belief that the land to which they are transferring their families, their capital, and their hopes, is a land flowing with milk and honey, where comforts and affluence may be obtained with little exertion.

The ladies to whom the letters are actually addressed, over the shoulder of her mother, should

brace their minds to the task, and thus avoid the repinings and discontent that are apt to follow unfounded expectations and fallacious hopes . . .

Like others who had made the voyage up the St. Lawrence into Lake Ontario, Catharine was deeply moved by the natural beauty of the shore, which she found "rising in waving lines of hill and dale, clothed with magnificent woods, or enlivened by patches of cultivated land and pretty dwellings." But she is also a candid commentator on the realities lying behind these lakeside beauties.

To the mere passing traveler, who cares little for the minute beauties of scenery, there is certainly a monotony in the long and unbroken line of woods, which insensibly inspires a feeling of gloom almost touching on sadness. And the thought that it must take years of hard labour ere a farm can be cut out of such a maze of timber—at first sight it seems impossible . . .

In a lovely passage, full of rapture for the new land, she notes the "fantastic bowers" of Virginia creeper, "forest trees, mingling their hues with the splendid rose-tipped branches of the soft maple, the autumnal tints of which are unrivalled in beauty by any of our forest trees at home." In a letter dated October 25, 1832, Catharine provides an especially affecting evocation of the land—and a tender warning and consolation to her female readers fearing the voyage out.

As I sat in the wood in silence and in gloom, my thoughts gradually wandered back across the Atlantic to my dear mother and to my old home; and I thought what would have been her feelings could she at that moment have beheld me as I sat on the cold mossy stone in the profound stillness of that vast leafy wilderness, thousands of miles from all those holy ties of kindred and early associations that make home in all countries a hallowed spot.

It was a moment to press upon my mind the importance of the step I had taken in voluntarily sharing the lot of the emigrant—in leaving the land of my birth, to which, in all probability, I might never again return. Great as was the sacrifice, even at that moment, strange as was my situation, I felt no painful regret or fearful misgiving depress my mind. A holy and tranquil peace came down upon me, soothing and softening my spirits into a calmness that seemed as unruffled as was the bosom of the star-lit water that lay stretched out before my feet.

Those not prepared to make the sacrifices necessary had better think of another way to make the peace with life. In her letter of April 18, 1833, she records a humorous exchange between a "very fine lady, the reluctant sharer of her husband's emigration," and her spouse, a captain.

The lady proclaims her son is "degrading" himself making an axe-handle. "My boys shall never work like common mechanics," she says.

"Then, madam, they will be good for nothing as settlers," her husband replies, "and it is a pity you dragged them across the Atlantic."

"I should like to know, then, what Canada is good for?"

"In short," came the answer, "the country is a good country for those to whom it is adapted; but if people will not conform to the doctrine of necessity and expediency, they have no business in it. It is plain that Canada is not adapted to every class of people."

22

THE COFFIN SHIPS

THE ERA OF PEACEABLE ARRIVALS, when the Moodies and the Traills and thousands of less grandly prepared and educated people came out and settled, persisted through the first decade of Queen Victoria, but not long past it. The Irish who began to arrive in Ontario during the black year 1847 had been nearly overwhelmed by horror at home, and it seemed to dog their steps as they made their escape.

Their journey had begun with a blight that destroyed the Irish potato crop, acre by acre. The price of food skyrocketed and the value of money collapsed in the famine, reducing millions of Irish tenant-farmers to destitution, and leaving them to feed off carrion, sicken of it and die. Cholera and typhus, the dire twin angels of every great human calamity, took whole villages down to death. The dead were left to rot in the ditches, or put into the ground without coffins, because there was neither timber for making them nor money to pay for the making.

Then came the tragic, vicious evictions, when landlords turfed hundreds of thousands of peasants from their homes, sentencing them to eke out a living in disease-ridden workhouses or simply to die. Landlords of more benevolent temperament paid the fare of tenants to emigrate, in their hundreds of thousands, across the seas. The death toll of the Irish Famine of 1846–50 has been estimated at more than one million, all from hunger and disease.

But the devastation did not cease to follow the luckless Irish once they had taken leave of their island home. For many of them, the ships they hoped would mean deliverance became floating coffins as fever swept the filthy quarters below deck.

Some 90,000 souls set sail from Ireland for Canada in the summer of 1847. Of those, 16,000 died of typhus or other diseases on ship or after arrival. An attempt was made to stop the fever at Grosse Isle, in the Gulf of St. Lawrence. But nothing kept it from moving inland. An estimated 50,000 Irish made it as far inland as the Kingston docks, many already very ill. Several thousand victims of typhus were put into rickety, quickly built fever sheds on the Kingston waterfront. How many of them died of disease and want will never be known. Some of the townspeople, including leaders of Church and civil society, maintained aloof indifference to the plight of the newcomers. Others in this mainly Protestant town went out to help these wretched Catholic newcomers. Hundreds of helpers died, and despite their ministrations at least 1,400 Irish perished, and today lie in a mass grave on the grounds of Kingston General Hospital. Monuments have been raised in honour of the fallen, but Kingston's dead will not stay quiet.

Bodies have continued to turn up, as though rising to remind the city of the infinitely weary, sad story. As recently as 1990, two bodies were uncovered during an excavation on the hospital grounds. "There was a marsh area and that's where a large number of typhus victims were buried," said Susan Bazely, a Kingston archaeologist. "The immigrants were quite poor and, in many cases, entire families were wiped out by the disease. With no family member left to bury the dead, common graves were used. We shall never know their names."

Robert Whyte, an eyewitness, captures the atmosphere of dread that followed the sick Irish along the St. Lawrence and into Ontario.

That the system of quarantine pursued at Grosse Isle afforded but a very slight protection to the people of Canada is too evident from the awful amount of sickness and the vast number of deaths that occurred amongst them during the navigable season of 1847 . . . an aspect of universal gloom—the churches being hung in mourning, the citizens clothed in weeds and the newspapers recording daily deaths by fever contracted from the emigrants.

Neither was the pestilence stayed here, for the inhabitants of Kingston, Bytown [Ottawa], Toronto and other places were infected and a great number died of the fever, amongst whom was the Rev. Dr Power, R[oman] C[atholic] Bishop of Toronto who contracted the disease in the discharge of his sacred functions among the sick. The following extract taken from the *Toronto Standard* serves to the manner in which the people of Canada suffered, and their sympathy for those who brought so much woe amongst them:

> The health of the city remains in much the same state as it did several weeks ago. The individual cases of fever have abated nothing of their violence and several families have caught the infection from having admitted emigrants into their houses. The greatest caution should be observed in this respect as it does not require contact alone, to infect a healthy person with the deadly virus of the fever. Breathing the same atmosphere with the infected or coming under the influence of the effluvia rising from their clothes is, in some states of the healthy body perfectly sufficient for effecting a lodgement of the disease in the human frame . . .

That disease is communicated by the sick to the healthy by "bad air" or "the effluvia rising from their clothes" is a belief of great antiquity, and of great tenacity. Microscopes had existed since the late seventeenth century, though it took two centuries for anyone to grasp the connection between disorders and microbes—which was too late for the victims of ship fever. Today we know the disease travels from body to body, with the louse as go-between. Lice thrive in filthy, crowded conditions, or in earthquake or war zones, or concentration camps, or anywhere sanitation has collapsed and people find themselves plunged into squalor.

Once infected by the microbe *Rickettsia prowazekii*—like most horrible microscopic bugs, it bears a name like that of a circus performer—the victim suddenly begins to suffer headaches and chills, exhaustion, excruciating muscular pain and high fever. The whole body is quickly covered by ugly dark spots, signalling the damage to vessels being done as the disease spreads. About a quarter of those infected will die of these ravages.

But when one steps back from the microscope and outside the clinic and looks at typhus as affliction, it assumes the guise of a hungry ghost, ever-present among us wherever we congregate, though usually slumbering. When awakened by catastrophe or crowding, typhus begins to stalk its easiest prey, those already victimized by other miseries and losses. Robert Whyte and the journalists of his day did not understand how typhus infection sneaks from body to body, but he knew very well the road it took. He also thought surprising the horror we can almost take for granted, after the ghastly twentieth century.

Nothing is known about Robert Whyte. The author's name may be an invention. *The Ocean Plague, or, A Voyage to Quebec in an Irish Emigrant Vessel,* published in the year 1848, purports to be the diary of the real voyage by which the author reached Ontario. It could have been cobbled together from eyewitness reports. But Whyte's *Journey* rings true, from its outset, on Sunday, May 30, 1847, the day he set sail from Ireland for Canada.

The balmy new-born day, in all the freshness of early summer was gladdened by the beams of the sun which rose above the towers of the city, sunk in undisturbed repose. It was a morning calculated to inspire the drooping soul with hope, auguring future happiness.

Too soon I arrived at the quay and left my last footprint on my native land. The boat pushed off, and in a few minutes I was on board the brig that was to waft me across the wide Atlantic.

Within three days of departure, Robert witnessed the discovery of a stowaway and the sternness of shipboard discipline—and the condition of those who had chosen to undertake the voyage out.

. . . The captain was summoned from below and a council immediately held for the trial of the prisoner, who confessed that, not having enough of money to pay for his passage, he bribed the watchman employed to prevent the possibility of such an occurrence. He had been concealed for three days, but at night made his way into the hold, through a breach in the partition; his presence was therefore known to some of the passengers. He had no clothes but the rags he wore nor had he any provisions. To decide what was to be done with him was now the consideration, but the captain hastily terminated the deliberation by swearing that he should be thrown overboard.

The wretched creature was quite discomfited by the captain's wrath, and earnestly begged for forgiveness. It was eventually settled that he should be landed upon the first island at which we should touch; with which decision he appeared to be quite satisfied. He said that he was willing to work for his support but; the captain swore determinedly that he should not taste one pound of the ship's provision. He was therefore left to the tender mercies of his fellow passengers.

In consequence of this discovery, there was a general muster in the afternoon, affording me an opportunity of seeing all the emigrants—and a more motley crowd I never beheld—of all ages, from the infant to the feeble grandsire and withered crone.

While they were on deck, the hold was searched, but without any further discovery, no one having been found below but a boy who was unable to leave his berth from debility.

Many of them appeared to me to be quite unfit to undergo the hardship of a long voyage; but they [had been] inspected and passed by a doctor, although the captain protested against taking some of them. One old man was so infirm that he seemed to me to be in the last stage of consumption.

As the ship slowly made its way west, and Ireland dropped under the horizon, Robert notes,

many of these emigrants had never seen the sea nor a ship, until they were on board. They were chiefly from the County Meath, and sent out at the expense of their landlord without any knowledge of the country to which they were going, or means of livelihood except the labour of the father of each family. All they knew concerning Canada was that they were to land in Quebec, and to go up the country; moreover they had a settled conviction that the voyage was to last exactly three weeks.

Gradually, the observations began to be tinged by a slowly darkening anxiety. At first, the most conspicuous sickness he sees around him is homesickness. Turning his gaze from the far horizon to the craft he and his fellow passengers are sailing in, he notes "a sensation akin to that of the 'Ancient Mariner'. . . . 'Alone, alone, all, all alone. Alone on a wide, wide sea.'"

His reveries are interrupted, however, when a boy is struck down by fever. With no doctor on board, Robert and the captain's wife inspect the medicine chest to see what remedies, if any, are

available. What they find are specifics against constipation and excruciating pain—"castor oil, Epsom salts, laudanum, hartshorn, etc; also a
book of directions, which were by no means explicit . . ." Despite the
lack of effective medicine, the boy recovered—but just as others were
sinking into disease. On Thursday, June 10, new cases of illness are
reported; by Sunday, "the reports from the hold became very alarming."
Eight more passengers come down with "serious illness—six of them
being fever and two dysentery. The former appeared to be of a peculiar
character and very alarming, the latter disease did not seem to be so
violent in degree." But the number of those fallen ill continued to
increase. By Tuesday, June 15, the reports had become "very afflicting,"
and the captain understandably alarmed.

On June 23, death claims its first typhus victim, a woman covered
with "black putrid spots," the telltale signs of the disease. The next day,

> some young men and women got up a dance in the evening,
> regardless of the moans and cries of those who were tortured by the
> fiery fever. When the mate spoke to them of the impropriety of
> such conduct, they desisted and retired to the bow where they sat
> down and spent the remainder of the evening singing. The mo-
> notonous howling they kept up was quite in unison with the scene
> of desolation within and the dreary expanse of ocean without.

The agony and convulsions and stupor associated with typhus strike
down one victim after another. Excrement and vomit seethe in the
hold, and the darkness deepens. Almost exactly a month after embark-
ing on the voyage to Canada, Robert notes the following scene, which
he would witness again and again in the days to come.

> Passing the main hatch, I got a glimpse of one of the most awful
> sights I ever beheld. A poor female patient was lying in one of the
> upper berths—dying. Her head and face were swollen to almost
> unnatural size, the latter being hideously deformed. I recollected
> remarking the clearness of her complexion when I saw her in

health, shortly after we sailed. She then was a picture of good humour and contentment, now how sadly altered! Her cheeks retained their ruddy hue but the rest of her distorted countenance was of a leprous whiteness. She had been nearly three weeks ill and suffered exceedingly until the swelling set in, commencing in her feet and creeping up her body to her head. Her afflicted husband stood by her holding a "blessed candle" in his hand and awaiting the departure of her spirit.

Death put a period to her existence shortly after I saw her. And as the sun was setting, the bereaved husband muttered a prayer over her enshrouded corpse, which as he said, "Amen," was lowered into the ocean.

And a few days later:

. . . The brother of the two men who died on the sixth instant followed them to-day.

He was seized with dismay from the time of their death, which no doubt hurried on the malady to its fatal termination. The old sails being all used up, his remains were placed in two meal-sacks and a weight being fastened at foot, the body was placed upon one of the hatch battens from which, when raised over the bulwark, it fell into the deep and was no more seen. He left two little orphans, one of whom—a boy, seven years of age—I noticed in the evening wearing his deceased father's coat. Poor little fellow! He seemed quite unconscious of his loss and proud of the accession to his scanty covering.

wearing his deceased father's coat . . .

On July 10, Robert saw for the first time a sign of hope: Anticosti Island, which stands at the mouth of the Gulf of St. Lawrence. But another island lay before them: Grosse Isle, in the St. Lawrence proper, which was being used as a quarantine point, to stop the ships. Robert's description of this place, which should have been a welcoming point, is ghastly. An "inspecting physician" comes aboard, and decides there has been fever on the ship; then declares that he will report momentarily whether the ship will be allowed to pass.

The day wore away before we gave up hope. I could not believe it possible that here, within reach of help, we should be left as neglected as when upon the ocean—That after a voyage of two months' duration we were to be left still enveloped by reeking pestilence, the sick without medicine, medical skill, nourishment, or so much as a drop of pure water—for the river, although not saline here, was polluted by the most disgusting objects thrown overboard from the several vessels. In short, it was a floating mass of filthy straw, the refuse of foul beds, barrels containing the vilest matter, old rags and tattered clothes, etc., etc.

While they wait, two Canadian priests come aboard to visit the sick and administer the Last Rites of the Church to a dying woman and an elderly man and baptize a baby. Robert learns from them how things stand with the other ships being held in quarantine.

They stayed a short time talking to us upon deck, and the account they gave of the horrid condition of many of the ships in quarantine was frightful. In the holds of some of them they said that they were up to their ankles in filth. The wretched emigrants crowded together like cattle, and corpses remaining long unburied, the sailors being ill, and the passengers unwilling to touch them. They also told us of the vast numbers of sick in the hospitals, and in tents upon the island, and that many nuns, clergymen and doctors were lying in typhus fever, taken from the patients. . . .

At high water this portion was detached from the main island and formed a most picturesque islet. However, this scene of natural beauty was sadly deformed by the dismal display of human suffering that it presented; helpless creatures being carried by sailors over the rocks on their way to the hospital—boats arriving with patients, some of whom died in their transmission from their ships. Another, and still more awful sight, was a continuous line of boats, each carrying its freight of dead to the burial ground, and forming an endless funeral procession.

The quarantine at Grosse Isle does nothing to save the immigrants from the ravages of typhus, and perhaps even exacerbates it, by keeping people in filth and hunger for days on end, awaiting bureaucratic medical inspection. "The inefficacy of the quarantine system is so apparent that it is needless to particularize its defects," writes Robert, "neither need I repeat the details of the grievous aggravations of their trials heaped by it upon the already tortured emigrants." After coming ashore permanently, at Toronto it seems, Robert set out on a tour of Ontario, where he found everywhere the ongoing ravages of typhus, the misery of those who had come, the failure of hope that would afflict so many in that fatal year of 1847, and the years to come.

Would that I could represent the afflictions I witnessed at Grosse Isle! . . . A large proportion of the emigrants who arrived in Canada crossed the frontiers in order to settle in the United States. So that they were to be seen in the most remote places. At St Catharines upon the Welland Canal, 600 miles from Québec, I saw a family who were on their way to the western part of the state of New York. One of them was taken ill and they were obliged to remain by the wayside with nothing but a few boards to protect them from the weather.

There is no means of learning how many of the survivors of so many ordeals were cut off by the inclemency of a Canadian winter so that the grand total of the human sacrifice will never be known but by "Him who knoweth all things." . . .

If any class deserve to be protected and assisted by the government, it is that class who are banished from their native land in search of the bare means of subsistence. All that could be done for those poor people by the great compassion and humanity of the captain and officers, was done but they require much more. . . .

My heart sickens when I think upon the fatal scenes of the awfully tragic drama enacted upon the wide stage of the Atlantic Ocean in the floating lazar houses that were wafted upon its bosom during the never-to-be-forgotten year 1847. Without a precedent in history, may God grant that this account of it may descend to posterity without a parallel . . . humanity in administering their disagreeable duties which consisted not in relieving the distress of the emigrants but in protecting their country from contamination. Still, it was most afflicting that after combating the dangers of the sea, enduring famine, drought and sickness, the wretched survivors should still have to lie as uncared for as when in the centre of the Atlantic Ocean. . . .

On their way [from Grosse Isle] to Montreal many died on board the steamers. There, those who sickened in their progress were received into the hospital and the survivors of this second sifting were sent on to Kingston, 180 miles further, from thence to Toronto and so on, every city and town being anxious to be rid of them. . . .

However, it may be thought that the immolation of so many wretched starvelings was rather a benefit than a loss to the world. It may be so. Yet—untutored, degraded, famished and plague stricken, as they were I assert that there was more true heroism, more faith, more forgiveness to their enemies and submission to the Divine Will exemplified in these victims, than could be found in ten times the number of their oppressors.

23
UNCLE TOM

LYMAN BEECHER, A CONGREGATIONALIST PREACHER in Litchfield, Connecticut, as the nineteenth century commenced, was a dogmatic, utterly unambiguous man of the sort who tends to father rebels. He believed that everyone was either damned or saved. When faced with injustice, such as American slavery, he came down on it with the wrath of an avenging angel. There was much room in his household for discussion of current affairs, and none for irony.

Happily for him and American democracy, Mr. Beecher's eleven children turned their strong wills against the blights of their age— slavery and the denial of the vote and advanced education to women. Most members of this formidable swarm sought to change the status quo in Jacksonian America. But Harriet helped change history.

Josiah Henson, escaped slave and Ontario author, met this most remarkable of Lyman Beecher's offspring in 1851, on his way home to Canada from the International Exposition in London. "I was in the vicinity of Andover, Mass., where Mrs. Harriet Beecher Stowe resided," Josiah recalled.

> She sent for me and my traveling companion, Mr. George Clark, a white gentleman, who had a fine voice for singing, and usually sang at my meetings to add to their interest. We went to Mrs. Stowe's house, and she was deeply interested in the story of my life and misfortunes, and had me narrate its details to her. She said she was glad it had been published, and hoped it would be of great service, and would open the eyes of the people to the enormity of the crime of holding men in bondage. She manifested so much interest in me, that I told her about the peculiarities of many slaveholders, and the slaves in the region where I had lived for forty-two years. My experiences had been more varied than those of the majority of slaves, for I was not only my master's overseer, but a market-man for twenty-five years in the market at Washington, going there to sell the produce from my master's plantation.
>
> Soon after, Mrs. Stowe's remarkable book, *Uncle Tom's Cabin*, was published, and circulated in all parts of America, and read openly in the North, stealthily in the South. Many thought that her statements were exaggerations. She then published the key to the book to prove that it was impossible to exaggerate the enormities of slavery, and she therein gave many parallel cases, and referred to my published life-story, as an exemplification of the truth of the character of her Uncle Tom.
>
> From that time to the present, I have been called "Uncle Tom," and I feel proud of the title. If my humble words in any way inspired that gifted lady to write such a plaintive story that the whole community has been touched with pity for the sufferings of the poor slave, I have not lived in vain; for I

believe that her book was the beginning of the glorious end. It was a wedge that finally rent asunder that gigantic fabric with a fearful crash. . . .

The weight of Mrs. Stowe's contribution to the overthrow of slavery in the United States can never be measured exactly. Most people who have thought carefully about the links between reading and war believe *Uncle Tom's Cabin* was crucial. It provided a compelling image of slavery as absolute evil and emancipation as absolute good. It portrayed a range of responses to enslaved men and women—ranging from kindly maternalism to the villainous cruelty of the taskmaster Simon Legree. Here was a vision of slavery vivid enough to outrage slavery's defenders and inspire its opponents to holy war. As Mrs. Stowe's chapters appeared in serial form during 1851 and 1852 in the abolitionist journal *The National Era,* the fame of her writing spread rapidly (as Josiah notes) throughout America, North and South. Everybody was talking about it. When the chapters were collected in two stout volumes, the book became nineteenth-century America's first runaway best-seller, then captured audiences in Europe and Asia.

Josiah Henson believed himself to be the original of Uncle Tom. But the creation of a fictional character is never that simple. The figure of Tom was created from tales heard by Mrs. Stowe during her sojourn in Cincinnati, popular penny-dreadful stories in magazines, newspaper reports garnered first-hand from escapees from slavery. But of all Mrs. Stowe's known informants, none more than Josiah Henson possessed the full repertoire of traits that we also find in Uncle Tom: gratitude for kindness, sweetness of temper under torment, a notable unwillingness to hold grudges. In her preface to his autobiography, Mrs. Stowe praises Josiah for these traits.

To the great Christian doctrine of forgiveness of enemies and the returning of good for evil, he was by God's grace made a faithful witness, under circumstances that try men's souls and make us all who read it say, "Lead us not into such temptation." We earnestly commend this portion of his narrative to those who, under much smaller temptations, think themselves entitled to render evil for evil . . .

In his own words, we sense the famous gentleness of spirit that characterizes Stowe's fictional Uncle Tom and that made the character's name a byword for Black complaisance under oppression. When on a special mission from Maryland to Kentucky on behalf of his master, Henson had ample opportunities to flee. But it was not a move he could make.

"Freedom had ever been an object of my ambition," he writes.

. . . I had a sentiment of honour on the subject. The duties of the slave to his master as appointed over him in the Lord, I had ever heard urged by ministers and religious men. Entrancing as the ideas were, that the coast was clear for a run for freedom, that I might liberate my companions, might carry off my wife and children, and some day own a house and land, and be no longer despised and abused, still my notions of right were against it. I had promised my master to take his property to Kentucky, and deposit it with his brother Amos.

Pride, too, came in to confirm me. I had undertaken a great thing; my vanity had been flattered all along the road by hearing myself praised; I thought it would be a feather in my cap to carry it through thoroughly, and had often painted the scene in my imagination of the final surrender of my charge to Master Amos, and the immense admiration and respect with which he would regard me . . .

Eventually, of course, he repented, acknowledging an "error of judgment" rooted in "the degrading system under which I had been nurtured," and making his way to freedom in Ontario. Yet his account of obligation and pride are true and persuasive—so much so that the "Uncle Tom" sobriquet seems almost too apt.

Josiah Henson remained an admirer and friend of Harriet Beecher Stowe from their first meeting, in 1851, until his death thirty-two years later, at Dresden, Ontario. Of her fantastically successful book, he writes:

> Mrs. Stowe's book is not an exaggerated account of the evils of society. The truth has never been half-told; the story would be too horrible to hear. I could fill this book with cases that have come under my own experience and observation, by which I could prove that the slaveholder could and did break every one of the ten commandments with impunity . . . I could give statements of facts that would appal a generous and kind-hearted soul.

Reading the 1849 autobiography that stirred Mrs. Stowe, one can only wonder what more appalling things Henson knew but did not tell. To see them, we must read with especially close attention, for Henson had neither the flair nor inclinations of the sensationalist writer.

Yet of the people whose arrivals in Ontario are recorded in this book, that of Josiah Henson is among the most poignant, and personally important. At the time of his departure for Canada, my ancestors owned slaves in the American South. I do not know their names, or whether they were treated badly or well by their masters. As we find in Henson's writings, cruelty and kindness came and went, according to differing times and places—with enough gentleness to ensure the loyalty of an intelligent man such as Josiah Henson, and with quite enough savagery to send him, first, to the free states, then to southern Ontario. He speaks for thousands, and his story is the story of thousands.

Josiah was born in 1789 on the Maryland farm of one Francis Newman, about a mile from Port Tobacco, on the broad estuary of the Potomac River, south of Washington. Among the most impressive events he recalled from childhood involved the punishment of his father in a scene of enforcement of the slave system. The father, it appears, had attacked an overseer after the white man struck Josiah's mother. Cruelty need not be direct. Josiah Henson and other slaves were being educated in the severity of the system without a hand being laid on them.

> The negroes from the neighbouring plantations were summoned to witness the scene. A powerful blacksmith named Hewes laid on the stripes. Fifty were given, during which the cries of my father might be heard a mile, and then a pause ensued.
>
> True, he had struck a white man, but as valuable property he must not be damaged. Judicious men felt his pulse. Oh! he could stand the whole. Again and again the thong fell on his lacerated back. His cries grew fainter and fainter, till a feeble groan was the only response to the final blows. His head was then thrust against the post, and his right ear fastened to it with a tack; a swift pass of a knife, and the bleeding member was left sticking to the place. Then came a hurra from the degraded crowd, and the exclamation, "That's what he's got for striking a white man." . . .
>
> Previous to this affair, my father, from all I can learn, had been a good-humoured and light-hearted man, the ringleader in all fun at corn-huskings and Christmas buffoonery. His banjo was the life of the farm, and all night long at a merry-making would he play on it while the other negroes danced. But from this hour he became utterly changed. Sullen, morose, and dogged, nothing could be done with him. The milk of human kindness in his heart was turned to gall. He brooded over his wrongs. No fear or threats of being sold to the far south—the greatest of all terrors to the Maryland slave—would render him tractable. So off he was sent to Alabama. What was his after-fate neither my mother nor I have ever learned; the great day will reveal all. This was the first chapter in my history.

This unfolding history is free of the polemical caricaturing we find in *Uncle Tom's Cabin*. The extreme punishment of his father revealed to young Josiah the wickedness of one man and the iniquity of the mob of onlookers. But Josiah never loses his sense that there are good and bad whites, with good ones probably in the majority. Indeed, if one personal failing is to be found on almost every page of his book, it is an optimistic view of human nature. But if he has one virtue outstanding above all others, it is gratitude for all the good done to him by people of whatever race.

At age eighteen, he was brought to Christian conversion by the preaching of a baker named John McKenny, who lived nearby. McKenny, Henson writes, "was noted especially for his detestation of slavery, and his resolute avoidance of the employment of slave-labour in his business. He would not even hire a slave, the price of whose toil must be paid to his master, but contented himself with the work of his own hands, and with such free labour as he could procure."

The sermon was more than a call to conversion. It was also a decisive moment in the evolution of Josiah's sense of himself and of the culture of racism into which he had been born. In the baker's sermon, Henson learned that "Jesus Christ, the Son of God, tasted death for every man; for the high, for the low, for the rich, for the poor, the bond, the free, the negro in his chains, the man in gold and diamonds." As Josiah listened to McKenny preach, he felt

his heart was filled with the love of Christ, and by the power of the Spirit of God he preached a universal salvation through Jesus Christ. I stood and heard it . . . Again and again did the preacher reiterate the words "for every man."

These glad tidings, this salvation, were not for the benefit of a select few only. They were for the slave as well as the master, the poor as well as the rich, for the persecuted, the distressed, the heavy-laden, the captive; even for me among the rest, a poor, despised, abused creature, deemed by others fit for nothing but unrequited toil—but mental and bodily degradation. Oh, the blessedness and sweetness of feeling that I was LOVED!

It was this conviction that he was *entitled* to love, and under obligation to love others, that stayed him in the difficult years to come. Around age twenty, he was maimed irreparably by a cruel taskmaster, but he forgave. In 1825, his master fell on hard times and, finding himself no longer able to maintain his plantation, he commanded Henson to take his eighteen slaves, Henson's wife and two young children, and deposit them with a brother in Kentucky. As we have seen, he declined the temptation to break free.

Henson's loyalty, as well as his intelligence and talents for leadership, earned him notable permissions usually denied to slaves. He was allowed to study theology and accept ordination as a Methodist minister. He was mobile, and obviously not shackled to the laborious toil of working the land of his master's brother. One imagines him happy in his state, unjust though he knew it to be—and content, having mastered the elaborate codes of deference necessary to maintain entitlement under the essentially cruel system of slavery. During the few years he and his family lived in Kentucky, if he saw this system grinding most dreadfully, he accepted its operation as reality, final and unchangeable. Wicked men must be opposed; the wicked system could be lived with.

That life could become better appears to have occurred to Josiah Henson only during a journey down the Mississippi River to New Orleans with his old master, now recovered. He knew that, when the South's greatest slave market was reached, he would be put up for auction—yet still he persisted in loyalty.

On our way down the river we stopped at Vicksburg, and I got permission to visit a plantation a few miles from the town, where some of my old companions whom I had brought from Kentucky were living.

It was the saddest visit I ever made. Four years in an unhealthy climate and under a hard master had done the ordinary work of twenty. Their cheeks were literally caved in with starvation and disease. They described their daily life, which was to toil half-naked in malarious marshes, under a burning, maddening sun, exposed to poison of mosquitoes and black gnats, and they said they looked forward to death as their only deliverance . . . Their worst fears of being sold down South had been more than realized.

I went away sick at heart, and to this day the remembrance of that wretched group haunts me . . .

For the first time in his life, Henson began to feel rage seething inside him, as his craft slowly descended the river.

All outward nature seemed to feed my gloomy thoughts.

I know not what most men see in voyaging down the Mississippi. If gay and hopeful, probably much of beauty and interest. If eager merchants, probably a golden river, freighted with the wealth of nations. I saw nothing but portents of woe and despair.

Wretched slave-pens; a smell of stagnant waters; half-putrid carcasses of horses or oxen floating along, covered with turkey-buzzards and swarms of green flies,—these are the images with which memory crowds my mind.

My faith in God utterly gave way. I could no longer pray or trust. I thought He had abandoned me and cast me off for ever. I looked not to Him for help. I saw only the foul miasmas, the emaciated frames of my negro companions; and in them saw the sure, swift, loving intervention of the one unfailing friend of the wretched,—death!

Yes; death and the grave!

As hopelessness gathered in his mind, anger "turned my blood to gall, and changed me from a lively, and, I will say, a pleasant-tempered fellow, into a savage, morose, dangerous slave. I was going not at all as a lamb to the slaughter; but I felt myself becoming more ferocious every day . . ."

Whereupon he made up his mind to murder his four companions, take whatever money he can find, scuttle their river boat and flee north.

One night, he got the chance he had been waiting for—only to have his raised hand held back by a seizure of conscience. He tried to explain to his master what he felt. Henson's record of the way the white man responded is typical of his manner and his psychological insight into the grand entrapment of all by custom, history, institutions.

Sometimes he would shed tears himself, and say he was sorry for me. But still I saw his purpose was unchanged. He now kept out of my way as much as possible, and forestalled every effort I made to talk with him. His conscience evidently troubled him. He know he was doing a cruel and wicked thing, and wanted to escape from thinking about it.

I followed him up hard, for I was supplicating for my life. I fell down and clung to his knees in entreaties. Sometimes when too closely pressed, he would curse and strike me. May God forgive him! And yet it was not all his fault; he was made so by the accursed relation of slave-master and slave. I was property,—not a man, not a father, not a husband. And the laws of property and self-interest, not of humanity and love, bore sway.

At length everything was wound up but this single affair. I was to be sold the next day, and Master Amos [his owner's brother] was to set off on his return in a steamboat at six o'clock in the afternoon. I could not sleep that night; its hours seemed interminably long, though it was one of the shortest of the year. The slow way in which we had come down had brought us to the long days and heats of June; and everybody knows what the climate of New Orleans is at that period of the year.

Then "occurred one of those sudden, marked interpositions of Providence, by which in a moment, the whole current of a human being's life is changed . . ." Without warning, Amos fell ill and rapidly became worse. By this time there was nobody on board the ship drifting south to help the stricken white man—except for Josiah.

> The tables were now turned. I was no longer property, no longer a brute-beast to be bought and sold, but his only friend in the midst of strangers. Oh, how different was his tone from what it had been the day before!
>
> He was now the supplicant, a poor, terrified object, afraid of death, and writhing with pain; there lay the late arbiter of my destiny. How he besought me to forgive him! "Stick to me, Sie! Stick to me, Sie! Don't leave me, don't leave me. I'm sorry I was going to sell you."

Thus by a twist of fortune, Henson was rescued from the auction block—and his mind about the vagaries of human fate was never to be the same again.

O my God! how my heart sang jubilees of praise to Thee, as the steamboat swung loose from the levee and breasted the mighty tide of the Mississippi! Away from this land of bondage and death! Away from misery and despair! Once more exulting hope possessed me, and I thought, if I do not now find my way to freedom, may God never give me a chance again!

Returned to Cincinnati, he at last devised a plan to free himself of slavery's chains forever. His destination: Canada, the nearest nation where slavery had been abolished.

His wife was terrified: "We shall die in the wilderness," she protested. "We shall be hunted down with bloodhounds; we shall be brought back and whipped to death." But for all her entreaties, Henson had at last come to the point at which the break was inevitable. But the danger was not over yet. Runaways were still subject to harrying by bounty hunters and by officials with the power to deport the escapees back into bondage. Eventually, however, the Hensons arrived at a place within sight of what had become for Josiah the Promised Land.

The next evening we reached Buffalo, but it was too late to cross the river that night. "You see those trees," said the noble-hearted captain, next morning, pointing to a group in the distance; "they grow on free soil, and as soon as your feet touch that, you're a man. I want to see you go and be a freeman. I'm poor myself, and have nothing to give you; I only sail the boat for wages; but I'll see you across. Here, Green," said he to a ferryman, "what will you take this man and his family over for—he's got no money?" "Three shillings." He then took a dollar out of his pocket and gave it to me. Never shall I forget the spirit in which he spoke. He put his hand on my head and said, "Be a good fellow, won't you?" I felt streams of emotion running down in electric courses from head to foot. "Yes," said I; "I'll use my freedom well; I'll give my soul to God." He stood waving his hat as we pushed off for the opposite shore. God bless him! God bless him eternally! Amen!

It was the 28th of October, 1830, in the morning, when my feet first touched the Canada shore. I threw myself on the ground, rolled in the sand, seized handfuls of it and kissed them, and danced around, till, in the eyes of several who were present, I passed for a madman. "He's some crazy fellow," said a Colonel Warren, who happened to be there. "Oh no, master! don't you know? I'm free!"

Josiah quickly discovered three facts. One was that in the Niagara frontier were "several hundreds of coloured persons," and "in the first joy of their deliverance, they were living in a way, which, I could see, led to little or no progress in improvement." They were, that is, working for white Ontarians in the same spirit of underdog deference that they had when working for American slave-holders. Very much in character, he immediately set himself a humanitarian task. "It soon became my great object to awaken them to a sense of the advantages which were within their grasp . . ."

He also experienced attitudes that stop at no river and pause at no boundary.

Though Canada was the land of freedom to the fugitive slaves, yet they met with so much prejudice at first, on account of their colour, that it was with difficulty they could procure the common comforts of life.

When they endeavoured to have their corn ground they found it no easy matter. A man would often walk three and four miles with two or three bushels on his shoulders, through paths in which the mud was knee-deep, leave his corn at the mill, and then go repeatedly after it in vain; he would be put off with a variety of excuses till he was quite discouraged, and would conclude that it was almost useless for him to raise any grain; and yet there was no other way for him to have a bit of bread or corn-cake.

I was tired of hearing these complaints, which became real grievances, and without having a spare dollar in my pocket, I determined that, as the only remedy was to have a grist-mill, independently of any already established, I would erect one and help the coloured people out of their difficulties.

With that goal in mind, he set out with other former slaves in the autumn of 1834, walking the Canadian coastlines of Lakes Ontario, Erie and Huron until he found a situation that suited him. On a plot of ground east of Lake St. Clair and the Detroit River, he and his fellow refugees from slavery found land enough to support themselves in independence. "This plan was followed," he relates, "and some dozen or more of us settled upon those lands the following spring, and accumulated something by the crops of wheat and tobacco we were able to raise."

Like most of southwestern Ontario before the great clearings of the mid-nineteenth century, the two hundred acres he and his comrades bought on the Detroit River were shaded by black walnut and softwood timber. His compatriots, he tells us, were inclined "to cut them down and burn them on the ground, simply to get rid of them." But Henson shrewdly saw a lucrative resource and the raw material for a timbering operation. In a bid for investment, he travelled back to New York and to New England to study mill operation and the market for black walnut, white wood and other lumber, "such as abounded and was wasted in Canada." He quickly found investors in Boston and others in Canada, including leaders of Toronto's Family Compact such as John Robinson. With that money, he was able to build and launch the mill, charter a ship for transport, load it with 80,000 feet of black walnut lumber sawn in the mill he had created and hire a captain to haul the cargo across Lake Ontario and deposit it at Oswego, New York. Henson's account of his successful enterprise glows with pride of the sort only a man who never imagined such a thing possible can know.

The next season I brought a large cargo by the River St. Lawrence, which came direct to Boston, where, without the aid of any agent or third party whatever, I paid my own duties, got the lumber through the Custom House, and sold it at a handsome profit.

A little incident occurred when paying the duties, which has often since afforded me a great deal of amusement. The Fugitive Slave Law had just been passed in the United States [in 1840], which made it quite an offence to harbour or render aid to a fugitive slave. When the Custom House officer presented his bill to me for the duties on my lumber, I jokingly remarked to him that perhaps he would render himself liable to trouble if he should have dealings with a fugitive slave, and if so, I would relieve him of the trouble of taking my money.

"Are you a fugitive slave, sir?"

"Yes, Sir," said I; "and perhaps you had better not have any dealings with me."

"I have nothing to do with that," said the official; "there is your bill. You have acted like a man, and I deal with you as a man." I enjoyed the scene, and the bystanders seemed to relish it, and I paid him the money.

I look back upon the enterprise related in this chapter with a great deal of pleasure, for the mill which was then built, introduced an entire change in the appearance of that section of the country, and in the habits of the people.

Nor did Henson miss the opportunities for export trade even farther afield. His momentous meeting with Harriet Beecher Stowe took place as he was on his way back from exhibiting the co-operative's timber at the famous Crystal Palace exhibition of 1851.

[T]he first idea which suggested to me the plan of going to England, was to exhibit, at the World's Great Fair, in London, some of the best specimens of our black walnut-lumber, in the hope that it might lead to sales in England . . . The boards which I selected were four in number, excellent specimens, about seven feet in length and four feet in width, of beautiful grain and texture. On their arrival in England, I had them planed and perfectly polished, in French style, so that they actually shone like a mirror.

The history of my connection with the World's Fair is a little amusing. Because my boards happened to be carried over in the American ship, the superintendent of the American Department, who was from Boston, insisted that my lumber should be exhibited in the American department. To this I objected. I was a citizen of Canada, my boards were from Canada, and there was an apartment of the building appropriated to Canadian products. I therefore insisted that my boards should be removed from the American department to the Canadian.

But, said the American, "You cannot do it. All these things are under my control. . . ."

This was quite a damper to me. I thought his position was rather absurd, and for the time it seemed impossible to move him or my boards. A happy suggestion, however, occurred to me. Thought I, if this Yankee wants to retain my furniture, the world shall know who owns it. I accordingly hired a painter to paint in large white letters on the tops of my boards: "THIS IS THE PRODUCT OF THE INDUSTRY OF A FUGITIVE SLAVE FROM THE UNITED STATES, WHOSE RESIDENCE IS DAWN, CANADA."

Flabbergasted at Henson's cheek, the American agent demanded the timber be removed at once from the American exhibition.

"I beg your pardon, sir," said I, "when I wanted to remove it, you would not allow it, and now . . . it shall remain."

In the meantime the crowd enjoyed it and so did I. The result was, that by the next day, the boards were removed to their proper place at no expense to me, and no bill was ever presented to me for carrying the lumber across the Atlantic.

Even as he was developing his successful agricultural co-operative near Windsor, Josiah Henson was being stalked by memories from his past.

The degraded and hopeless condition of a slave can never be properly felt by him while he remains in such a position. After I had tasted the blessings of freedom, my mind reverted to those whom I knew were groaning in captivity, and I at once proceeded to take measures to free as many as I could. I thought that, by using exertion, numbers might make their escape as I did, if they had some practical advice how to proceed.

To that end, he embarked on extensive preaching campaigns in Canada and in New England, and was, he tells us, "cordially welcomed as a speaker in the pulpits of the liberal Protestant denominations, for the most part—Congregationalists, Presbyterians, and Universalists, holding meetings on slavery." His observations on his audiences are, as usual, candid and shrewd.

At that time, slavery was considered to be a permanent institution of the South, and it was supposed that nothing but an earthquake would have the power to break up the foundations of the system. It is a mistaken idea that the majority of the slaveholders would have sold their slaves if the government had offered to buy them. They liked the system, had grown up with it, and were not disposed to part with it without a struggle.

Anti-slavery ideas were not popular at the South, nor generally at the North. On this account, those who had sufficient moral courage to discuss the merits and demerits of the system were accustomed to hold meetings and conventions for this purpose. I was constantly traveling and doing all I could to help to change the public sentiment at the North.

The great upswing of popular opposition to slavery among the northern American population can be traced back to the publication of *Uncle Tom's Cabin,* which at last created a myth people could hold on to, believe in, live for—and, if necessary, die for. To that end, the life of Josiah Henson is crucial—for had he not escaped to Canada, lived and prospered in Ontario to the extent that he could go back and crusade, he would not have contributed to that book.

Yet he seems destined to remain problematic for those who want the past to resolve itself nicely into a conflict between angels and demons. Henson shares that unattractive distinction with most members of the Family Compact. In the Rebellion of 1837, he had no problem deciding which side to support. "The coloured men," he writes, "were willing to help defend the government that had given them a home when they had fled from slavery." During the brief conflict, he served the Crown as a captain to the 2nd Essex Company of Coloured Volunteers and fought the rebels valiantly.

Sometime both American slave and soldier for the Crown, defender of liberty, entrepreneur and visionary—Josiah Henson was all of these. He passed in one lifetime through many histories, the heritage of the Age of Revolution and the inheritance of British traditions—both the racism, which has still not been wholly eradicated in Ontario, and the hope of liberty.

AM I NOT A MAN AND A BROTHER?

24

THE LAST INVASION

Though Canadians occasionally complain about the insidious effects of American popular culture above the 49th parallel, nobody north of the border lies awake at night awaiting the rumble of American tanks through the streets of Toronto or the scream of American bombs falling from the sky on Ottawa. The scenario is hardly thinkable, given the economic and political intimacy that has long existed between the two largest nations on the continent.

Were he alive today, John A. Macdonald—veteran of the last American invasion of Canada and military historian—would think us naïve to the point of lunacy. Writing in 1910, he decried the ignorance of "the great mass of the young Canadian boys and girls" about U.S.-Canadian military engagements he remembered vividly. Though the American Civil War had ended only months before, another menace to continental peace arose immediately, to "cast dark shadows over this fair and prosperous Dominion . . . It was a period of great peril to this rising young Nation of the North, which might possibly have ended in the severance of Canada from British dominion." He was annoyed that so few Canadians knew about the invasion of Canada by Americans in 1866, and that so many thought it could never happen again.

After all, for almost a century after that gaggle of gentleman farmers, fanatical ideologues and farmer soldiery led Britain's southern Atlantic colonies to independence, the threat of an invasion of monarchist Canada by republican America was there, and was real. There was the rekindling of old hostilities after 1812, when John Strachan stopped the American looters in Toronto and later cheered on the Redcoats as James and Dolly Madison scampered from the burning White House. Then came the American Civil War, and a rekindling of hostilities between Washington and London. While it declined to give the rebellious South the dignity of diplomatic recognition, Her Majesty's Government did recognize that a state of "belligerence" persisted between the United States and the entity headquartered at Richmond. The mere acknowledgement of a rebellious "entity" on U.S. soil was enough to cause friction. For President Abraham Lincoln and official Washington, it's worth remembering, the Confederate States of America never existed outside the fantasies of Jefferson Davis and other Southern dreamers, politicians, fighters. The South was United States territory under rebel rule, period. Britain would have been playing with fire to defy that doctrine openly.

But in the view of many, Britain and British North America had been playing a dangerous diplomatic game during the Civil War. In 1862, an editorialist at *The Times* of London wondered:

And when the time has at last arrived when, either from the termination of civil strife or the failure of money and credit, the United States are no longer able to support their vast army, what is to prevent that army from marching towards the Northern frontier, and satiating its revenge, its love of plunder and of conquest, in the rich and unwasted provinces of Canada?

A firm *nothing* to that question could have extinguished British rule on this continent forever. Speaking in Montréal in 1862, the Canadian politician Thomas D'Arcy McGee declared of the volley that sparked the Civil War:

> That shot fired at Fort Sumter was the signal gun of a new epoch for North America, which told the people of Canada, more plainly than human speech can ever express it, to sleep no more, except on their arms—unless in their sleep they desire to be overtaken and subjugated.

As things turned out, Whitehall waffled and demurred until 1865, when the Union put an end to Britain's dithering by crushing the rebellion of the South. If anti-British sentiment still rumbled occasionally in the popular American press, British North Americans felt they could rest easy. Their worst fear—invasion by the vastly more powerful armed forces of the United States—had not materialized. But as the first anniversary of peace approached, in the spring of 1866, Ontario was threatened more urgently by invasion from the United States than at any time since the War of 1812. The invaders called themselves Fenians.

George Denison, a Canadian officer who had served in the defence of British North America on the Niagara Frontier during the Fenian raids, opens his 1866 memoir with a reminder of the long, miserable chain of misfortunes and tumults he believes led up to the onslaught he witnessed.

> About seven hundred years ago, Strongbow, Earl of Pembroke, at the head of his English archers, effected a landing on the coast of Ireland . . . From that time until the present day, Ireland, or the greater part of it, has been an appendage of the British

Crown. Looking back through the long course of years that have since elapsed, we find that the history of Ireland is little more than an account of a continual series of wars and insurrections, in which the native Irish, or the Celts have endeavoured to throw off the yoke of their Saxon conquerors . . .

The Irish race in America, living under republican institutions, and thriving in a country far richer and more prosperous than the land they had left, naturally became imbued with republican ideas and tendencies, and soon imbibed a hatred to England and the British Empire . . .

Denison, though a loyal Queen's man, sympathized with those wretched Irish immigrants to the United States

who believed that by uniting their race in Ireland and America they would be in a position to realize their day-dream of having their country an independent republic . . . In order to carry out this idea, a few of these men organized a small society in New York, which afterwards, enlarging in its dimensions, became the Fenian Brotherhood.

The year of the Brotherhood's founding was 1863, at New York's Tammany Hall. In their hurt nationalist pride, their outrage at the continuing subjugation of Ireland by autocrats, the New York Irish shared much frustration with radical Austrians, Hungarians, Italians and French who had passed from hope to despair during the failed revolutionary outbreaks of 1848 and 1849. But even against the background of that mid-century tumult, the Irish, about to unite as the Fenian Brotherhood and draw thousands to their cause, were extraordinary in their wild romanticism. A key figure in all this was John O'Mahony, veteran of an Irish uprising ten years before and living in exile in the United States at the time the South went down to defeat. The Brotherhood's name came to O'Mahony from the Irish legends popularized during the romantic nationalist revivalism of Victorian times. In these old stories, the hero Fiann headed a band of warriors, dangerous children of the world of faery and fantasy, known as the *fianna* ("band of hunters" in Irish), and dedicated to the defence of Irish soil. O'Mahony was as treacherous a figure as any of the mythical *fianna*, though less effectual—at first.

For a couple of years after the launch of their paramilitary organization, the Fenians made very little headway among Irish immigrants. Their activities were rarely remarked upon in the press. The Brotherhood seemed to be merely another of those wild little conventicles, religious and political, that had always (and would always) be brought by newcomers to these shores from the lands they were forsaking. Major Denison knew that the invasion of Canada in 1866 was officially condemned by the U.S. government. But he believed the Civil War and the impending raids on Canada were fed by the same poisoned stream, running underground in American culture.

When the war broke out in the United States, it gave a great impetus to the Fenian organization. Up to that time the present generation had not undergone any experience in war. After a lengthened peace men get so accustomed to peaceful pursuits, and the idea of war becomes so hateful to them, that the military spirit of a nation becomes almost extinct, or at least exceedingly sluggish in its action. When a people are in that condition, it is useless to attempt to get them to embark on any undertaking likely to lead to war and bloodshed.

After, or during a war, on the other hand, the military spirit is awakened, and in some instances even created, and after a time becomes very active: men who have left peaceful pursuits, and have become accustomed to the bustle of camps and the excitements of a soldier's life, return to their usual avocations with reluctance, and abandon their military duties with regret . . . The leaders of the Fenian Brotherhood, fully appreciating this feeling, sought to turn it to their own advantage as well as to the benefit of the cause for which they were working.

By 1865, an estimated ten thousand Civil War veterans had joined Fenian military brigades, or "circles." The central organization had a huge war chest of about $500,000. But as romantic ideological movements tend to be, the Fenian movement was riven by factionalism. The dominant tendency, led by the Civil War veteran Thomas W. Sweeny, was not content merely to found a fraternal organization to help Ireland from afar. After the Fenians had invaded and captured key points on the Niagara Frontier in the spring of 1866, Sweeny justified his attacks in a proclamation addressed to the Irish people in Canada, and luminous with the flamboyance characteristic of the movement.

We have taken up the sword to strike down the oppressors' rod, to deliver Ireland from the tyrant, the despoiler, the robber. We have registered our oaths upon the altar of our country in the full view of Heaven, and sent up our vows to the throne of Him who inspired them. Then, looking about us for the enemy, we find him here—here in your midst, where he is most vulnerable and convenient to our strength; and have sworn to stretch forth the armies' hand of Ireland and grapple with him. The battle has commenced and we pledge ourselves to all the sacred memories of struggling liberty, to follow it up at any cost to either of two alternatives—the absolute political independence and liberty of Ireland or the demolition of our armies.

The Fenians "have no issue with the people of these provinces," Sweeny declares, adding that his "weapons are for the oppressors of Ireland . . . Against England, upon land and sea, until Ireland is free!"

Along with other thoughtful British North Americans, George Denison feared and expected this offensive by the considerable Fenian force against Canada in 1866, and he resolved to be its scribe.

At the suggestion of a friend I had decided, early this spring [1866] to write, if possible, an account of the Fenian Raid which we both felt confident would take place on the Niagara Frontier during the summer; consequently, on being ordered to the front to aid in repelling the invaders I kept the idea constantly in view, and was continually gathering up information of what was passing around me, in every quarter in which I could obtain it . . .

But before the incursion actually took place, Major Denison and other apprehensive observers in Canada and elsewhere found themselves isolated. The victorious Union, after all, had not turned a great and victorious army against its northern neighbour in the summer of 1865. The prevailing view in the press held the Fenian leaders to be clowns and ruffians, and their rhetoric so much hot air and smoke. As late as April, 1866, the Chicago *Tribune* (in an editorial reproduced soon thereafter in the Toronto *Globe*) stated:

Amidst the atmosphere of falsehood, deception and fraud that envelops the whole Fenian humbug, it is difficult to tell what that organization may or may not be doing. We only know that the leaders connected with it are without brains, and the followers are very generally without character.

Around the same time, *The Times* of London proclaimed that

the Fenian Conspiracy [was] rendered harmless for the present by the proved imbecility or roguery of some of the ringleaders . . . who are eating green turtle and drinking madeira at the expense of stupid servant girls and waiters of New York and other cities.

Denison nevertheless persisted in this belief that there was ample reason for apprehension (and the thoroughness of his narrative shows the fruits of mental preparation). While officially opposed to Fenian movements, U.S. agents seemed to become suddenly absent-minded when the Brotherhood made an inflammatory speech, or even a military move. Invasion had been noised about in Canada late in 1865, prompting a call-up of Canadian militia and their dispatch to the border just before Christmas. A Fenian rally in New York in March, 1866, had featured enough incendiary speeches and threats against Canada to cause the colonial administration to put ten thousand militia on alert. If the Fenian warriors and General Sweeny were fanatical dreamers, increasing numbers of Canadians began to realize these seasoned veterans of the American Civil War could inflict serious damage on Canada, should they attack—and, just possibly, strike a blow of calamitous magnitude to the world at large. George Denison correctly understood that the invading Fenians had to be stopped at once.

General Sweeny considered that by attacking Canada he was attacking England, and attacking her in her weakest point, in a point far removed from her base, and along a frontier of a length difficult to be guarded . . . Again, if he was able to take a sufficient portion of Canada to enable him to form a belligerent government, one recognized by the United States, vessels could be sent to prey upon British commerce, and the offer might be made to the United States to give up Canada to them on condition of their giving assistance in freeing Ireland. Again, by attacking Canada, they might have better opportunities of fomenting a war between the United States and England . . .

Thus would British troops be siphoned off to do battle in the New World. The idea was to leave the English overlords in Ireland without adequate defence, hence vulnerable to the uprising Sweeny believed would inevitably ensue. The plan was a recipe for world war.

Denison got his chance to be both recording angel and soldier in the closing days of May, 1866. On May 30, the news flashed by telegraph across the world.

Toronto, Canada West.—Intelligence has been received from Buffalo of Fenian movements in progress. The military are on the alert, and every preparation being made for emergency.

The next afternoon:

New York, May 31, p.m.—A Toronto despatch says the Mayor of Buffalo yesterday telegraphed to the Mayor of Hamilton, that six hundred Fenians had left Cleveland for that city. Rumour has it that the Government will tomorrow call out the volunteers again.

Major Denison had correctly predicted that the principal thrust of a Fenian invasion would be at the short Niagara River, which empties the waters of the upper Great Lakes into Lake Ontario. It was, and is today, a nexus of vital road and rail transportation, a centre of population density, and a perfect place for international spies, like old East and West Berlin. It was also a vulnerable juncture, with open waters on two ends, a swift but navigable river between. However obvious a crossing-place this neck of land might have been to Major Denison, it was not self-evident to most Canadian military men, who expected the attack, if it came at all, to occur along the long border between Québec and New England. To be on the safe side, the American navy had put its warship *Michigan* in the area, to watch out for Fenians attempting a passage over. But most observers did not seriously expect a raid from Buffalo, even though an unusual number of men were grouping there, for reasons unknown to all but themselves.

During the last two or three days of May 1866, the telegraphic despatches brought rumours of bodies of men moving northward, along the various railroads leading to the lake borders. These men traveled, for the great part, unarmed; and, if interrogated as to their destination, stated that they were going to California, to work in the mines. When they stated this intention while moving northward, they had some colour for the statements; but, when they continued the story after turning eastward from Cleveland, toward Buffalo, the impudence of the falsehood was unparalleled . . . It had long been anticipated by those who took the trouble to think upon the matter, and by those who, contrary to the general opinion, believed the Fenians intended to attack Canada, that Fort Erie would be the first and most likely place to be attacked.

Though contrary to the general opinion, such was Major Denison's opinion; and such was the fact. The massing of some three thousand Fenians in Buffalo was complete by Wednesday, May 30. Only by nightfall on Thursday, May 31, did "the authorities in Canada," says Denison, begin "seriously to apprehend an immediate crossing." It was almost too late. By next morning, telegraphic dispatches were chasing each other across the globe, hitting front pages of newspapers everywhere.

New York, June 1, p.m.—It is reported that Fort Erie, in Canada opposite Buffalo, has been captured by the Fenians, who are represented to be 3,000 strong, and 2,000 of which are said to be marching, unopposed, into the interior, and to have already cut one telegraphy line.

Buffalo, 11 a.m.—The Fenians have torn up the railroad tracks, and destroyed all the telegraph cables at the terminus of the Grand Trunk Railroad between Black Rock and Fort Erie.

Buffalo, N.Y., June 1—Notwithstanding the vigilance of the authorities the US steamer *Michigan* being under steam and having her ports open, and the fact that the city is swarming with Canadian spies, several regiments of Fenians crossed over into Canada last night, including troops from Kentucky, Tennessee, and Indiana, a regiment from Ohio, and a regiment from this city.

At this point they crossed in canal boats, drawn by tugs and, when nearing the Canadian shore, set up wild Irish cheers with the green flag floating. Col. O'Neil, of the 13th Regiment of Nashville, is in command of Fort Erie . . . All the telegraph wires are cut on the Canadian side, except those via the suspension bridge. The agent of the Associated Press has left for the scene of operations. The Fenians are reported to be marching towards the suspension bridge, 22 miles from here. Fort Sarnia, Canada West, opposite Port Hudson, was also captured this morning by a detachment of Fenian troops, and Windsor, opposite Detroit, is also in Fenian possession.

In Toronto, the Queen's Own Rifles—troops first mustered to fight the Fenians—were rallying for the boat ride across Lake Ontario to Niagara-on-the-Lake. The British consul at Buffalo and the U.S. District Attorney were on the *Michigan,* watching the Fenians on the Canadian side. The destruction of railway tracks and telegraph lines suggested the immediate aim was a strike against all lines of communication. But at first, nobody outside Fenian ranks appears to have had any idea as to exactly what the invaders planned to do.

For Major Denison, and for the Fenian leaders, there was no doubt about the immediate objective: the destruction of the locks on the Welland Canal, stopping ship traffic between Lakes Erie and Ontario, thereby striking a deadly blow to Canadian prosperity. As Denison reports in his memoirs:

To prevent the Fenians from carrying out their designs on the canal, the Canadian military authorities had called up 14,000 militia volunteers. None of them, however, were ready to go into action when the Fenians made their lightning raid on Fort Erie. But on June 1, as the Fenians made ready to march on toward the canal, the scattered and confused Canadian troops were forming themselves into a clenched fist. It was prepared to strike twice: at the north end of the Welland Canal, near St. Catharines; and at the south end, on Lake Erie.

When the opposing sides finally engaged, the largely inexperienced Canadian volunteers made one tactical error after another. Their only experience was the drill-field, if that; and they were opposing experienced Civil War veterans, used to cruel and hard fighting. The Canadians fell back, then broke and ran.

But behind them and the Niagara River, and their only chance to retreat back into friendly territory, stood a far more experienced Canadian force. The Fenians' commanding officer ordered his soldiers to board the transports he had arranged to have waiting on the banks of the river. But also waiting for them was the USS *Michigan,* which took the barges and their cargo of men into custody.

In the next hours and days, any hopes that the Fenians might have harboured about victory or solace quickly collapsed. The tribute for Canada's salvation cannot really be given to the valiance or military superiority of the British North American troops deployed against the enemy. The honour has to go, instead, to the United States for bringing the Fenian caper to a swift end.

Though Washington had no warm feelings about Canada, it wanted no new confrontation with Britain. On June 5, President Andrew Johnson decided that the United States would abide strictly by the Neutrality Laws of 1818 and that the Fenians would no longer be tolerated, even in a country with a rich history and a future of tolerating all manner of oddities, eccentrics, fanatics. Remarkably, several more Fenian raids took place on Canadian soil, but these were desultory, accomplished nothing and were quickly repulsed.

The Fenians immediately tried to regroup. The disgrace of being beaten back by an ill-equipped and inexperienced Canadian force could perhaps have been overcome. But the withdrawal of popular American support seems to have dealt the final blow to their crippling exhaustion. Within days of the Niagara raid, the Philadelphia Fenian "Senator," John Gibbons, received a letter from a comrade calling him to a meeting of leaders arranged to set the Brotherhood's liberationist work in train once again. His reply, with its small cry of despair, may have been typical of such responses. He writes:

I received your dispatch this morning to attend Senate meeting on Wednesday. Circumstances prevent my attending. I have dispatched to that effect and, laying my resignation of Senator and State Centre before you, you will of course accept it, as I will not serve longer in that position . . .

Our career, in a military sense, has been nothing but a series of blunders since I left New York. Our Colonel had orders to leave on the 25th [May, 1866]. I sent a man to Cincinnati to see about transportation, when he was told by Mr Fitzgerald that we should be in Cleveland on the night of the 28th after dark. I went to Indianapolis and made arrangements accordingly. Once got to Cleveland on Monday night, the 28th, no arrangements there to go further. By then I had spent 20 hours with 300 men.

Got orders from headquarters to go to Buffalo. Got there Wednesday evening. Got orders there from Hynes to cross the river on Thursday night, which we did, and, as the sequel shows, made a beautiful fight of it. Our men were made into a forlorn hope—some in prison, some in strange locales wounded, and some killed. The balance got home again. We have no plan nor programme to follow. Done as best we could, thought we were doing right but probably done all wrong, for all we know. The people here blame me for not being better-posted and refuse to give another dollar . . .

Your Senate should have met in Washington and hurled your anathemas against those who deceived and betrayed us . . .

Britain's empire in America had survived extinction again—though certainly not because of its internal strength, political or military. The Canadian forces carried obsolete weapons and knew how to fight in ways that were out of style. The colony had survived by accidentally dropping into a safe spot between the grinding mountains of great powers. Britain did not want to send out a military force to Canada (which it eventually had to do), but it could not be seen to waffle in the face of Irish armed force, even when the force was somewhere else and exerted against a colony Britain did not want to the bothered by.

The solution to everybody's problem would be an efficient domestic militia and a measure of political independence greater than the Canadian territories had enjoyed since the coming of Cartier. There was clearly a matter of priorities in these tasks, in an order clearly outlined by the American historian P. G. Smith.

The first task was to rearm the militia. Most soldiers sent to defend the border in 1866 carried antiquated, muzzle-loading rifles, many of which lacked ramrods and had damaged firing mechanisms. Colonel Patrick MacDougall filed this report on the state of Canadian weapons in 1867: "It is very difficult to enforce proper cleaning of their arms by volunteers; they take pride in turning out on parade smart and clean and soldier-like so far as regards the outward appearance; but it is too often the case that their rifles are so fouled within that they cannot be fired."

Steps were quickly taken to acquire newer breech-loading weapons. The Canadian government purchased three thousand Peabody rifles, with bayonets, from the Providence Tool Company of Providence, R.I. Starr carbines and Spencer repeating rifles were also acquired in the United States. The farmers of the St. Armand area, concerned about their lack of defence during the Fenian raid of 1866, sent two representatives south to Massachusetts, where they bought forty Ballard sporting rifles. The U.S. government took no steps to impede those arms sales to a foreign government with whom relations were strained. The British government, however, assumed the lion's share of strengthening Canada's arms. In 1867, thirty thousand breech-loading Snider-Enfield rifles, complete with all necessary equipment, were shipped to Canada for immediate issue to the militia.

But no amount of military hardware could compensate for the ignominious political position Canada found itself in: hugely wealthy, yet politically dependent; vast, but vulnerable—not wanting domination but needing strong friendships.

The era of Confederation was right for nation-building. Historians believe that the union of Canadian provinces into a nation would have occurred eventually, Fenians or no Fenians. But within days of the invasions, the newspapers had grasped the importance of the raids for the future of Canada. "The Fenian invasion has had the effect of not only rallying all classes of our Canadian people to the defence of the country," declared the *Niagara Mail* on June 27, 1866, "but it had the additional effect of Uniting the North American Colonies, as one, for the defence of the whole."

Lest one become too serious about the invasion that inspired Confederation, as Canadian historians are inclined to do, it's worth remembering yet again how lost in fantasy the raiders were. This is not to diminish the real harm they did or the potential of their little raid for touching off a conflagration that could have spread across oceans and ended Canada's own dreams of independent nationhood forever. But if Canada had to be invaded by anyone, thought the soldier George Denison, better the Fenians than any other Americans. Neither the comedy nor the tragedy of the Fenians escaped him.

> I spent three weeks in Fort Erie and conversed with dozens of the people of the place, and was astonished at the universal testimony borne by them to the unvarying good conduct of this rabble while among them . . . They have been called plunderers, robbers and marauders, yet, no matter how unwilling we may be to admit it, the positive fact remains, that they stole but few valuables, that

they destroyed, comparatively speaking, little or nothing, and
that they committed no outrages on the inhabitants, but treated
every one with unvarying courtesy.

It seems like a perfect burlesque to see a ragged rabble without
a government, country or flag, affecting chivalrous sentiments
and doing acts, that put one in mind of the days of knight
errantry . . .

It perhaps does not come with good grace from a Canadian to
give any credit to the Fenians, who without any ground of
complaint against us invade our country, and cause the loss of
valuable lives among us, but as a truthful narrator of facts, I must
give them credit on the only ground on which they can claim it.

V
DOMINION

25
NIAGARA

NOTHING PROVIDED A MORE EFFECTIVE VISUAL SYMBOL for the new, energetic Ontario that emerged from colonialism into nationhood in 1867 than Niagara Falls. The only trouble with the Falls as a defining image is that it's never as awe-inspiring as the first-time visitor expects it to be. (This fact long ago gave rise to a joke, to the effect that the Falls is every honeymooner's second big letdown.) Despite disappointment with the cataract, we have verbose travel writers of the last three centuries to thank, beginning with the sly, purple-prosed Franciscan priest Louis Hennepin. (We caught him lying, back in the seventeenth century, about his great "discoveries" in the far-flung reaches of Louisiana.) After visiting the Falls in November, 1678, he wrote the earliest known account of it in *Description de la Louisiane* (1683), then retold the story again in his fabulously popular travel memoir *Nouvelle Découverte d'un très grand pays Situe dans l'Amérique, entre le Nouveau Mexique et la Mer Glaciale,* published at Utrecht in 1697 with a dedication to the English king William III. The first English translation appeared in 1698.

Betwixt the Lake Ontario and Erie, there is a vast and prodigious Cadence of Water which falls down after a surprising and astonishing manner, insomuch that the Universe does not afford its parallel. Tis true, Italy and Suedland boast some such Things; but we may well say they are but sorry Patterns, when compar'd to this of which we now speak. At the foot of this horrible Precipice, we meet with the River Niagara, which is not above a quarter of a League broad, but is wonderfully deep in some places. It is so rapid above this Descent, that it violently hurries down the wild Beasts while endeavouring to pass it to feed on the other side, they not being able to withstand the force of its Current, which inevitably casts them above Six hundred foot high. . . .

This wonderful Downfal, is compounded of two great Cross-streams of Water, and two Falls, with an Isle sloping along the middle of it. The Waters which fall from this horrible Precipice, do foam and boyl after the most hideous manner imaginable, making an outrageous Noise, more terrible than that of Thunder; for when the Wind blows out of the South, their dismal roaring may be heard more than Fifteen Leagues off. . . .

The River Niagara having thrown itself down this incredible Precipice, continues its impetuous course for two Leagues together . . . with an inexpressible rapidity: But having past that, its impetuosity relents, gliding along more gently for two other Leagues, till it arrive at Lake Frontenac [Lake Ontario]. . . .

If one isn't playing to the market, as Father Hennepin surely was, the belief that the waters are magnificent tends to increase with unfamiliarity, meaning those most overwhelmed by all that water are people who have never been there. In 1825, the Philadelphia sign-painter and Quaker visionary Edward Hicks, who never went anywhere, created a reverential image of Niagara Falls with a border inscription meant to celebrate the spiritual exaltation he was trying to capture in art. (The poem painted into the margins is by Alexander Wilson, nineteenth-century America's most famous birdwatcher.)

This great o'erwhelming work of awful Time
In all its dread magnificence sublime,
Rises on our view, amid crashing roar
That bids us kneel, and Time's great GOD adore.

Mrs. Simcoe went, and as far as I know did not kneel or think about God. She was dismayed by the scarcity of snakes, as you will recall, and was bitten by a bug. But while on the topic of dismayed visitors—what list would be complete without Anna Jameson? "Well!" she exclaims, with a typical harrumph, in *Winter Studies and Summer Rambles*.

I have seen these Cataracts of Niagara, which have thundered in my mind's ear since I can remember—which have been my "childhood's thought, my youth's desire," since first my imagination was awakened to wonder and to wish. I have beheld them, and shall I whisper it to you?—but, O tell it not among the Philistines!—I wish I had not! I wish they were still a thing unbeheld—a thing to be imagined, hoped, and anticipated—something to live for—the reality has displaced from my mind an illusion far more magnificent than itself—I have no words for my utter disappointment yet I have not the presumption to suppose that all I have heard and read of Niagara is false or exaggerated—that every expression of astonishment, enthusiasm, rapture, is affectation or hyperbole. No! It must be my own faith. . . . What has come over my soul and senses?—I am no longer Anna—I am metamorphosed—I am translated—I am an ass's head, a clod, a wooden spoon, a fat weed growing on Lethe's bank, a stock, a stone, a petrifaction—for have I not seen Niagara, the wonder of wonders; and felt—no words can tell *what* disappointment!

But that's enough of that. The temptation every writer about Niagara Falls must confront and defeat—and no book about Ontario arrivals would be complete without some reference to the breathless, exasperated or otherwise delicious observations about the province's most illustrious natural landmark—is to simply keep listing them, page after page. Some literary raves are very funny; most are hackneyed and predictable. Some reported conversations are absurd and turn out to be sad, like the last words of people about to risk a tightrope walk over the Falls or a plunge in a barrel.

Then there is the plethora of accounts that are nothing more than ghoulish voyeurism hiding behind a mask of objective reporting. When Joseph Avery got himself trapped on the edge of the gorge for thirty hours in 1853— he was eventually swept to a horrible death—the ordeal made the front pages of New York newspapers. The local tourism industry was upset by Marilyn Monroe's 1952 film *Niagara,* because it recalled the darker aspects of the Falls experience—the danger and violence, murder, suicide, sleaze. But headlines and compassionate newspaper stories about a real cliff-hanger—that turned out badly for him who hung—is different. It's news of the kind the people who make money off the Niagara Falls tourists have always welcomed.

The hucksters had taken over both the New York and Ontario sides of the Niagara River gorge by the time of Confederation. By the turn of the twentieth century, each nation that shared the great ditch was trying to curb the riverside squalor and ramshackle development as best it could. But the restoration of something like natural beauty along the gorge was still a haphazard affair when the British utopian author H. G. Wells swung by in 1905.

In much the same spirit of hope that took conservative Edwardian intellectuals to continental baths and spas, there to soak away their angst, the radical socialist Wells had crossed the Atlantic to have his quasi-religious faith in Modern Technology bolstered by America's "growth invincible" (as he calls it). Beauty and the Sublime had no part to play in so commonsensical a pilgrimage. Where better to have that secular religion of Progress confirmed than among the new temples to divine and practical Electricity?

"As a waterfall," writes Wells in *The Future in America: A Search after Realities* (1906),

Niagara's claim to distinction is now mainly quantitative; its spectacular effect, its magnificent and humbling size and splendour, were long since destroyed beyond recovery by the hotels, the factories, the power houses, the bridges and tramways and hoardings that arose about it. It must have been a fine thing to happen upon suddenly after a day of solitary travel; the Indians, they say, gave it worship; but it's no great

wonder to reach it by trolley-car, through a street hack-infested
and full of adventurous refreshment places and souvenir shops
and touting guides.

Interestingly enough, it is in these "extremely defiling and ugly"
developments, the "human accumulations" crowding the rim of the
gorge, that Wells finds confirmation of a rosy technological unfolding.

> They stood for the future, threats and promises, and the water-
> fall was just a vast reiteration of falling water. The note of growth
> in human accomplishment rose clear and triumphant above the
> elemental thunder. . . .
> [T]hese represent only the first slovenly onslaught of
> mankind's expansion, the pioneers' camp of the human growth
> process that already changes its quality and manner. There are
> finer things than these outrages to be found.
> The dynamos and galleries of the Niagara Falls Power
> Company, for example, impressed me far more profoundly than
> the Cave of the Winds; are, indeed, to my mind, greater and
> more beautiful than that accidental eddying of the air beside a
> downpour. They are will made visible, thought translated into
> easy and commanding things. They are clean, noiseless, and
> starkly powerful . . . They are altogether noble masses of machin-
> ery, huge black slumbering monsters, great sleeping tops that
> engender irresistible forces in their sleep. They sprang, armed like
> Minerva, from serene and speculative, foreseeing and endeavour-
> ing brains. First was the word, and then these powers. . . .

If readers are so minded, they can insist at this point that I return to
my topic, which is Ontario. Wells was probably looking at (and
swooning over) generating plants on the New York side of the Niagara
River.

But here I must invoke again a privilege that has elsewhere determined the direction of this writing, sometimes obviously, sometimes

not. It has to do with the fact that Ontario's geographical boundaries, beginnings and endings are notably fluid. I would never argue that Niagara Falls is in Louisiana, though Father Hennepin's *Description de la Louisiane* is where we first find the cascade written up. Indeed, at certain places, by reason of geography and the fiat of politicians or generals, the borderline between Ontario and its neighbouring juris-dictions is quite clear. The Niagara Frontier is such a place. A danger-ous, fast-running river rushing through a canyon stands between two nations and can be crossed only over easily policed bridges. When the Fenians barged across the Niagara River and invaded Ontario with a view to setting up a tiny pirate outpost, everybody agreed they had violated an international boundary.

But at some places—and even there, not always—the border can become virtually non-existent. Neither the water that rushes north from Lake Erie into Lake Ontario nor the turbines it turns nor the electricity it produces has passport, national loyalty or political prefer-ence. As telephones had already begun to abolish the distances sepa-rating people, the launch of electrical production on both sides of the Niagara River a century ago began the gradual process, still continuing today, of vaporizing boundaries. Within the informational and electric commonwealth that began to emerge from the old system of nation states in the Victorian period, those lines on maps have never really stopped declining in importance. Something occasionally happens to remind us how porous they actually are.

One such event took place at 5:16 on the afternoon of November 9, 1965, when electrical supply to a vast swath of the United States and parts of Ontario was abruptly interrupted. The culprit turned out to be a misbehaving switch at the Sir Adam Beck No. 2 Generating Station at Queenston, Ontario, that had accidentally flipped and sent a tsunami of unexpected electrons crashing into the Canada–United States Eastern Grid. The result was an automatic shutdown that affected 30 million people immediately, and untold millions indirectly. Of course, the faulty circuit breaker could as easily been at the Robert Moses Generating Station, across the river on the New York side, and connected to Sir Adam Beck by high-voltage lines and a little tramway. That the faulty breaker was in the Canadian half of Niagara's trans-border hydroelectric zone did contribute, potentially anyway, to the world's knowledge of Ontario history.

Before that November night in 1965, most Americans had never heard the name of Adam Beck. Ontarians, if they'd heard of him, had forgotten who he was. A beautiful Art Deco fountain dedicated to this remarkable man's memory stands on University Avenue, Toronto's grandest boulevard, though the waterspouts have not been turned on for years. It is to be hoped that at least some people, back in 1965, wondered about the man after whom the guilty power station had been named. Had they pressed on, the search would have led them to a German immigrant's son who was obsessed by electricity and by the vision of making sure it flowed freely over the length and breadth of Ontario.

He was born plain Adam Beck in 1857, in the same narrow, short corridor of southern Ontario countryside wherein Alexander Graham Bell was to make the first long-distance telephone call a few years later—of which, more presently. First and foremost a remorseless politician and operator, Beck was no equal to Bell, the visionary. But both men breathed the same air and enjoyed the same Victorian climate of adventure that inspired dreams of unlimited industrial progress and prosperity, of bounding upward and forward. It hung brightly over Ontario throughout the late half of the Old Queen's reign. Since 1867 and Confederation, in the view of many, a new freedom from old pieties was blowing in the wind.

"I've just returned from the Old Country," writes an anonymous wag about England in 1884 to a Toronto satirical magazine. "Miserable old place—seems so small and pokey after this 'boundless continent of ours.' You can't throw a stone without winging a noble-man; the place is fairly crowded with 'em. . . ." But the worst thing about English folk "on their own soil" is their "density and opaqueness in the matter of seeing a joke or a pun." They could all stand to have "their brains oxygenated and ozoned by a trip to Canada." The author might just as readily have been sending up the "density and opaqueness" of the Brits in the matter of can-do personal initiative. Ontarians were feeling superior on all counts.

In the late Victorian world where Adam Beck came of age, the last vestiges of famously dense, forbidding Ontario bush were being chopped back to make way for rich, rolling croplands. The British feudal fealties taken for granted by old Thomas Talbot had vanished. There were rich farmers in the countryside, and rich merchants in the towns. At last, hard-working families had time, leisure and money to enjoy themselves and to pursue their curiosities about the great world suddenly being shrunk by new communications technologies. The world's oldest annual agricultural and industrial showcase, now called the Canadian National Exhibition, was launched as a small rural Ontario show of farm machinery and such in 1849. By 1852, when the travelling fair swung into Toronto, it had metamorphosed into a spectacle and showcase of marvels—telegraphy and astronomy, fine art and agricultural machinery, breeding stock becoming ever better and more efficient. Writing in the 1852 brochure, the fair's promoters themselves seem awestruck by the changes that had swept Ontario in the six decades since John and Elizabeth Simcoe set up Captain Cook's tent exactly where the fair stood, on the flat lakeshore site of old Fort Rouillé.

Sixty years ago, an Indian wigwam stood alone on the spot now occupied by a city containing thirty-two thousand inhabitants, and furnished with nearly all the requirements of modern civilization, and much of the energy and skill which characterizes the age.

Sixty years ago, the population of Upper Canada consisted of a few thousand families, dispersed over a territory containing upward of forty-six thousand square miles, enjoying but a very limited means of communications between themselves, and deriving few advantages from the chequered intercourse with the world beyond their own great lakes.

At the time we write, this extensive province is peopled with one million freemen, in possession of those civil and religious blessings, which can alone be won and enjoyed by an enterprising and vigorous people . . .

But the "enterprising" people celebrated by this fluorescent propaganda were ready, not merely for the uplifting and progressive aspects of the New, but for Modernity itself—which is a decidedly more complex reality than Victorian fair-promoters were able to acknowledge or emphasize. In the fifty-one years of its nineteenth-century career, and well into the twentieth century, the Canadian National Exhibition played to the unpurified, indiscriminate taste for the technically progressive and the psychologically monstrous that always seem to accompany the uplifting. The same visitors who came to the Exhibition to marvel at scientific discoveries and mechanical innovations also came to gawk at JoJo the Dog-Faced Boy, and the Pinheads, pathetic freaks dressed in Mother Hubbards. They came to look at the latest in appliances, but also to gaze at wonders and take pleasure in the extreme—the world's fattest man, the tattooed Mexican, the bearded lady. They also came expecting thrills. The program for the 1888 CNE included "parachute descents from a balloon," which were billed as "the most daring and marvelous feat ever performed by human beings."

From the dizzy height of 5,000 feet, a man will drop from a balloon and go rushing down through space at the velocity of a railroad train, depending on the atmospheric resistance of his big umbrella to keep him from being dashed to pieces.

Of course, there was always the chance that he would be dashed to pieces. In this situation, the consumer and producer of spectacles are always in secret collusion to want the worst to happen. As mentioned earlier, the dreadful fate of the man who hung for thirty hours on the Niagara gorge made world headlines. So did the death of Jumbo, P. T. Barnum's world-famous elephant, struck and killed by a train at St. Thomas, Ontario, in 1885, during a tour of the pleasure-hungry countryside. It was a terrible thing, of course, for the huge and much-loved elephant, but great business for Barnum.

There is still a slight ghoulishness about the annual air shows held each summer at the Canadian National Exhibition. Planes crash; and a show of daring swerves and swoops by the Canadian Forces' Snowbirds, a headlining act at every air show, can and does very occasionally end in a spectacular collision. But I have no intention of portraying the nineteenth-century visitors to the Exhibition (or their twentieth-century followers) as ghouls. They were simply embodiments of a new sensibility and culture, foreign to agricultural Ontario, being instilled here by mechanical wonders that seemed to offer freedom from all the contingencies of rural life. The world's first automobile shows were held at the Exhibition, after all—along with the first demonstrations of phonograph recordings and a very early display of television, presenting fighter Jack Dempsey and chanteuse Jessica Dragonette on little screens before rapt audiences. Things relished for a single summer day at the fair were also harbingers of the ceaseless surprises and emancipation from toil and sensuous limit that Modernity promised to bring in its train.

The nineteenth-century marvel around which more liberationist fantasies, hope of wealth and sheer dreaming swirled than any other was electrification. Electricity had the virtue of being both a fabulous novelty and, as almost everyone saw at once, a tremendous advance over smokestack energy in industrial production. Electrical supply sprang up in Ontario, as everywhere, as so many aggressive private enterprises, generating voltage with coal or oil-fired installations, and marketing the energy to industrial operations employing the new electric motors. Young Adam Beck may well have come up from the country for the 1882 Canadian National Exhibition and witnessed the world's first lighting of a fair by electric power. In 1885, the Ottawa Electric Company announced that it had created the first dinner made entirely with electricity. (Historian Robert Bothwell says the menu included Consommé Royal, Saginaw trout with potato croquettes, beef tongue and sugar-cured ham, larded sweetbreads with mushrooms and, for dessert, black-currant tart and coconut drops.)

But to return to Adam Beck. Surrounded by evidences of Progress, electrical and industrial, he was having none of the rampant private enterprise associated with so many of these ventures, despite his own success as a cigar box manufacturer. He had become wealthy in business and successful in public life (as mayor of London, Ontario), when he got it into his head to put Ontario's rivers—particularly the short, tremendously powerful Niagara River—to work producing electricity for sale to industries and homes across Ontario, thereby replacing costly imported coal. He was able to look at the torrent of water and neither wax romantic about it nor hunger for spiritual uplift nor cynically turn away to worry about his mosquito bites nor lust after all the money one could make by harnessing the waters. For reasons not clear—and unlike other hugely energetic entrepreneurs such as Thomas Edison—Adam Beck looked at the Falls without any thought of reaping the potentially gigantic profits for himself.

In 1903, he began campaigning for the construction of huge generating facilities at Niagara and the creation of a provincial public utility to manage the distribution of power at cheap rates. The private power companies scattered across the province rose up in outrage, but found in Beck a granitelike foe. In the midst of the pitched battles with private interests, the curiously disinterested Adam Beck never flinched. In 1906, the year H. G. Wells's *The Future in America* appeared, the Hydro-Electric Power Commission of Ontario—Canada's first publicly owned power authority—was created, with Beck installed as chairman and de facto Grand Emir of Electricity. He immediately bought out the generating interests of the Ontario Power Company, a powerful rival, at Niagara Falls. In May, 1917, construction began at Queenston on the facility that was later to be known as Sir Adam Beck No. 1. In 1920, he won his last battle for public power in Ontario by buying up the Toronto Power Company. When he died in 1925, Sir Adam had spent the best years of his life battering private electrical companies out of existence and creating the largest publicly owned supplier of electricity in the world.

For some reason, the twentieth century enjoyed debunking the Victorian era as the heyday of hypocritical prudes, imperialist monsters and so forth. We are, or should be, now beyond all that. We should be glad to have more men like Adam Beck among us. He was an instance of that Victorian bird (rather more common than previously believed), the immensely practical, tyrannical and profoundly humane dreamer. The twentieth-century worship of Progress and such found its embodiment and finest expression in men of Adam Beck's cast; its most ghastly incarnations in men such as Lenin.

The Victorians and Edwardians were wrong about almost everything they believed in and hoped for. Religious faith did not die out as our reliance on gadgets increased; for reasons not exactly clear, God and technology have enjoyed a parallel rise as objects of mass-cultural worship. The futuristic enthusiasts before the Great War, and many during and after it, would never have believed that the great northeastern blackout of 1965 could happen, because the Machines of the Future would not allow it. Believers in Man's essential goodness, for which there is absolutely no evidence, they certainly had no idea that the culminating, most costly and most intricate technological accomplishments of the twentieth century would be not practical and liberating appliances but useless space stations and weapons of mass destruction. The new machines, for Wells, were goodness incarnate and the sacraments for communicating goodness to all humankind. So what if a little industrial nastiness and tourist sleaze were uglifying the once-dramatic beauty of the Niagara gorge?

I, at least, can forgive the loss of all the accidental unmeaning beauty that is going for the sake of the beauty of fine order and intention that will come. I believe—passionately, as a doubting lover believes in his mistress—in the future of mankind. And so to me it seems altogether well that all the froth and hurry of Niagara at last, all of it, dying into hungry canals of intake, should rise again in light and power, in ordered and equipped and proud and beautiful humanity, in cities and palaces and the emancipated souls and hearts of men . . .

The dot-dot-dot at the end of the quotation, incidentally, is Wells's doing—as though he wanted to, but dared not, go on and on with this flapdoodle humanistic twaddle. Because he is a good writer, however, he stops before embarrassing himself and us, and does a quiet, attractively old-fashioned critique of the powerhouse architecture rising beside the gorge. "It hasn't caught the note," he writes. "There's a touch of respectability in it, more than a hint of the box of bricks."

26
ELECTRIC EMPIRE

THOUGH THE PASSENGER SERVICE provided by Canadian railways had been in decline for decades and the tracks were not all ripped from the ground, the scheduling cuts of the mid-1980s brought sharp pain to many who never rode the rails at all. Canada had turned from political fiction to continuous geographical fact in 1885, with the completion of the transcontinental railway. To question the current usefulness of the link because of something so philistine as cost was viewed as an attack on a hallowed, uniquely identifying institution, like the monarchy, the national health scheme, the beaver. Pierre Berton's popular history *The Last Spike* gave opponents a stake to drive into the hearts of vampiric railway executives—without, however, the effect stakes are said to have on real vampires.

There was an element of historical fact in favour of the romantic-nationalist argument. British Columbia was persuaded to join the Dominion in 1871 on condition that a transcontinental railway be constructed within ten years. The promise of a great system of rail lines actually did create a nation that was much larger than Canada had been from the time of Jacques Cartier to that of John A. Macdonald.

And from almost the time of Confederation until the service cutbacks began—and though the national railways never really paid for themselves—the shining steel ribbon served as a visible expression of the national motto *A mari usque ad mare*. But by the time of Confederation and the launch of the Canadian Pacific Railway, a far more potent instrument of nation-building was rapidly spreading across Canada, linking not only the large cities and ports but villages, outports, remote stations in the west and north. The messages flew on wires at close to the speed of light, instead of being pulled along by locomotives. The instrument and true tool of Canada's nation-building was not the train but the fleet spark, dot-dashing its way back and forth across continental and intercontinental distances.

The problem with the telegraph for young Alexander Graham Bell, of Brantford, Ontario, was that it did nothing for his deaf mother. He imagined that some combination of sparks and wires might be able to help her. To make the deaf hear was the longing that inspired his inventive spirit from his earliest days. It was also a desire that ran in the family.

Alexander's father, Melville, had chosen as his wife a woman who had been deaf all her life. Eliza Symonds was wife and mother—but also experiment. Both Melville and his own father had been fascinated by sound, the voice, the spoken word. Grandfather Bell, after whom Alexander Graham Bell was named, had used his glorious and powerful voice to forge a career as an orator and (usually unemployed) actor in his native Scotland. Most actors believe, forgivably, that being able to speak one's lines well is good enough. Not the elder Alexander. He was fascinated by the voice itself, and by the various maladies that prevent one from producing or hearing a voice. So he set about working on methods to unlock the bound tongues. By 1838, *The Practical Elocutionist, Stammering and Other Impediments of Speech* had earned Grandfather Bell the accolade of "celebrated Professor of Elocution."

He was never really a professor of anything, but he possessed hugely infectious enthusiasm. Both his sons, David and Melville, grew up enchanted by speech and elocution and articulation. Fortunately for them, there was a market for this fascination. Then, as now, as in the time of Professor Higgins and Eliza Doolittle, people thought movement from lower to higher social classes could be facilitated by adopting the "correct" intonation and accents. But for David and Melville Bell, speech and speech pathologies were mechanical matters of great interest in their own right. Intelligent, deaf Eliza, a gifted painter of miniatures, was a constant reminder of the place audible sound ended and was dashed and killed, on the stone cliffs of deafness.

Not that Eliza Grace Bell resigned herself glumly to deafness. She became a pianist with a reputation for "accomplishment," and she never gave up the belief that she would be able to hear music, voices, the infinite variety of sounds continually falling on the ears and passing into the minds of the unimpaired. As it happened, the silence in which Alex's mother lived was never broken by sound. But her condition did inspire her son with a determination to penetrate this wall of quiet—a goal pursued with energy and determination akin to that of other great Victorian explorers. The Victorian frontiers to be overcome, however, were usually conceived in terms of hugeness and great distance. For Alexander Graham Bell, the obstacle was as thin as an eardrum, as tiny as the delicate tubing of the inner ear.

Everything about sound and silence appears to have entranced Bell from earliest days. While in London with his father, he witnessed a demonstration of a "speaking machine" designed by Charles Wheatstone. The nephew and apprentice to a London maker of musical instruments, Wheatstone (who invented the concertina) educated himself in the new electrical science and engineering of the times and, in 1837, was among the patent-holders of the first British electric telegraph. Wheatstone's speaking machine—half science and half vaudeville, as most scientific inventions tend to be in their infancy—inspired Alexander's brother to make a similar contraption, mimicking the creation of words. And it worked. He also found that by manipulating the throat of his terrier he could make barks sound like syllables. He had discovered a stunt, a gimmick, a party trick—but hardly an invention with any practical uses.

He began with the view that the creation and communication of sounds are both parts of one, continuous process. But were they? Common sense, that besetting devil of all inquiry, said *yes*. The true answer is *no*—but Alexander only learned the truth by accident, while studying at the University of London.

During his student work on waves, sound, electricity and such— voguish topics at the time—he encountered a book by the famous German physicist Hermann von Helmholtz, *On the Sensations of Tone*. Bell was fascinated by the parts of von Helmholtz's book that had to do with generating vowel sounds by a contraption of electric tuning forks and resonators. He did not, however, understand what he was reading. Bell's almost non-existent German led him to think the physicist was making an argument for taking audible sounds, translating them into electrical impulses, then recreating these impulses at the other end as audible sounds. (Which is how a telephone works.) He later said this misreading—surely one of the most fortunate muddles in the history of communications technology—gave him confidence he needed to understand the behaviour of waves. "If I had been able to read German," he reminisced, "I might never have begun my experiments in electricity."

His experiments in England did not last long. By twenty-three, two of Alex's brothers had died of tuberculosis, and the young inventor was seriously ill with the devastating illness. So it was that Melville and Eliza decided to take their son to Canada. Why anybody would think the humid valley of Ontario's Grand River would be particularly healthy is beyond me. Perhaps Melville and Eliza thought anywhere on earth would be an improvement over smoggy Dickensian London.

While Brantford people like to make much of the inventor's time there, and while he did indeed accomplish a magnificent feat in Ontario, A. G. Bell, like other people in this book, came and went. His working life was spent teaching Visible Speech at the Boston School for Deaf Mutes. Like his father, he married a deaf woman, a student, and determined to accomplish what he had failed to do for his mother. As in his university days in London, Bell imagined that breaching the towering wall of deafness would be made possible by some hitherto unrealized combination of wires and electricity. That he was already thinking about how to put Samuel Morse's equipment to work in his scheme can be divined from the name— "harmonic telegraph"—he gave an early technical sketch of what he had in mind.

It was an idea seething in his mind and rapidly coming closer to some practical realization when he came home to his dreaming place for the summer holiday season of 1876.

Bell had been working for the past year with a Boston technician named Thomas Watson, who shared with him the conviction that a contraption capable of carrying syllables on electrified wires could be built. On June 2, 1875, Bell and Watson had been working in separate rooms in Boston, when Watson, wrenching free a tiny element from an electromagnet in which it was stuck, did something that sent a twanging sound over a wire into an adjoining room where Bell was at work. The accidental twang sounded enough like a syllable to satisfy Bell that he could send speech over a wire.

But a twang isn't a word, or even a syllable. It's just a sound. The first instance of the real thing—voice transmission—took place on March 10, 1876, when Bell and Watson were again at work together. Bell, so the famous story goes, accidentally knocked over a container of battery acid onto some wires and exclaimed: "Mr. Watson, come here. I want you!" The words reached Watson unexpectedly over a wire, not through the air. The first telephone call had been made.

That summer, Bell unveiled the telephone at the Centennial Exhibition in Philadelphia, where the Emperor of Brazil, upon hearing Bell reading Hamlet's famous soliloquy through the machine from thirty metres away, remarked, "My God, it talks!"

THE KEY EARLY EXPERIMENTS COMPLETED, the notion of transmitted speech had graduated from notion to novelty. The Emperor Dom Pedro had been impressed, everybody had been impressed. But the telephone was still not an appliance with a practical use. To become something more than a gadget, the cheerful device had to mature into a serious machine, capable of detecting vocal vibrations and translating them into electrical codes that could be reconstructed mechanically into human-sounding noises at distances greater than thirty metres. And it was the job to which Bell set his hand in the summer of 1876, when he escaped the Boston heat, which he found insufferable, and sought refuge at his dreaming place on the cool Grand River overlook known as Tutela Heights.

Alex had left his deaf wife, Mabel, in Boston, and wrote wistfully homesick letters to her. Sensible woman that she was, she wrote back that he should be paying more attention to his telephone experiments, using available telegraph wires. "Try the lines between Brantford and Paris [Ontario]," she suggested, "and do your utmost to induce someone to take up your foreign patents and to allow you to go on working." Bell complied; and in late July rigged up wires between Brantford and the tiny village of Mount Pleasant, some eight kilometres away, and connected the wires to his sophisticated voice-relay devices.

All Mount Pleasant, such as it was, gathered in the store where the reception equipment had been placed to receive a recitation by Alex's uncle David. The results were barely intelligible. A second experiment at transmission, this time run out from Tutela Heights toward Mount Pleasant on iron stove-pipe wire strung along the roadside, worked better. With the same amazement we all feel when thinking about the littleness of world-changing events, Bell's biographer James Mackay has described this more successful attempt at long-distance telephony.

> At the telegraph office David Bell recited Shakespeare while one of his daughters and a local singer went through their repertoire of popular ballads. The successful transmission and reception was duly recorded by the *Brantford Expositor*, even if the reporter was more impressed by the list of dignitaries assembled for the occasion than the demonstration itself. The *Toronto Globe*, owned and edited by George Brown, relegated the event to the trivia column on page three, merely repeating the *Expositor* account. What would soon be hailed as the miracle of the age was dismissed as an entertainment which "afforded much pleasure and information to those present."

But the world at large had downplayed the power of the telephone for the last time. On August 10, 1876, Alex rigged up his receiving mechanism at the nearby Ontario village of Paris to a transmitter in Brantford, using the extant telegraph wires. Again, the whole community turned out, and the Paris telegraph office was crammed with wonder-seekers. The wonder turned out to be a little spectacle of crackles and pops—at first, anyway. Then, at last, the crucial thing about long distance happened. It was possible for the listener to determine who was calling, despite the electromagnetic haze of rattle and buzz. James Mackay again:

Hitherto only disembodied, rather metallic voices had been heard. Alec discerned Uncle David, but then he heard the voice of his father who was not supposed to be at the Brantford office. An enquiry sent by telegraph elicited the response that Melville had just walked in off the street. Others came for the speak and listen, and what had been planned as a one hour demonstration stretched to three.

Ninety-three summers later, U.S. President Richard M. Nixon made a long-distance telephone call to the moon.

THERE'S AN OLD STORY about the first long-distance telephone call that goes like this.

Among those on hand in Paris to witness the events of August 10, 1876, was a boy, ten years old, from the village of Fergus, Ontario. He was the son of an Anglican minister, and his name was Reginald Fessenden. After the demonstration, the lad went up to the great Bell, tugged at his sleeve and asked the inventor a question. If a voice could journey to a distant location over a wire, could it do so through the air? To which Bell replied: Not a chance.

Though he was small and Dr. Bell was big and famous, Reginald did not believe the scientist had given him the right answer. So he went back home to Fergus, grew up, migrated to the United States, invented the radio and, on Christmas Eve, 1906, made history's first wireless broadcast of voices and music, caught on Marconi telegraph equipment by merchant seamen on Caribbean banana boats.

While I would love to relate that the pleasant tale about little Reggie at Bell's side is gospel truth, it is almost certainly apocryphal. That Reginald Fessenden heard and read about what happened in Paris and Brantford, however, is probable. That he made the first true radio broadcast—as opposed to the transmission of dots and dashes—is certain.

The event, radio historian Mervyn Fry has written, began at exactly nine o'clock that Christmas Eve, from transmission towers at Brant Rock, Massachusetts. To alert the Marconi operators on the ships that something unexpected was about to happen, Fessenden dispatched the letters "CQ CQ CQ,"

meaning *general call* to all stations within range, sent out in dots and dashes. Then, over the microphone, Reginald himself gave a brief speech as to the program to follow. This was immediately followed by one of the operators switching on the Edison phonograph and a solo voice singing Handel's "Largo."

The first case of "mike fright" was registered when Mr. Stein, an assistant, backed away unable to utter a word! However, Fessenden grabbed his violin and "fiddled" through "O Holy Night," singing as well as playing. Helen, his wife and his secretary, Miss Bent, endeavoured to read parts of the Bible text, "Glory to God in the highest and on earth peace to men of good will," but, like Mr. Stein, they suffered stage fright.

Concluding the program, Fessenden wished his listeners "A Merry Christmas." The success of this first broadcast was verified by operators, not only from those on the ships of the United Fruit Company but also from vessels all over the south and north Atlantic, amazed at the magic and miracle of this first wireless radio broadcast.

In fidelity to the rule I laid out at the beginning of this book—to tell the stories of people who came to Ontario, not those who grew up here and achieved fame elsewhere—I will leave the remarkable (and unfortunate) story of Reginald Fessenden to be told by other writers about notable Ontarians.

The fact that the inventor of radio grew up where he did, however, reinforces the ancient, stubbornly inexplicable notion of *genius loci*. Places do seem to create people of certain sorts. In the gently rolling landscapes and under the beautiful skies of a small part of south-central

Ontario—along a ninety-kilometre line that could be drawn between Toronto and Brantford—a century of worldwide theory and thinking about electrical communication converged and condensed, and the basic communications technologies by which the contemporary world lives and dies were either born, or first demonstrated and first understood. Alexander Graham Bell's phone call is one instance; Reginald Fessenden's launch into an obsession to throw the voice without wires is another. Marshall McLuhan, an Alberta-born professor who thought and taught at the University of Toronto, improbably turned from a conventional English scholar into a pioneer witness to the prophetic messages embodied in the appliances of communication. McLuhan's brilliant, hugely controversial thought, in turn, rested on the research of Harold Innis, his colleague at the University of Toronto. Innis was a lifelong student of the role played in the architecture of the modern world by mass communications. As it happened, he was born on that magical ninety-kilometre axis of invention, almost exactly halfway between Toronto and Brantford.

It could be argued that the invention of the inter-city phone call and radio and the first theories to make sense of their world-changing impact could have taken place anywhere. But they didn't. It all happened in Ontario, of all places, among a few people who had come to this place on the waves of arrival.

27
THE SWAMP MURDERER

F ROM AN OFFICIAL REPORT in Ontario, 1855:

> Houses are being erected in almost every town, city, and village in Upper Canada; and as the farmers have enjoyed a very unusual degree of prosperity for several years past, farm improvements, and extended as well as superior cultivation, have become almost universal. I am therefore of the opinion that all mechanics, such as blacksmiths, wheelwrights, tailors, carpenters, masons, bricklayers, shoemakers &c., as well as agricultural servants, who are likely to seek employment in Upper Canada in 1856, will be able to obtain it, and that farmers who know how to cultivate their own land will find farms suitable to their means, and, if prudent and industrious, will be sure to succeed.

Anyone growing old in Ontario during the latter half of the Victorian age would have seen Ontario change from the colony of settled yeoman farmers described in this notice into a province in a newly independent country, engaged in international manufacture and trade, and dotted with sizeable and prosperous cities. The railways had come at mid-century, opening up gleaming steel rivulets through the bush, linking cities and ports and markets hitherto accessible only by mud roads. The influx waxed and waned in the second half of the nineteenth century, but never ceased. Skilled labourers, especially, were in great demand, as all the advertisements abroad made clear. A government report from 1856 declares that "good farm servants, male and female [have] every prospect of their finding employment at good wages."

It is tempting to garland the years between 1850 and 1914 with roses, and view these sixty-odd years as a golden age. Surely from the 1920s until almost the present day, a distinct nostalgia for the Edwardian and Victorian periods has lingered in the air of urbanized Ontario. The Group of Seven paintings recollect the pre-war Northern Sublime, as it was before the vexations of tourism and heavy mining transfigured the landscape. By 1890, the small towns were being emptied of young people eager for jobs in the burgeoning Great Lakes cities, and the truly wild regions were being tamed by great mining companies. But the myth of a nourishing northland continued to strengthen its hold over the urban populations, who needed it more than ever before. It provided spiritual roots as whole populations were being uprooted and finding the world strange.

John Simcoe had grasped the need for roots when he travelled through the province in 1793, naming every river and future townsite after a British city or lord or king or principality. As the nineteenth century progressed, with republicanism in decline and the patriotic longing for Ontario *not* to be the United States on the rise, yet other symbols were needed. And, as it had the place names, so Britain now provided a sprinkling of minor *milordi* to strengthen the ties to the motherland. Working Ontarians were impressed by these second sons of second sons of knights and earls and such. For their part, these gentlefolk scattered in small towns throughout the province had little to do but impress the locals, which they appear to have done successfully.

Of the upper-class Britons to ride out to Ontario, Reginald Birchall was among the most bewitching—in the most concrete, sinister sense of that word. During his stays in Woodstock, London and Niagara around 1890, he apparently reassured British working folk with memories of the country-house ascendancy back home. He had the style and flair to bring it off.

But Reginald had spent most of his brief life bewitching people. The younger son of a prominent Anglican vicar, scion of an ancient Lancashire family with connections both to the land and to Oxford University, he was not quite titled, but handsome, suave, smart, delightful and a nuisance to the stuffy. In the proper British public schools he was sent to, Reginald seemed always inclined to rebellion. He was usually in transit from one school to another.

But in 1888, he travelled up to Oxford in the spirit young men quite often went to England's great universities in Victorian times: briefly, less to study than to carouse; to fuss over one's horses and throw expensive parties for one's friends. He was a clever student, when he found time to put his nose into a book. On paper, he was studying for the Church. In practice, he spent much time worrying over his flamboyant wardrobe and planning pranks and parties. Which was nothing out of the ordinary, he claims in the autobiographical memoir he wrote, at age twenty-four.

Go to any college porter of any long standing,
to any hotelkeeper who can date back twenty or thirty years, or
to the old inhabitants of the neighbourhood, and to those who
lived when the Bullingdon Club was in its prime, and ask them

to tell you their experiences and recollection of the "free spirits" of their time; and then you will see into what utter insignificance and shade nay of my so-called "wild ways" will sink.

It's all quite plausible. Victorian gentlemen of Birchall's sort, having tippled and wildly overspent their way through university, went on to become, promptly and somewhat miraculously, sober and upright British subjects, ready for dispatch to hold court, administer justice, preach the Gospel, or provide some other service in a corner of history's vastest empire. But in his college days, the handsome and bright young man quickly got himself into a spot of bother by neglecting to pay bills—yet another fault for which he can forgive himself.

A man goes up to Oxford. He enters college, be it which it may. He no sooner enters his rooms, which have been set apart for him, than he finds his table covered with letters from tradesmen who vie with each other for the honour of supplying him all manner of things, necessary and unnecessary; and letters . . . He can get credit unlimited from the wine merchant, the grocer, cigar merchant, who deems it a personal favour to be privileged to keep in condition a dozen boxes of the best Havanas for his use . . .

Persecuted by creditors, he decided precipitously to decamp with a wife across the seas, to the edges of the Empire. He took, in other words, a route to refuge already well travelled by elegantly turned-out, affluent and indolent young Englishmen in financial difficulties. But in doing so, his misfortunes were multiplied considerably, and turned aside not at all. In his autobiography, he tells a tearful tale of his brutal disillusionment, in 1888, by the international land-granting brokers Ford & Rathbone, which, as it happened, had an office in Woodstock, Ontario, Canada.

From my own experience I should say that Fraud & Rathbone would be a more fitting description of that firm. . . . I called upon them, and they assured me of the comfort and ease of the farmer's life, and of the quantity of sport of all kinds and the absence of much work. I was taken with the idea, and after my marriage, as I had some money to spare, I thought it presented a good opening in life.

His assurance of a good position by these scoundrels, for which he paid £500 in advance, came in the form of a photograph of a grand farm "which never existed at all," he says, "save in their fertile imagination (the photograph being simply of some very fine and rich man's house and nothing like a farmhouse out there.)"

Words fail me entirely, dear reader, to give you any idea of my impressions of farm life in Canada conducted in the style in which I saw it . . . A dirty house, dirty children, a filthy bedroom, a bed that even the commonest gaol beds would give points to, were not calculated to increase one's faith in Fraud & Rathbone's gilded statements. So on the following day I left this human pig sty and returned to Woodstock, and demanded an explanation of Mr. McDonald [the land agent]. He explained the matter by saying he did not understand what I wanted, and that what he said was true, as usual. I soon decided that farming was "off," and very much "off." However, as I had until the following May on my hands I set to work to make the best of it.

The "work" to which he set himself, he tells us, was much sporting and riding with Woodstock friends who, like him, had been duped and temporarily inconvenienced by the unscrupulous Ford & Rathbone agents. They all got on famously.

For if his choice of a real-estate broker had been unfortunate, his pick of a refuge had been shrewd. Woodstock was used to ex-pat nobs. By the end of the Victorian age, the town had grown into a prosperous agricultural centre from a mere spot on the map, put there by John Graves Simcoe on his 1793 trip between Toronto and Windsor in search of places easy to use in defence of his new British Empire from American attack. His name for both the town and district was Oxford. The county in which Woodstock stands still bears that name. Though hardly one of Victorian Canada's centres of population or cultivation—or perhaps for this reason—Oxford County had been a favoured destination for upper-class Britons of the sort nobody wanted under foot since the 1830s. They had quite often brought with them piles of money and vast dreams, both of which vanished as their business schemes collapsed.

The persistent problem was, apparently, that the immigrants had simply no idea of where they had come to. An old story in Woodstock tells of a certain Admiral Vansittart, who arrived in 1834 with a large ship in pieces, ready for reassembly and commercial deployment on Ontario's river Thames. He had assumed the waterway to be as grand as its European namesake, only to find Ontario's Thames a shallow stream. (If John Simcoe had had his way, everything in Ontario would have been named for a good English spot, and the province would resemble a map of England, with the same rivers, cities, towns, roads.)

A contemporary account by another hand casts a curious light on Birchall's stay in Woodstock. He had indeed arrived in 1888. But in the view of this witness, certain details of his arrival and stay had been soft-pedalled or ignored.

His name was not Birchall then. He was Lord Somerset, Frederick A. Somerset, some day to be one of the lofty lords of England. His wife was Lady Somerset. They boarded at Mrs. John McKay's in Woodstock, lived gaily, dressed loudly, and became familiar figures in the country round about. They seemed to have money like the lord and lady they were supposed to be. They were fond of driving and picnics, and one of the spots Lord Somerset visited on various occasions was Pine Pond, with the Blenheim Swamp around it. This was eight miles from Woodstock and Lord Somerset came to know it well. When they left Woodstock to return to England, Lord and Lady Somerset were called away suddenly and left numerous unpaid bills behind them. Lord Somerset, from across the sea, wrote to a Woodstock acquaintance as follows:

MY DEAR MAC,

You must have been surprised to find me gone. I went down to New York for the wife's health and while there got a cable the governor was suddenly taken ill. I rushed off, caught the first steamer over, and got here just too late, the poor chap died. So I have been anyhow for some time. I am coming out to Woodstock shortly, I hope, as soon as I settle up all my governor's affairs. I owe you something I know. Please let me know, and tell Scott, the grocer, to make out his bill, and any one else if I owe anybody anything. I was in too much of a hurry to see after them. I have several men to send out to you in August. Tell me all news and how you are. Many thanks for all your kindnesses.

FREDK. A. SOMERSET.

Thus did Lord Somerset, né Birchall, leave Woodstock behind. For a while.

He would almost certainly have gotten away with the skip. The small-town merchants would probably never have chased down Birchall in London to recover their losses. Everybody in town knew that the young English aristocrats who drifted through were given to doing such things. They were soft, pampered men, best quickly and gently fleeced, then quietly forgotten when they ran out of money.

And young Reginald almost certainly would never have returned— had not this clever, if unfocused, young man finally hit on a way to make his fortune.

He decided to become a killer.

THE FIRST VICTIM WAS DISCOVERED with his brains shot out in February, 1890, in the bleak, dank tangle of Blenheim Swamp, near Woodstock. The find was almost pure serendipity. While tourists occasionally ventured in, to savour the romantic melancholy of so desolate a place, almost nobody ever had business in it. In that cold week, however, three people did have business there: two local farmers, out to chop wood, and the murderer. John Wilson Murray, the founder of Ontario's provincial police and the detective who solved the swamp murder, describes the event in his autobiographical book of famous trials.

> The body was found by the Elridge brothers, Joseph and George. They lived in that vicinity, and were out chopping on Friday, February 21st, and one of them, in the tangle of the bog, amid a snarl of logs, and vines, and briars, and brush, stepped on the body, slipped, and almost fell upon it.
>
> They bore it out of the swamp, and, in response to a telegram to the Department of Justice, I went immediately to the township of Blenheim, in the county of Oxford, and saw the body. It was the body of a young man, smooth shaven, of refined appearance, and clearly a gentleman. The clothing was English in style and cut, with a check caped mackintosh. The underclothing was of English make, for I had ordered some of the same kind and make in England some months before. There was no clue to his identity. The name of his tailor and the label on his clothes had been cut out carefully. The label of his brown Derby hat had been removed. Even a possible tell-tale button had been severed.
>
> I sat down with the body, placing it in a sitting posture opposite me. I looked at it as if it were a man asleep. He was little more than a big boy, a gentle lad, a youth just out of his teens, a refined son of refined parents. In the back of his head was the purplish black hole of the bullet, and near the nape of the neck was another. He had been shot from behind; perhaps he never knew who shot him. Death crashed upon him from the rear, and he fell without a glimpse of his murderer . . .

"Who are you?" I asked the dead body as it sat facing me; but, in answer, it lurched forward and fell on its face.

When Murray visited the site of the discovery, he found the swamp notably reluctant to yield any but small and unhelpful evidence. A trail of blood suggested the young man had not been killed where he was discovered—but whether near or far, Murray could not say. With no substantial leads, with only the well-preserved corpse of a young English gentleman to work from, Murray had the dead man photographed and the pictures dispatched to newspapers across Canada, the United States and England, with an appeal for identification. Somewhere, someone had known the man in life, and would recognize his countenance in death, if he or she happened to see it in a newspaper.

After the passage of five days without a response, Murray released the body for burial at the village of Princeton, a short way from the swamp where the unfortunate man was found. But the very next day, Murray's hopes came true. A man arrived with his wife at Princeton, claiming he had seen the picture in a Niagara newspaper and was almost certain he had seen him alive. After the body was exhumed, the living man and his wife quickly identified the dead one as a fellow passenger on a recent crossing from England. And the name? "'I think it was Bentwell, or Benswell, or Benwell,'" said he. "'I knew him very slightly.'"

The gentleman who had come to Princeton instantly impressed Detective Murray, who had a knack for spotting class and money.

He was dressed in perfect taste. He was handsome and easy in manner, with a certain grace of bearing that was quite attractive. He came toward me, and I saw he was about five feet nine inches tall, supple, clean cut, well built. His hair was dark and fashionably worn; his forehead was broad and low. He wore a light moustache. Two dark-brown eyes flashed at me in greeting. Clearly he was a man of the world, a gentleman, accustomed to the good things of life, a likeable chap, who had lived well and seen much and enjoyed it in his less than thirty years on earth . . .

"When did you last see the young man alive?" I asked.

"He was on his way to London, Ontario, and as we were traveling to the Falls our way was the same. I last saw him at the Falls. He had a great deal of luggage down there. He left some of it, in fact."

"I'm very glad to know this," said I gratefully. "You will be able to point out his luggage?"

"Yes," said he. "I'll be very glad to aid you. I am returning to the Falls to-day. We came, you know, because we saw the picture in the paper."

"Will you take charge of the luggage for me?" I asked.

"Gladly," said he.

"Your name, so that I may find you at the Falls?" I asked.

"Birchall," said he. "Reginald Birchall, of London—London, England."

In the memoir he wrote during his murder trial in Woodstock, Birchall emphasizes flamboyantly his propensity for fallibility and youthful folly. As for the detective, writing some years after the fact, he can hardly emphasize too often his infallible forensic instinct. Murray recalls that everything seemed right, but something was unmistakably wrong about the sudden appearance of the Birchalls so soon after the murder.

Why had they come? This story of seeing the picture in the paper was quite plausible. If he were telling the truth I could understand it, but I was satisfied he was lying . . . I wanted a few hours to investigate it and make sure. So I entered the [Princeton] telegraph office and sent a telegram to the Falls, describing Birchall and telling of his return to the Falls later that day.

"'Shadow this man,'" I telegraphed. "'Do not arrest him unless he tries to cross the river to the States. I will be there Sunday night.'"

Murray quickly "scoured" London, Ontario, and concluded that the victim had not been there. He had Birchall and his wife arrested—for misdeeds unspecified—at Niagara Falls, Ontario, on March 2, 1890.

When Birchall was taken, yet another figure, apparently innocent, enters the story. He was Douglas Raymond Pelly, "a handsome young fellow, about five feet nine inches tall, slight build, small light moustache, and a decided English accent"—and, Murray could have added, about as much alertness as a fence-post. Upon interviewing this newest player, Murray got quick confirmation of his suspicion that Birchall had known Benwell better than he was prepared to admit at the graveside. Pelly and Frederick Benwell, and the Birchalls, had come out to Canada via New York on the same ship. It had been Pelly, alarmed upon seeing Benwell's dead face in a newspaper, who had persuaded Birchall to go to Princeton and identify the body.

Murray also discovered the familiarity among the three men was not the result of a casual shipboard acquaintance.

Douglas Pelly, who escaped the murder planned for him, and Benwell, who did not, were young men with much in common. Each was well-connected to the English aristocracy, educated at an ancient British university, in his mid-twenties, well-off (or blessed with parents who were), in love with the picture of the leisured landed gentry, with neither drive nor the faintest clue about what to do with his life. Both Pelly and Benwell were instantly attracted by this advertisement in London's *Daily Telegraph* in 1889.

CANADA.—University man—having farm—wishes to meet gentleman's son to live with him and learn the business, with view to partnership; must invest five hundred pounds to extend stock; board, lodging, and 5 per cent. interest till partnership arranged.—Address, J.R. BURCHETT, Primrose Club, 4, Park Place, St. James', London.

In his prison memoir, Birchall explains in detail the confidence game he decided to play, under the name "Burchett," after his return from the Lord Somerset caper in Woodstock:

> I cast about for some new idea which might help me, and after a good deal of thought, planned out a great scheme which I thought would land safely upon the shore of comparative afflu-ence and comfort. I spoke of it to others, who agreed and entered into it warmly. This scheme was, in short, to make a pile of money out of the English Derby, which would be run in 1890, and about which we had certain information that would have put us right, and as the race turned out we should have landed a big *coup*. But none of us had sufficient ready capital to work this scheme, and the question came up how *were* we to get it? After a good deal of thinking my former experience with Ford & Rathbone came up in mind.

Like those nefarious land brokers, Birchall would find a gullible young man or two, sell them on investment and partnership in a beau-tiful, prosperous horse farm near Niagara Falls, and take a hefty advance before they caught on to the game. After winning the Derby, Birchall tells us, he would give them a little money "to appease them, and say farewell to them in good part." Birchall knew his marks. He knew they would be too embarrassed ever to admit to having been taken. Birchall was, after all, the kind of man he was after.

> It was a poor fraud, without doubt, but I thought so long as we repaid them afterwards it covered the fraud to a large extent, as far as my conscience, at any rate, was concerned. I may here state most emphatically, with all the force that my poor nature is capable of, that the idea of murder was never for a moment thought of or planned, and that it was a pure and simple fraud for the time being. If it failed, it failed on its own merits, said we, but as we had the thing down pretty fine, it wasn't likely to do that.

Birchall could be confident of success so long as Benwells and Pellys existed in the world. Pelly told the detective of Birchall's blandishments: he said a number of Englishmen lived around Niagara Falls, and that a club had been created in which the members lived in English style and had English servants. J. R. Birchall said he organized the club. The country was an earthly paradise, with wealth to be had for simply sojourning in the land.

Being either an accomplice—which Murray did not believe—or extraordinarily stupid, Pelly carried on with Benwell and the Birchalls to Niagara Falls. Birchall and Benwell were soon off together to see the non-existent farm; Benwell did not return. After this, Pelly testified at the trial, Birchall tried twice to murder him with a shove into the Niagara River—a fact Pelly did not realize until after Birchall's arrest.

With only scanty physical evidence to go on, Murray interviewed everyone who had knowledge of the movements of accused and victim on the day of the murder, checked railway timetables, went over the murder scene fastidiously, cross-referenced every clue he could nail down. "Thus," he writes, "I traced them, step by step, to the swamp and to the very hour of the murder."

> Then comes an interval when the murderer is alone in the swamp with his victim . . . Benwell was a credulous young fellow and innocently entered the swamp and started up the abandoned winding trail, Birchall readily finding a pretext for dropping behind a moment and Benwell eagerly pressing on for a sight of the farm—the farm he never was to see.

Though there were no eyewitnesses to the killing, Murray got the condemnation he sought at the inquest held at Woodstock in March, 1890. Pelly was absolved, Birchall's wife was dismissed, Reginald Birchall committed to trial.

Begun in September, Birchall's legal ordeal attracted attention across Canada and around the world. "The verdict," writes Murray, "was inevitable—guilty. The evidence simply was overwhelming. Birchall was sentenced to be hanged on November 14th." On which day he was indeed hanged. The Dominion Hangman bungled the job, so, instead of dying quickly, as planned, Birchall was slowly strangled while the gawkers looked on.

In the end, there were two important accounts of the career and deeds of Reginald Birchall. One is John Murray's detailed narrative, published in 1904. In it, Murray asserts that Birchall was not only the murderer of Benwell, but a mass murderer whom only "fate" and "providence"—words much liked by Murray—prevented from seducing many other aimless English aristocrats into coming to Ontario, then killing them. "Birchall had embarked in business as a murderer," Murray writes.

He had adopted life-taking for revenue as a profession promising rich returns. He had become deliberately a professional murderer. For a year he had planned the crimes, and fitted himself for the practice of his profession. While masquerading as Lord Somerset he had selected the bottomless lake, known as Pine Pond, for the grave that would tell no tales. The Blenheim Swamp he selected as the place of slaughter, his chamber of death . . .

He conceived the idea of taking rich young men instead of poor emigrants. He created an imaginative farm, and he went back to England to select a victim. He made the mistake of taking two instead of one. Even then his plans were well laid. He would kill Benwell in the swamp and shove Pelly into the rapids at the Falls to be pounded to pieces . . .

He was relying on water to hide both his victims. Neither body was to be found. The two young men were to vanish from the face of the earth. The professional murderer would have collected, by bogus letters to fond parents, the sum still due from the victims, and would have gone back to England for more victims . . .

Eventually he might become rich. No bodies could be found, and lost dead men are as good as live men whom no one can find, he reasoned. As he increased his capital, he might buy a farm with a bottomless lake and a dismal swamp, and kill his victims without trespassing on other people's property. He could vary his name and address and keep the families of his victims far apart, and thus minimize the risk of detection while the bottomless lake swallowed the victims one by one and kept their bones icy cold through endless years.

The second key report was the Toronto *Globe*'s compilation of articles, news reports and (most important of all) Birchall's prison apologia, which was in print almost before the killer's body was cut down. I have already quoted enough from this autobiographical statement (illustrated by Birchall's drawings and caricatures) to give a general sense of how the accused defended himself. He freely admits to being a lout, rowdy, scoundrel and fraud. He presents his life as a warning to other young men about the dangers of debt and loose living. He offers detailed rebuttals to every allegation Murray brings against him in court. He never confesses in the autobiography, nor did he ever admit to having committed the crime. But in the end, Murray could confidently say "that, while Birchall went to his death without a public confession, the last possibility for doubt of his guilt was swept away before he was executed."

Having studied the documents, I believe Birchall did kill Benwell on the day and at the place the prosecution specified—if only because nobody, other than the accused, who was in Ontario in February, 1890, had any motive for shooting the unfortunate, credulous young Englishman in the head twice, then dragging the body into Blenheim Swamp. That said, both leading popular sources of information about the murder—Murray's book and Birchall's memoir—leave the careful reader uneasy. One feels close to an inner sickness of Ontario's culture during its Victorian high noon—the shadows of mendacious remittance men from the old country and wily self-made folk (murderers and detectives) spawned by the metropolitan civilization taking root here and by an increasingly bureaucratic, positivistic world view that came with the wealth of this industrializing province.

In his self-portrait, Murray shows an obsessive and vainglorious face to the world. He was famous, and proud to be. He is prone to give glory to "providence" or "fate" in one paragraph, then snatch the glory back for himself, and his stunning powers of detection, in another. (The account of his life-work in which this case appears is entitled *Memoirs of a Great Detective*.) As he makes clear, he believed Birchall to be a liar from their first encounter—though, like other tributes to himself, this one may well be a conclusion drawn after a career of cease-less flattery and notoriety. We are never told what made him believe Pelly's every word, or why Birchall's wife was so quickly exonerated and allowed to vanish, when she was almost certainly an accessory, if not an outright accomplice. Birchall probably did have a career in deception and death planned out—though we are shown no hard evidence. In these accusations, Murray repeatedly changes roles, from self-styled "great detective" to clairvoyant.

For his part, Birchall's text is exceedingly sly and seductive, calcu-lated to create reasonable doubt, and unreasonable sympathy for a gifted, well-read young English gentleman of the sort who could *never* have done so horrible a deed. It works. At the end of his short book, we are left with a clear choice. Either this man of twenty-four is telling the truth; or he possessed a criminal mind of extraordinary agility and a penetrating knowledge of contemporary opinion. He knew, for example, that then (as now) everybody "hates lawyers"—other than his own, of course. Birchall liked his lawyer, and found him generous to a fault. But as for the others—he reels off a humorous list of exorbitant legal charges clearly intended to make us think him clever indeed.

"Getting into and out of cab—$6 . . . Going up stairs—$10 . . . Speaking to you—$50. Hearing you speak to me—$60 . . . Shaking hands with gaoler—$5 . . . Cigar for self—$5. Thinking of your case while smoking—$10." By his calculation, these frivolous legal items add up to $190 per visit. He concludes this story with a bit of world-wise advice to us readers.

This is just by way of warning those who have not yet had any experience in such matters. Beware of the law. It is very unsavoury.

28

THE DISENCHANTMENT

WE MET CATHARINE PARR TRAILL a few chapters back, in an account of gentlefolk's landing and settling in Ontario. Like some other people in this book—Bishop John Strachan, for instance, and Champlain—Catharine did a thing that can be inconvenient for writers of books such as this one. She simply lived too long, over-staying her usefulness as a convenient epitome of a certain point in time and history—in her case, the 1830s, when numerous proper English gentlewomen like Catharine were being swept by imperial interests into the eastern Ontario bush. She lived long enough, in fact, to witness the end of early English Ontario and the dawn of the populous, industrial Ontario that exists today.

And I'm very glad she did.

Catharine had been a young bride in the 1830s, recently landed in Upper Canada with her husband Thomas, a half-pay officer in the colonial service of His Britannic Majesty. This member of the "literary Stricklands"—a pack of writing offspring that included the poet Susannah Moodie, Catharine's sister and next-door neighbour in Canada—had made a gentle arrival in the New World, and settled comfortably into her surroundings. She also got down to work at once on a dutifully up-beat and very lovely imperialist tract entitled *The Backwoods of Canada: Being Letters From the Wife of an Emigrant Officer, Illustrative of the Domestic Economy of British America.* It was published in London in 1836, and in Paris, in French, in 1843.

The agenda is clearly set out in the introduction, where she warns her upper-crust readers to prepare themselves mindfully for the hard, creative work lying before them.

> The writer is as earnest in recommending ladies who belong to the higher class of settlers to cultivate all the mental resources of a superior education as she is to induce them to discard all irrational and artificial wants and mere useless pursuits. She would willingly direct their attention to the natural history and botany of this new country, in which they will find a never-failing source of amusement and instruction, at once enlightening and elevating the mind . . .
>
> To the person who is capable of looking abroad into the beauties of nature, and adoring the Creator through his glorious works, are opened stores of unmixed pleasure, which will not permit her to be dull or unhappy in the loneliest part of our western wilderness.

Catharine lived on, long past the launch of her popular book. She remained on her farm near Lakefield, Ontario, through the brief Rebellion of 1837, through the coronation of the great Victoria (and throughout almost the whole of Victoria's reign). She was alive when Josiah Henson came, and Jefferson Davis, Confederation, and the swamp murderer. And she was quite alive when the world's first long-distance telephone call was placed, between Brantford and Paris. She lived long enough to have seen the birth of the movies and, almost, the first airplane flight. None of these things appear to have mattered to her, if she took notice of them at all. *The Female Emigrant's Guide* appeared in 1854. It was her final work of old-fashioned optimistic propaganda, whereafter she devoted herself to her most durable intellectual passion, botany. At an appropriately great old age, past ninety, she issued her memoirs; then died at Lakefield in 1899.

Catharine also saw the lakeshores of Ontario and Erie change from deserted coasts into a necklace of burgeoning cities. These transformations appear to have held little fear for Mrs. Traill or, in fact, for anyone who actually lived through them. Once upon a time, it was stylish in academic literary circles to make much of what Northrop Frye (and Margaret Atwood) called the "garrison mentality" in Canadian writing—its intrinsic defensiveness, its liking for barricades against the fearful wilderness. In his anthology *Treasures of the Place: Three Centuries of Nature Writing in Canada,* Wayne Grady looks for traces of anxiety in the books, and finds little of it. In fact, an insistent theme in the experience of newcomers is delight at the wilds, and curiosity about what lies in wait there. Cartier gazed with fascination westward from Mount Royal, toward what he believed was the strange, opulently rich kingdom of Saguenay. In 1702, Antoine Laumet Cadillac, fur trader and founder of Detroit, described it as a land "so temperate, so good and so beautiful that one can justly call it the earthly paradise of North America." In the nineteenth century, Susannah Moodie said much the same thing about Ontario, as émigrés have always pronounced far-flung places different from the metropolitan capitals of their empires—as Gauguin said of Tahiti, and others of fabulous Shangri-La: "True independence greets you here." In a poem called "The Backwoodsman," Susannah summons inbound newcomers to

breathe a purer, freer air
. . . Indulgent heav'n has blessed the soil
And plenty crowns the woodman's toil.

Catharine, too, summons us through her letters in *Backwoods* to plunge in: "How often do I wish you were beside me in my rambles among the woods and clearings: you would be so delighted in searching out the floral treasures of the place."

Ontario writer Wayne Grady has observed that

. . . Canadians and Americans shared a similar experience of nature, but a hundred years apart. Once newcomers to Canada realized they were not sailing up the backside of Asia, they calmed down and took a good look around.

Then came the opening of the land to farms, with the early deep-woods vision of things giving way to pastoral, then industrial landscapes. "Even as this view of the land was arriving at the apex of its influence," writes historian Allan Smith, "new realities were beginning to erode the foundations on which it rested." Miners and timber harvesters were going north, while the southern Ontario cities, especially Toronto, were beckoning to new immigrants for the mills and factories. The children of yeomen farmers were being drawn remorselessly to the new industrial enterprises along Lake Ontario.

Catharine, like Susannah, gave little emphasis in her writings to these drastic changes. One might be tempted to say that, tramping the boggy land around Peterborough in her ceaseless search for new wildflower specimens, Catharine was simply not interested in the new, late-Victorian world of industry and urbanization coming into existence all around her. True, she never wrote a book about it, pro or con. But *Backwoods of Canada,* published long before any of these changes began to reshape the Ontario countryside, is haunted by clues to Catharine's thinking. They appear as footnotes, inserted into one of the many editions published decades after its debut in 1836.

trillium

Catharine occasionally dates a footnote. In an aside about the town of Peterborough, which was nothing but a little clearing in the bush when she arrived in 1832, she writes: "The whole of this ground is now covered with buildings . . . all on those grassy plains where I used to ramble gathering wild flowers thirty-seven years ago—now divided by streets, houses and flower gardens."

It is a double view—or double take. In one book—the amended edition of Catharine's best-known work—two minds are present: one the early immigrant propagandist, and another, that of the older, observant settler. Exploiting the characteristic modesty of footnotes, which usually remain hidden at the bottom of pages in small type, Mrs. Traill revises the backwoods, or at least the representation she had given of it many years before.

arrowhead

Some things, she believes, have notably improved. On the way out to Upper Canada, in 1832, she and Thomas stopped over in Montréal. Her hostile reaction is very much like that of every European traveller who bothered to jot down his or her memories of our Canadian cities in the early nineteenth century. Staying at the Nelson Hotel, she writes:

yellow water lily

> I was greatly disappointed in my first acquaintance with the interior of Montreal; a place of which travelers had said so much. I could compare it only to the fruits of the Dead Sea, which are said to be fair and tempting

to look upon, but yield only ashes and bitterness when tasted by the thirsty traveler.

She makes sure to insert a revision here: "Since the date of this letter Montreal has improved in every way in cleanliness, in buildings, in size and population. It may be ranked the finest city in Canada."

In another letter, she notes the establishment of a new grist-mill closer to her own homeplace than Peterborough, destined to "prove a great comfort" to the grain-growers in her remote district, by saving the time and money required to ship corn to the miller farther away. To this remark she appends this note:

More than half a century has gone by since this was written, and now all and more than all these hopes have been verified. The writer has lived to see greater changes even than this take place in her adopted country.

The job she set herself in the footnotes is to record these changes— often without an indication to her feelings. One senses that she had no strong feelings about most changes, or generally felt them to be good.

In 1832, the Traills' way leads west, up the St. Lawrence River to Lake Ontario, to Cobourg. Her admiring prose recalls that of other writers from the same period. "The shores of the Ontario are very fine, rising in waving lines of hill and dale, clothed with magnificent woods, or enlivened by patches of cultivated land and pretty dwellings."

In October, 1832, Thomas and Catharine came ashore at the final dock, then began their trek inland, in the northerly direction toward their dwelling place at Lakefield. The lover of nature is immediately drawn to the glory of the forests, the swags of vines, the flowers. The view she crafts in words is drawn from Romantic painting, with its deep glooms and radiant lights.

On October 25, 1832, she notes:

As the day was particularly fine, I often quitted the wagon and walked on with my husband for a mile or so.

We soon lost sight entirely of the river, and struck into the deep solitude of the forest, where not a sound disturbed the almost awful stillness that reigned around us. Scarcely a leaf or bough was in motion, excepting at intervals we caught the sound of the breeze stirring the lofty heads of the pine-trees, and wakening a hoarse and mournful cadence . . .

There is a want of picturesque beauty in the woods. The young growth of timber alone has any pretension to elegance of form, unless I except the hemlocks, which are extremely light and graceful, and of a lovely refreshing tint of green. . . . There is no appearance of venerable antiquity in the Canadian woods. There are no ancient spreading oaks that might be called the patriarchs of the forest. A premature decay seems to be their doom . . .

Then the footnote to this melancholy and romantic passage:

With the exception of a few blocks of noble forest trees through which the new macadamized road lies, the last remnant of this forest through which we journeyed that day has gone. Far and wide spread out the richest fields of that and other farm crops; over hill and dale far as the eye can reach presents a varied and agreeable landscape.

But she is also able to see beyond, to the industrial abolition of both farms and the picturesque and melancholy grandeur of the forest primaeval. In the cold, early Ontario spring after her arrival at Lakefield, Catharine writes to her mother about a ramble along the Otonabee River during the winter just ending, and the discovery, beautifully described, on that rocky waterway.

Just below the waterfall I was mentioning there is a curious natural arch in the limestone rock, which at this place rises to a height of ten or fifteen feet like a wall . . . the arch seems like a rent in the wall, but worn away, and hollowed, possibly, by the action of the water rushing through it at some high flood. . . . Hemlock firs and cedars are waving on this elevated spot, above the turbulent waters, and clothing the stone barrier with never-fading verdure . . .

To this lovely sketch of a natural wonder of precisely the sort J. M. W. Turner (along with other painters of the Sublime) would have admired, she attaches an observation that is flat but telling.

The limestone arch has long ago disappeared, the rocky wall has been utilized to build the mill-dam. A timber slide has usurped the ridge of rock which caused the waterfall. Down this barrier the waters of the upper lakes now rush; below the wild Otonabee rushes the foams in its rocky bed. . . .

If there is no sadness in this note, or in many others, it is perhaps because Catharine was always a modern woman—educated, well-to-do, a daughter of privilege—and with a contempt for the showing-off stylish among the country-house élite of Georgian times. We have already seen her lofty disdain for *nouveaux riches* offended by the roughness of Ontario life. Two years after her arrival, she writes to her mother of the Georgian finery she sees in the bush, "where I see a ridiculous attempt to keep up an appearance that is quite foreign to the situation of those that practice it . . ."

Now, we *bush-settlers* are more independent: we do what we like; we dress as we find most suitable and most convenient; we are totally without the fear of any Mr. and Mrs. Grundy; and having shaken off the trammels of Grundyism, we laugh at the absurdity of those who voluntarily forge afresh and hug their chains.

Then, in a note to these lines, she records the following:

I am obliged to confess after many years sojourn in Canada that this primitive style of living has greatly disappeared from among us—a new order of things has replaced the simplicity of the old: luxury and fashion prevail even in our farm houses. We, like our neighbours across the water, are a progressive people.

I doubt she had ever believed Canada could remain quietly distanced from the busy world beyond.

In its celebration of natural beauty and charting of social change, Catharine's prose represents a significant step forward in Canadian descriptions of nature. Many of the earlier so-called nature writers were nothing of the sort, but scientific reporters. Samuel de Champlain, in 1603, notes that, eighty kilometres upriver from Québec City,

there are plenty of grapes, pears, hazel-nuts, cherries, currants and gooseberries. They also have certain small roots, the size of a nut, that taste like truffles and are very good either roasted or broiled.

Wayne Grady points out that this is not nature writing. "The earliest voyages of discovery did not produce nature writing for the same reason that most corporate board meetings do not produce poetry. It's not their business." Grady could have gone on to note where the minds of these literary explorers and adventurers were formed: in the cloister, the laboratory, in the barracks—places with little time for beauty, or the new music, art, theatre. There is strict piety and abstinence and the abstemiousness of Cartesian science, in those early representations of the New World. But for Mrs. Traill, as early as 1834, the quotidian and empirical method appears to have been an appropriate way to understand and write up the new land.

As to ghosts or spirits they appear totally banished from Canada. This is too matter-of-fact country for such supernaturals to visit . . . We have neither fay nor fairy, ghost nor bogle, satyr nor wood-nymph; our very forests disdain to shelter dryad or hamadryad . . . No Druid claims our oaks; and instead of poring with mysterious awe among our curious limestone rocks, that are often singularly grouped together, we refer them to the geologist to exercise his skill in account for their appearance; instead of investing them with the solemn characters of ancient temples or heathen altars, we look upon them with the curious eye of natural philosophy alone.

We have neither fay nor fairy, ghost nor bogle, satyr nor wood nymph.

29
COSMIC CONSCIOUSNESS

O NE EVENING IN THE EARLY 1890S, at the exclusive Rittenhouse Club in Philadelphia, Sir William Osler—brilliant Canadian physician, medical educator and prankster—gathered his friends for some fun at the expense of an acquaintance from school days at Montréal's McGill University. His name was Richard Maurice Bucke.

Dr. Bucke, head of the London, Ontario, Hospital for the Insane, had earlier asked Osler to look in on the ailing and elderly American poet, Walt Whitman, then living in nearby Camden, New Jersey. Dr. Osler dutifully did so. He liked old Walt, as those who met him always had. And like everyone else who knew Dr. Bucke, Osler had also gotten wind of the psychiatrist's intense, peculiar devotion to the Good Grey (and gay) Poet. Bucke's attraction to Whitman had apparently never been sexual. It was something else, or something more. Anyway, the dinner party was a set-up. Here is Sir William's recollection of it:

> Of the two men [Whitman and Bucke], Bucke interested me more. Though a hero-worshipper, it was a new experience in my life to witness such an absolute idolatry.

Where my blurred vision saw [in Whitman] only an old man, full of common sense and kindly feelings, Bucke felt himself in the presence of one of the world's great prophets. One evening after dinner at the Rittenhouse Club . . . I drew Bucke on to tell the story of Whitman's influence. The perfervid disciple . . . is not often met with in these matter-of-fact days. It was an experience to hear an elderly man—looking a venerable seer—with absolute abandonment tell how "Leaves of Grass" had meant for him spiritual enlightenment, a new power in life, new joys in a new existence on a plane higher than he had ever hoped to reach. All this with the accompanying physical exaltation expressed by dilated pupils and intensity of utterance that was embarrassing to uninitiated friends. This incident illustrates the type of influence exercised by Whitman on his disciples—a cult of a type such as no other literary man of our generation has been the object. . . .

The fanatical rhapsody provoked by Dr. Osler would not have turned out very differently, I imagine, had Sir Adam Beck been the target of this mock-solemn teasing, and electric power, not electrifying poetry, been the topic. Both Beck and Bucke were serious Victorian eccentrics of a sort that prospered in Britain's colonies generally, but in Ontario, for some reason, especially. Both men had sprung from immigrant stock, so could not take their social standing in conservative Ontario for granted. Both were also boundlessly optimistic, remorseless, obsessed by the notion of electrifying the province and the world—of liberating the flows of natural force for the benefit of all humanity. For Beck, the visible incarnation of that energy was the Niagara cataract. For Bucke, it was Walt Whitman. Both Beck and Bucke were determined to possess these visible manifestations of invisible graces; and each, in his own way, did so.

A twisting path had led R. M. Bucke to Whitman, and to the malicious evening at the Rittenhouse Club. It began in Norfolk, England, where he was born to a Church of England clergyman in 1837. Why the curate abruptly upped and moved himself, his wife and son Maurice, then one year old, and his magnificent library of six thousand books, to a homestead near the future site of the madhouse at London, Ontario, is not known. None of the Reverend Mr. Bucke's children went to school. In the pastor's view, his own tutoring and huge library offered resources quite good enough for his offspring's intellectual cultivation.

In one sense, he was proved right. All the Bucke children went off to good Canadian universities, did brilliantly and enjoyed solid, conventional careers. Richard Maurice, however, required some time to achieve a settled position in the world. At age sixteen, he left London for California, where he intended to make a gold-mining fortune. Instead, he was trapped and overwhelmed by a mountain snowstorm, and fell victim to frostbite, which he survived minus a foot. His wilderness adventuring at an end, he did medical training at McGill (where he met Osler) and finished with high honours.

His lifelong work as a psychiatric hospital administrator was distinguished by its competence and unexceptional reformism. He swam energetically with the tide of asylum revamping that was all the rage in North America, never falling behind or moving conspicuously ahead. By 1880, when he had consolidated his control over the nine hundred patients at London's Asylum for the Insane, beatings and starvation and chaining down the unruly were *démodé* in progressive medical circles, but still controversial, even among intellectuals. (Edgar Allan Poe hated the idea of "progressive" psychiatric reform, and wrote a nastily funny story about it.)

Dr. Bucke immediately moved to change things. He took a strongly optimistic stand on treatment, downplayed restraint and old-fashioned heroic assaults on misbehaving patients, abolished dosing the insane with alcohol and allowed greater freedom of movement for patients. Good psychotherapy, not sedation, he believed, was the way to inner calmness. His convictions (and the modest recognition that not every psychiatrist would share his view) is summed up in a dignified one-sentence manifesto. "The object of treatment in the case of insanity," he wrote, "is (to my mind) not so much the cure of disease as it is the rehumanization of the patients." R. M. Bucke remained head of the London hospital until his death in 1902, respected, as people are inclined to say about prominent public figures who get through life without getting into trouble or causing it—and admired.

So much for his public career. In his off-hours, the respectable psychiatrist pursued an eccentric course, immersing himself in Whitman's poetry, and studying a phenomenon he called "cosmic consciousness." To R. M. Bucke, by the way—not Timothy Leary or some other hippie guru of the druggy 1960s—goes the credit for coining this famous phrase.

Nobody nowadays would find anything out of line in Dr. Bucke's fascination with Whitman and his poetry. A doctor can be a fan, after all, just like anybody else. Bucke became one in 1867, shortly after marrying and settling into medical practice at Sarnia, Ontario. In Montréal, his friend T. Sterry Hunt, a chemist who invented the permanent green ink used on banknotes, suggested Bucke might like to read the American poet named Walt Whitman. There and then began the central enchantment of Bucke's life—a productive bewitchment, as it happens, which left us the first biography of the poet, posthumous gatherings of Whitman's important uncollected works, and the ten-volume "death-bed" edition of the writings, meant to promote Whitman's fame as widely as possible. I have an acquaintance who is that way about the Boswell Sisters: obsessed beyond all measure. Fandom happens. It is far too complex and pervasive a phenomenon to get into here, but usually it is harmless enough.

A doctor whose off-hours are devoted to the study of "cosmic consciousness," however, might be well advised to keep quiet about it, these days anyway.

But not in R. M. Bucke's era. It would hardly have been necessary. The startling inventions and discoveries of Victorian scientists and technologists, from Bell's telephone to the tomb-treasures of Egypt, aluminum and the colour mauve—had made anything mysterious fashionable. A person with a perfectly respectable career could indulge, without fear of public disapproval, in fantasias we would find crazy now. Rays and waves, racialism, emanations, "animal magnetism," vibrations, séances, ectoplasm, Darwinian evolution and so forth were topics for chat at bourgeois breakfast tables across the Empire and across the world. There is something bewildering about a wartime Canadian prime minister, Mackenzie King in this case, seeking counsel from his dead dog Pat via an Ottawa psychic; but Mackenzie King was a child of the era in which Bucke was an elder. William Osler's bemusement, it's worth remembering, had less to do with Bucke's personal intellectual pursuits, which were merely among the stylish ones of the day, than with his friend's wild-eyed Whitmania.

I believe that Bucke never understood what Whitman was doing as a literary artist. For the psychiatrist, Whitman was proclaiming a gospel, not making art. As for Bucke's main *intellectual* preoccupation, with cosmic consciousness—having never experienced anything I would identify as a mystical incident in my life, I cannot claim to understand exactly what Bucke meant by this phrase. But for what it's worth, here follows, considerably abridged, a description he delivered to a conclave of learned psychiatrists who were meeting at Philadelphia in 1894.

In the first place, does it not seem pretty certain that a race which has been enabled by its own inherent growth to advance from excitability to sensation, from that to simple consciousness, from that to self consciousness; that has been able to take on the human moral nature, color sense and a hundred other faculties—does it not seem pretty certain, I say: that this race, still as full of vitality as ever, will take on, as time passes, still other faculties? . . . The human mind is now in the very act of making this supposed step—is now in the very act of stepping from the plane of self-consciousness to a higher plane, which I call Cosmic Consciousness.

Since 1890, Bucke goes on to say, he had studied no fewer than twenty-three cases of "this so-called Cosmic Consciousness," and decided the usual age for attaining it is thirty-five. Among veterans of this phenomenon—

"not simply an expansion or extension of the self conscious mind, with which we are all familiar, but the superaddition of a function as distinct from any function possessed by one of the higher animals"—are Buddha, St. Paul, Dante, Balzac, William Blake and Walt Whitman. All these men underwent

certain phenomena connected with the onset, or oncoming, of the new faculty—which is usually, perhaps always, sudden, instantaneous. Among these the most striking symptom is the sense of being immersed in flame or in a brilliant light. This occurs entirely without warning or outward cause, and may happen at noonday or in the middle of the night . . .

Whitman, for example, reports his experiences in the following lines:

As in a swoon one instant,
Another sun, ineffable, full dazzles me,
And all the orbs I knew—and brighter, unknown orbs;
One instant of the future land, Heaven's land.

"The dazzling, sudden, unexpected, subjective light" produces alarm, a vision of someone speaking, occasionally the fear that one is going insane. Then this disconcerting hailstorm of sensory impressions fades, leaving in the initiate an ineffable, profound apprehension of the "life and order of the Cosmos." (Let us ignore the fact that Whitman was wildly effable about it.)

> With the intellectual illumination comes an indescribable moral elevation—an intense and exalted joyfulness, and, along with this, a sense of immortality; not merely a belief in a future life—that would be a small matter—but a consciousness that the life now being lived is eternal—death being seen as a trivial incident which does not affect its continuity. Further, there are annihilation of the sense of sin and an intellectual competency not simply surpassing the old, but on a new and higher plane.

Bucke draws his address to a close with a memorable image of the upward mental evolution already occurring in our midst, creating nothing less than a new race of human beings.

> The creature with simple consciousness only is a straw floating on a tide, moving freely every way with every influence. The self-conscious man is a needle pivoted by its center—fixed in one point but oscillating and revolving free only on that with every influence. The man with Cosmic Consciousness is the same needle magnetized. It is still fixed by its center, but besides that it points steadily to the north. It has found something real and permanent outside of itself toward which it cannot but steadily look.
> . . . [A] Cosmic Conscious race will not be the race which exists to-day, any more than the present is the same race which existed prior to the evolution of self-consciousness. The simple truth is, that a new race is being born from us, and this new race will in the near future possess the earth.

Did Bucke believe himself to be in the vanguard of the coming race of illuminated and elevated beings? In *Cosmic Consciousness: A Study of the Evolution of the Human Mind* (1901), his most developed argument and by far his most famous book, he admits only to having had, at the auspicious age of thirty-five—the year would have been 1872—the requisite catastrophic experience. It had taken place, apparently, during a visit to London, England, and was precipitated by Whitman's *Leaves of Grass*. The account of this occurrence is left, modestly but somehow curiously, in the third person.

> It was in the early spring, at the beginning of his thirty-sixth year. He and two friends had spent the evening reading Wordsworth, Shelley, Keats, Browning, and especially Whitman. They parted at midnight, and he had a long drive in a hansom (it was in an English city).
>
> His mind, deeply under the influence of the ideas, images and emotions called up by the reading and talk of the evening, was calm and peaceful. He was in a state of quiet, almost passive, enjoyment.
>
> All at once, without warning of any kind, he found himself wrapped around as it were by a flame-coloured cloud. For an instant he thought of fire—some sudden conflagration in the great city. The next he knew that the light was within himself. Directly afterwards came upon him a sense of exultation, of immense joyousness, accompanied or immediately followed by intellectual illumination impossible to describe.

Into his brain streamed one momentary lightning-flash of the Brahmic Splendour which has ever since lightened his life; upon his heart fell one drop of the Brahmic Bliss, leaving thenceforward for always an aftertaste of heaven. Among other things, he did not merely come to believe, but saw that the Cosmos is not dead matter, but a living Presence; that the soul of man is immortal, that the universe is so built and ordered that without any peradventure all things work together for the good of each and all; that the foundation principle of the world is what we call love and that the happiness of every one is in the long run absolutely certain.

ALL LONDON, ONTARIO, WAS UPSET in the late spring of 1880 about the impending arrival of Walt Whitman.

On one hand, nobody could fault the credentials of Whitman's host. Dr. R. M. Bucke was respected and respectable in a small city that had always—*has* always—cherished its provincial respectability and venerable foundation. Because Dr. Bucke was engaged in writing a biography of the journalist and poet, then sixty-one and famous, a visit to Ontario by the subject was hardly unreasonable.

On the other hand, there was Whitman's famous poem cycle *Leaves of Grass,* first published in 1855. The work celebrates, along with much else that is good in human life, carnality and the exuberance of good sex and other bodily pleasures. While there was surely as much erotic romping in the London of 1880 as there is today, talking about it publicly was novel. Walt Whitman not merely talked about it, but did so with exultation. Not that Londoners had actually read the book. Busybodies who like to denounce books for being smutty never read anything carefully or wisely. But everybody had heard about the poet's literary extravagances.

And everybody in London surely knew about the Harlan affair. Living in Washington in 1865, as the terrible rebellion of the South was sputtering out, Whitman got a job as a clerk in the federal civil service. He was fired almost at once, when his boss, Secretary of the Interior James Harlan, found out his new office help was "the author of an indecent book," that notorious *Leaves of Grass*. Whitman's friend and fan William Douglas O'Connor launched a pamphlet war against Harlan that failed to get Whitman reinstated but left the forty-five-year-old writer branded forever as a "Good Grey Poet." Londoners were prepared to believe their visitor would be grey. He was certainly a poet. But good?

Dr. Bucke went on the offensive some months before Whitman's arrival, by giving lectures on the poet's great personal virtues. The holy child born in 1819 was destined to exercise "as great an influence upon the human race as any man that the world has ever yet produced."

> Whatever he does or suffers becomes altered by its contact with him, so that by that contact poverty loses its meanness, old age its helplessness, and pain, sickness and death lose their terrors. As he says himself, "I make holy whatever I touch or am touched from." . . . The distinguishing feature belonging to this man, which as a key unlocks every apparent enigma about him, is his extraordinarily elevated moral nature, his exalted trust in God and his intense love for mankind. In a few years he will not be visible to our eyes, and if we wish to know him, whom to know is to love, we must go to his other self, which may be found in "Leaves of Grass."

The popular uproar and Bucke's attempts to damp it down combined, as usual, to inspire a media frenzy. In a bid to grab an impromptu exclusive, the *London Free Press* dispatched a reporter to jump on board Whitman's train at Paris, a couple of hours from London, and hunt the poet down.

"After searching in vain through several of the dining-room cars," the reporter tell us,

Mr. Whitman was found on the platform of the rear Wagner surveying the beautiful hills around Paris, in company with his personal friend, Dr. R. M. Bucke, Medical Superintendent of the London Lunatic Asylum. . . .

A card was handed to Dr. Bucke, who spoke a few words in private to Mr. Whitman. Without waiting for further formalities, the poet reached out his hand, and, with a slight American accent, said, warmly: "Most happy to meet you. I'm one of the fraternity myself. Been a newspaper man most of my life. You wish to have an item about me? Well, I never back out on a news-paper man. Come right into the car."

"Well, this is taking time by the forelock" said Dr. Bucke, with a laugh. "How did you know we were aboard the train?"

"Oh, you trust a newspaper man to know when an item is about to turn up," explained Mr. Whitman. "They know it by instinct."

This is the earliest glimpse of the poet in Canada we get, and also a picture of him as a warm, ordinary, unpretentious man, stripped of the metaphysical vapours in which Bucke always had, and always would, try to keep him fogbound. A *London Advertiser* interviewer, in a "Chat with the 'Good Gray Poet'" published the day after his arrival—there was to be no escape from that tag for poor Walt, even in Ontario!—is at pains to reassure Londoners of the poet's harmlessness.

He was told that his works had excited a good deal of interest in London, and that they had been severely animadverted upon by a clergyman of the city, Rev. Mr. Murray, and that that gentleman was on the platform as he arrived.

"Ah," said Whitman, "I should have liked to have met him. I wish he had come and spoken to me," and the manner in which he spoke showed that he was plainly in earnest . . .

The interchange quickly turned to Whitman's literary interests—
and for the first time, we see the author pulling a bit of warm and wily
charm on this obviously star-struck reporter:

He reads but little comparatively, so he said, but his favourite
works are those of Sir Walter Scott (some of which he has read
five or six times), George Sand, Shakespeare, Homer, and "that
best of all books, the Bible," the quoted words being spoken with
a reverence that one would scarce expect in a man denounced for
his immorality.

Then, suddenly, we glimpse a flash of the great Walt whom all who
love poetry will love forever—and around whom one must be always
ever so slightly on one's guard against complete seduction.

If Shakespeare and the Greeks wrote mainly of rulers and gods, it
had always been this poet's intention "to give expression to
Nature as we actually find it. The man, the American man, the
labourer, the boatman, and mechanic. The great painters were as
willing to paint a blacksmith as a lord. Why should the poets
only confine themselves to mere sentiment? The theologians to a
man teach humility, and that the body is the sinful setting of the
immortal soul. I wish men to be proud—to be proud of their
bodies—to look upon the body as a thing of beauty . . ."
The hour was late, and it was not well that the fatigue of the
journey should be supplemented by too much conversation, yet it
was learned that Walt Whitman is a man with whom any can
converse with distinct convictions on literature and religion, and
while it is not the province of the reporter to pronounce upon his
orthodoxy, there can be no doubt that he is a reverent man, with no
suggestion of irreverence or pruriency in his talk. It is probable that
he will remain with Dr. Bucke the great part of the summer, and
possibly he may deliver a lecture in the course of his stay in London.

Whitman remained with Dr. Bucke and his family continuously for what Bucke calls "three-and-a-half months' absolute intimacy" during that summer of 1880, in London or on pleasure trips that took them as far down the St. Lawrence as Chicoutimi. It was a time of companionship between a spectacular poet and quirkily brilliant psychiatrist that we can hardly believe could have stayed as utterly free of trouble or conflict as it appears to have done. Yet what choice do we have to believe that their time together was quite amiable?

Three and a half months of absolute intimacy.....

A couple of weeks after his arrival in London, Whitman wrote in a local paper that he had come to spend "the season half-indolently in Canada." Every jotting by Whitman, published and unpublished, that has survived from that summer suggests that he stuck by his resolve. He liked going on walks, and noted the wildflowers he saw. He was interested that many of the birds he had watched and enjoyed in New Jersey were to be found in Ontario. Of course, something would occasionally move the man who wrote the endless lines in *Leaves of Grass* to incandescent eloquence.

June 6.—Went to the religious services (Episcopal) Main Insane Asylum, held in a lofty, good-sized hall, third story. . . .

O the looks that came from those faces! There were two or three I shall probably never forget. Nothing at all markedly repulsive, or hideous—strange enough, I did not see once such. Our common humanity, mine and yours, everywhere; "The same old blood—the same red, running blood;" yet behind most an inferred *arriere* of such storms, such wrecks, such mysteries, fires, love, wrong, greed for wealth, religious problems, crosses—mirrored from those crazed faces (yet temporarily so calm, like still waters), all the woes and sad happenings of life and death—now from every one the devotional element radiating—was it not, indeed, that peace of God that passeth all understanding, strange as it may sound? I can only say that I took long and searching eyesweeps as I sat there, and it seemed so, rousing unprecedented thoughts, problems unanswerable. (How, sometimes, a flash of the living sight, magnetic, all previous statements, and reams, folios of argument) . . .

When not writing for publication (as he was, about the asylum service), his diary entries tend to go like this one datelined London, Ontario, June 18, 1880.

Calm and glorious roll the hours here—the whole twenty-four. A perfect day (the third in succession); the sun clear; a faint, fresh, just palpable air setting in from the south-west; temperature pretty warm at mid-day, but moderate enough mornings and evenings. Everything growing well, especially the perennials. Never have I seen verdure—grass and trees and bushery—to greater advantage. All the accompaniments joyous. Cat-birds, thrushes, robin, etc., singing. The profuse blossoms of the tiger-lily (is it the tiger-lily?) mottling the lawns and gardens everywhere with their glowing orange-red. Roses everywhere, too.

Whitman was obviously interested in the madhouse worship service. Why shouldn't he be? He was enjoying a miraculously beautiful southern Ontario summer. Who wouldn't? Every Ontario summer is like that. What I am suggesting is that I do not understand how a man—a deeply genial genius, but still a man—could spend almost four months with R. M. Bucke and not end his summer either mad or homicidal. Nor will I ever comprehend how nearly four months with Walt Whitman did not dim or qualify Dr. Bucke's "absolute idolatry," even a smidgen. Three years before Whitman's 1880 visit, Bucke had written to a British editor about the recent first encounter between the two men.

> I have never seen any man to compare with him—any man at least like him, he seems more than a man and yet in all his looks and ways entirely common place. ("Do I contradict myself?") He is an average man magnified to the dimensions of a god—but this does not give you the least idea of what he is like and I despair of giving you any idea at all however slight—I may say that I have experienced what I have heard so much about, the extraordinary magnetism of his presence . . .

And so on. Nearly four months with Whitman did not lessen this slavish adoration by so much as one scintilla. In November, 1880, just after the poet had taken the train back to New Jersey, Bucke wrote to a fellow fan:

> It is my dream to devote the rest of my life (not many years perhaps, but still a few) to the study and promulgation of the new religion ("The great idea") and I should hope to find younger men to pass on the work to when I laid it down.

In the pioneering 1883 biography, Bucke worries that no such younger men are coming forth, thereby putting the "New World Republic" in danger of success on only "the lower grounds" of philistine materialism. The only answer: a great awakening to the explosive message of the Prophet of Camden and his scriptures.

"I consider Walt Whitman's life and poems," writes Bucke, ever searching for the great hyperbole, "unspeakably important."

And if this is not bad enough, in *Cosmic Consciousness* Bucke's obsession finally takes him into the stratosphere of pure delirium.

Walt Whitman is the best, most perfect, example the world has so far had of the Cosmic Sense, first because he is the man in whom the new faculty has been, probably, most perfectly developed, and especially because he is, par excellence, the man who in modern times has written distinctly and at large from the point of view of Cosmic Consciousness, and who also has referred to its facts and phenomena more plainly and fully than any other writer either ancient or modern.

Whether Dr. Bucke himself was mad or not, I must leave to experts. The ones who have pronounced on this topic have found him odd, but sane. I am not prepared to argue with them. That said, the Victorian Ontario in which Richard Maurice Bucke came of age was one in which the population at large was inflicted sharply and heavily by the strange new culture of modernization—with curious results. The farming communities in Ontario were not emptied gradually. They were abandoned with breathtaking speed, as the population moved, hugely and rapidly, to the industrial and heavily urbanized stretch along the north shore of Lake Ontario. The disorientation was massive. Traditional values and pieties were suddenly overturned. No matter how quickly the neo-Victorian churches and faux-Gothic housing went up, the stark fact remained that traditional systems of belief and cultural continuity had been doused by the corrosive acid of modernity, and were dissolving.

A few young men and women did pick up Dr. Bucke's torch of Cosmic Consciousness upon his death in 1902—only to see it drowned in the soggy trenches of the First World War. Very little

Victorian and Edwardian optimism, whether of Beck's sort or of Bucke's, survived in Ontario past 1920. But there was one more development that Dr. Bucke could not have foreseen: the commercialization of Cosmic Consciousness; its sale for the price of a train ticket north.

30
THE MYSTIC NORTH

As THE VICTORIAN ERA CLOSED IN ONTARIO, with an explosion of lakeshore cities and desertion of the countryside, John Simcoe's founding vision of the place—conservative, un-American, aristocratic—found new and surprising expression in a popular nationalist myth that early attached itself to the North. The United States, in contrast, found its identity in distinction from the Latin and British cultures that bounded it, south and north. Ontario similarly defined itself—before the Great War, and especially after it—against the industrious, republican egalitarianism of its southern neighbour. Our northern boundary, however, was a huge, spectacularly beautiful desert of lakes and rocks stretching north forever. To go there was to escape the industrialized city and find our true identity as people grounded in the experience of intense loveliness and forbidding ruggedness of the North.

For Ontario painter J. E. H. MacDonald, the defining idea of the North came to him in 1913, while visiting an exhibition of Scandinavian canvases at Buffalo's Albright Art Gallery. Many years later, reminiscing about the day he first saw landscapes by the Swedish painter Gustaf Fjaestad, in the distant, Edwardian twilight of empire, he said: "We were so fond of these things ourselves that we couldn't but like the pictures, and we were well assured . . . that we would know our own snows and rivers better for Fjaestad's revelations. They . . . seemed to us true souvenirs of that mystic north round which we all revolve."

The flights to the "mystic north" that began to entice Ontarians in the early twentieth century began, of course, in the "secular south," where most people lived and worked. The city had become an unavoidable preoccupation of millions, as nineteenth-century industrialization turned into twentieth-century urbanization. How the all-important myth of the Mystic North came into its own before the Great War must be understood against this background of Ontario's first great crisis of metropolitan living.

There was no doubt among the citizens that the most rapidly expanding city in Ontario at the turn of the twentieth century was in trouble. It was girl trouble. And, if that weren't bad enough—boy trouble, to boot.

The "girl problem," as it was known, had become so grievous that the Toronto Vigilance Committee printed up a broadsheet recruiting the town's good folk into its fight to "usher in a 'Better Toronto.'" The crusaders' declared objectives included the curbing of Toronto's full-time white slavers, presumably combing the streets for young women to capture and slam into local "Chinese dens of infamy, kept for the purposes of ruining young Canadian girls." Next on the list was the "suppression of unduly obnoxious behaviour on the part of immoral women," especially where the vicious goings-on could be observed by children.

But it takes two to make vice—and the Committee was quite aware that certain young men of the town were up to no good.

Our representatives have followed a number of young girls, who were in the company of young men whom we suspected of being desirous of ruining the girls. We are always ready to step in and prevent any overt act.

Even the Toronto press was playing unwitting accomplice to the corruption of the city.

Recently a number of persons have been advertising for lady stenographers, waitresses, etc., and when the applicants called, they would be rudely treated by being asked such questions as:
"Do you wish to have a good time, and make big money?"
"Do you smoke, play cards, dance, stand on your head?"
"Do you desire to go to wine suppers?"
"What are your measurements from your hips down?"
One villain of a man induced one of the young girls to go to an establishment he operated on Bathurst Street, and there accomplished, possibly, the ruin of the girl. OUR SISTERS AND DAUGHTERS MUST NOT BE SUBJECTED TO THESE GROSS AFFRONTS!

Item number 7 on the Vigilance Committee's list of objectives— sandwiched between ridding the town of pimps ("so-called cadets") and breaking up Chinese dens of infamy—is the expenditure of "efforts to aid in preventing boys being led astray by moral perverts." But it was already too late to stop the subversion at the city gates. Sixteen years before, in the startling investigative exposé *Of Toronto the Good,* journalist Christopher St. George Clark had noted gaggles of "street boys," aged ten to sixteen, on the loose. "They are generally sharp, shrewd lads," he had observed,

with any number of bad habits and little or no principles . . . Some of the larger boys spend a considerable portion of their earnings for tobacco and drink, and they patronize all the theatres . . . When a newsboy gets to be seventeen years of age he finds that his avocation is at an end, it does not produce money enough and he has acquired lazy, listless habits . . . He becomes a vagrant and perhaps worse.

While Clark declines to identify this thing worse than vagrancy, he leaves no doubt at all about what he's talking about. "Men and their acts of indecency are the talk of boys all over the city," Clark says. Young lodgers in Chicago boarding houses, he has learned, are familiar with "it"—though if looking for evidence of "it," you don't need to look as far away as Chicago. "Consult some of the bell boys of the large hotels in Canada's leading cities, as I did, and find out what they can tell from their own experiences."

But anybody prepared to visit Toronto's working-class districts could have skipped the bellboys and witnessed for himself the dawn of Toronto's gay community. Between the publication of C. S. Clark's exposé in 1898 and the Vigilance Committee's call to moral arms in 1912, the number of music halls, burlesque houses, vaudeville theatres, movie palaces around the intersection of Queen and Bay jumped tenfold, from around 10 to 110. Police rap sheets suggest every gay man in town knew he could connect with a "street boy" at the theatres, and the new fast-food franchises—a place called Bowles was a favourite hangout for gay men and teenagers. There are records of straight-up male prostitution for money in Toronto the Good early in the last century. But quite often, it appears, theatre tickets were what the game was about. Vaudeville shows, movies—they were all the craze. In 1921, a fourteen-year-old lad had sex with an adult employee at the Star Theatre, and got arrested. Asked why he did it, his answer to the bewigged judge was refreshingly frank: "I got in free." (Interestingly, the court records studied by Steven Maynard—one of the very few historians interested in gay Toronto of old, and a principal source for what I'm telling you—suggest the usual reason for arrest was a complaint by a teenager who didn't get the *post facto* payoff he was promised.)

The Toronto police were openly complaining about the city's "boy question" or "boy nuisance" as early as 1891—a phenomenon Maynard sees as symptomatic of larger cultural prejudices. Maynard writes:

At the heart of the boy nuisance was the widely shared belief that working-class boys were responsible for a good deal of crime and vice in the city. Not surprisingly, much of the boy question was discussed with reference to the most visible boys—street boys—particularly the ever-present newsboy. Testifying before the 1889 Royal Commission on the Relations of Labour and Capital, former Toronto mayor and moral reformer W. H. Howland related his conversations with "respectable working people who told me that their boys were all right until they began to sell newspapers on the street at eleven and twelve o'clock at night, but then they got demoralized . . . I am satisfied that in every city a large portion of the petty crime is done by these boys."

The streets, for Howland, were at the heart of the "boy nuisance" and, he could have added, "the girl problem." These culprit streets were the crowded, noisy, busy thoroughfares of an industrial, working-class metropolis of exactly the kind Toronto was becoming. The police were sent in to harass street kids by middle-class politicians elected by middle-class constituents who remembered a very different kind of Toronto. Those whom Maynard called "social purity activists" were members of an international movement of turn-of-the-century white people menaced by urbanization and the inflow of immigrants different from any people Ontarians had ever seen before: neither white nor anglophone; or, if white, not Christian. Somehow, "purity" became the antidote to both impurity and anxiety. Methodist youth coming of age in Toronto around 1910 were sternly lectured about "sexual hygiene," by which was meant abstinence from masturbation and abhorrence of homosexuality. Created in 1911, the Toronto Vigilance Committee kept special watch over the doings of youth in the working-class entertainment area around Queen and Bay.

Toronto's blue-collar workers, however, might have been the only people in the city who were not being driven to distraction and absurdity by the unstoppable forces of urbanization. Catharine Parr Traill was in the last generation of immigrants who had come out under gentle conditions and taken her place in a rural colonial world. In the year of Confederation, many people were alive in Ontario who could remember the Rebellion of 1837, and the earlier times of Georgian colonial rule. But they were growing old; and like most of those who grow old, they began to fashion a history that suited them. In this visionary past, the sun over Victorian Ontario had been ever in the ascendant, rising toward the acme of heaven and shining benignly over a land once shrouded in dark bush, now farmland open to the sky. Here was the fulfillment of a promise, and Ontarians were grateful for the blessings of nature and the distant Queen.

By 1880 or thereabouts, it was becoming—or had already become—impossible for Ontarians to think of their land in quite the same, simple way. The new element crowding in upon the Virgilian pastoral of Ontario was Toronto.

The provincial capital had long been a nagging bother, or a pit of temptation for the predominantly agricultural colony. Early in the nineteenth century, Toronto—so the myth went—was the citadel of the Family Compact, that band of Anglican tyrants opposed to the honest yeoman farmer and Catholic or Non-Conforming stalwart. The latter were the *true* Ontarians. But as the century began to move toward its close and this notion reached its greatest persuasiveness, it was also becoming implausible. The strength of Ontario was in Toronto's mills and factories, in the strong arms of its new, non-British immigrants, Jewish and Gentile. But this change necessitated a change in the myth of Toronto. The notion of the Family Compact had become obsolete. A new wickedness about the city had to be constructed, and also a new sanctity for the countryside sliding into irrelevance.

In mid-Victorian mythology, writes historian Barry Dane, the "happy farm" had been opposed to the city, with its "busy hum of machinery, the regal mansion of the capitalist, and a background of squalid tenements where vice, and penury, and dirt, produce a diseased and vicious population."

By the 1880s, however, rural Ontario had subtly shifted from noble alternative to reassuring refuge. The country became "an alternative to civilization, a place where one could find solace, uplift, repose, tranquility and regeneration in a withdrawal from the constraints imposed by the new urban order . . ."

But north of the countryside lay the almost unthinkably vast and ancient sub-Arctic expanse called the Shield, with its countless brilliant lakes and trackless bogs, its mystery and magical remoteness. "By itself, alone, untouched by the arts and techniques of man," writes Dane, "the forest virtually compelled understanding of itself . . . as a barbarizing place, withdrawal into which produced a Caliban-like state of degradation. But the incursion of the railways into the rocky Shield gave a way in, and a way out, making it an altogether less frightening entity. . . ."

[Then] a sense of it as the venue of a terrifying encounter with an intractable force could be displaced by an understanding of it as the place where people might find a temporary, accessible and refreshingly different alternative to the kind of life they normally lived. The new order, in sum, might have created a special need for uplift and regeneration, but [it] also generated conditions which made it possible to seek those things in places once thought capable of providing only their opposite. . . .

The allure of the Mystic North as the place of revival was about to cast its spell over Ontario's urban south.

The more familiar pitch of Northern promoters of the North is well known, and effective down to the present day. In 1889, a moment of intense urbanization and urban expansion in southern Ontario,

propagandistic publications always began with lyrical seduction. Here follows a sampler of a huge onslaught. An author in 1889 writes:

> "Men and women cribbed in towns / with nerves over wrought and weak," the "weary, over-worked toiler of the city," and even the children of that confining place "would find their nerves being turned to healthful music" as a consequence of their time spent midst the splendors of the woods. . . . "By leaving an atmosphere tainted with sewer gas to inhale the tonic perfume of the pine bush" they would find "their cheeks flushing with freshened tints of purified blood." "The healing sunshine" and "fresh air" of the woods would, in fact, "work wonders."

Muskoka, land of enchantment! "Here," asserted a promoter, "the business and professional man finds rest from care and toil; [and] the feeble, health." "To the worker," insisted another, "this vacation life [in Muskoka] is a seduction." In that happy place, a third put it, one could spend "cool, healthy, happy days, as unlike those of busy town life as civilized men can devise." The commercial development of the Shield bounded forward in tandem with the industrial prosperity of Toronto. At another level, the invention of what Ontarians call "cottage country" proceeded in pace with the conviction that urbanization represented "a bewildering range of traits—progress, tolerance, culture, decay, sin, alienation as well as respectability and order." In both the United States and Canada, it was a climate ready for the simplifications represented by religious revivalism, which advanced with cottaging as Ontario cultural obsessions.

The characteristic incarnation of the new religious spirit was the camp meeting. These rural gatherings of evangelical Christians had begun in the United States in the late eighteenth century, long before urbanization was an issue. The first such event in Ontario was led by the Reverend John Carroll, a Methodist preacher, in 1825 at Cummer's

Mills, north of Toronto. An historian of these early camp meetings has written of them as follows:

A week before the revival, a large board tent and preaching stand were erected; slab seats were arranged in a gentle slope ringing the stand; and the whole encampment was surrounded by a high stockade to keep out intruders. During the meeting guards would be stationed at the gates to minimize rowdyism. Finally, the site was cleared of brush and arrangements were made for a supply of water and firewood.

The decline of this primitive camp meeting began around 1840. But with the rise of large cities and industrial emplacements, the Ontario camp meetings revived, though in a new form. They tended to "become more formal . . . Social refreshment, which came with a vacation from the routine of daily life, continued to keep them popular, but they bore little resemblance to the old-time revivals." By the 1870s, they had become permanent campgrounds with "the moral atmosphere of a park." The early evangelists who brought camp meetings to Ontario would hardly recognize what they had become by 1882, when the Methodist Episcopal Church's *Christian Guardian* described its place of Christian renewal as follows:

There is no more healthy and pleasant summer resort than Thousand Island Park, on the St. Lawrence. The scenery is picturesque and beautiful. The water is cool and clear. The air is pure and bracing. Good order and interesting services are maintained. Fishing, boating and bathing are available to any extent. The first of the series of services of the season was begun last Friday, under the direction of the Rev. Dr. Hibbard, and is now in full blast.

No wild enthusiasm here! It is a "coveted summer retreat from the extreme heat of city life and a favourite resort for amusement." It is a place of religion tamed, normalized, made into yet another bit of furniture for bourgeois living. It also left unfulfilled the spiritual yearnings of those who wanted more than cozy reassurance.

THE PAINTERS IN THE 1913 BUFFALO EXHIBITION inspired the future members of the Group of Seven, who declined to draw their topics from Paris, then the reigning world capital of art. They sought instead their ideas in the northern native ground. The Canadian artist Lawren Harris spoke of the ambitions, program and philosophical ground that he and other members of the Group of Seven discovered in those years before the Great War.

We, who are true Canadians imbued with the North, are an upstart people with our traditions in the making. Our day of scholarship has not yet arrived. We have not yet created a field for it to examine. We have no body of criticism of our own. Our days for such [are] in the future, when we have created much more for criticism to moil over. Whitman saw this and was therefore almost wholly a yea-sayer . . .

The modern European artist serves "a consciously held idea of art" derived from its great treasure-houses of art, its museums, galleries, palaces, and cathedrals. The Canadian artist serves the spirit of his land and people. He is aware of the spiritual flow from the replenishing North and believes that he should ever shed clarity into the growing race of America and that . . . working creative individuals will give rise to an art quite different from that of any European people. He believes in the power and glory, for the North to him is a single, simple vision of high things and can, through its transmuting agency, shape our souls into its own spiritual expressiveness . . .

The source of our art then is not in the achievements of other artists in other days and lands, although it has learned a great deal from these. Our art is founded on a long and growing love and understanding of the North as an ever clearer experience of oneness with the informing spirit of the whole land and a strange brooding sense of Mother Nature fostering a new race and new age.

Theosophy and Madame Blavatsky, the poetry of Walt Whitman and the speculations of R. M. Bucke, Symbolist painting and a drive to found an authentic painting of the metaphysical North—these influences arrived in Ontario by books and media and visits, and flowed into the stream of Harris's thought, and from him into the Group. The founding seven were Frank Carmichael, Lawren Harris, A. Y. Jackson, Franz Johnston, Arthur Lismer, J. E. H. MacDonald and F. H. Varley. Had he lived until 1920, when the Group staged its first controversial exhibition, Tom Thomson would certainly have been invited to join, making it a Group of Eight. Though Thomson died early, an array of his friends' landscape art would be unthinkable without him, and for this reason, he is almost always displayed with them, as one whose spirit sang in unison with theirs.

Conveying that urgency today, and expecting agreement that the Group represented the culminating cultural moment in Ontario so far, is never easy. The most famous topics of the Group of Seven and Tom Thomson—stormy lakes, a lone pine installed against a sunset, gloriously golden forests, deep woods, denuded mountains poised within emptiness and mystery—are altogether too familiar to Canadians through reproductions, and solemn school tours through museums. Anyone who has grown up in this country knows too well the brilliantly colourful, heavily swatched and scumbled Group style of painting. The Group must also overcome the prejudice that their fame rested upon their powers of vivid illustration of what rich cottagers in the newly opened Muskoka district wished to see. Simply because the paintings of the Group are so firmly etched into official national culture—that shelf of pieties and objects, like maple syrup, the beaver and other oddments, that presumably make Canada—dwellers in this country who take these paintings for granted, or ignore them, can hardly be blamed for doing so.

Yet, no body of art less deserves such casual indifference. In a dozen years on either side of 1920, Thomson and Group artists painted the most boldly inventive and resonantly beautiful modern landscapes ever made in this country until that time, or since. If it now takes an effort to see them with fresh eyes, then so be it. They are worth it.

Having said that, I admit the effort may be considerable. The official schoolbook portrait that's come down to us is off-putting. In it, seven brave men (plus Thomson) stand stalwartly against an uncomprehending and hostile nation that was destined to learn gratitude only belatedly. From this stylized portrait springs a habit of seeing the pictures as dusty allegory: the storms of Thomson or MacDonald symbolizing the torments unleashed by hostile critics, the mystic peace in Harris representing the spiritual aspiration that guided the artists through the dreadful storms.

The reality was more complex, and more interesting. To be sure, critical opposition to the brilliant, unusual coloration characteristic of the best Group work did erupt early and loudly. "Rough, splashy, meaningless, blatant plastering and massing of unpleasant colours in weird landscapes," blustered a flabbergasted Montréal critic in 1918. The stately official artists' organizations, notably the Royal Canadian Academy, tried for years to keep Group artists out of the museums and galleries. Even the politicians got in on the act, raising hell in the House of Commons when, in 1924, the National Gallery decided to include examples of the Group's "hot mush painting" in Canada's official entry at the British Empire Exhibition in England.

The important thing about the 1924 episode, however, is not the jawing of politicians but the strong support for the Group exhibited by the National Gallery, especially in the person of its far-seeing director, Eric Brown. But even as early as 1924, Brown was hardly a lone witness among knowledgeable Canadians. The liberal intellectual establishment of the Ontario art world quickly swung its weight behind the Group after its launch. Soon, wealthy Canadian businessmen and industrialists began to appear on the stage, playing roles as collectors, patrons and advisers. "By 1926," art historian Dennis Reid has written in his *Concise History of Canadian Painting,* "the Group of Seven were the acknowledged centre of serious art activity in Toronto, which in turn was the major centre of activity in the country. Followers and disciples were gathering. And even the broad public began to become aware of the Group of Seven as the 'national' school of art."

If some critics continued to harangue the Group well into the late 1920s—"the greatest abortion of a work of art ever seen in 'our fair city,'" wrote an Ottawan; "a group of freaks," snarled a Vancouver writer—they were outside the mainstream of Canadian opinion. But they were not without usefulness to the Group, which throughout its existence thrived on philistine attacks. I do not think it's an accident that, once such attacks stopped and the Group attained its maximum fame, it merely fell apart. No avant-garde movement in art seems able to survive without at least a few token puffsters to keep it militant and on the move.

However strong its penchant for publicity and self-dramatizing, the Group invented the first Canadian art of our century to command support across the spectrum of public opinion, taste, class and economic standing. They created symbols for a disparate country hungry for unifying symbols, images of mystic union for a nation and province tugged this way and that by regional interests, colonial hankerings for the British motherland, the centrifuge of industrialism, the gravitational pull of America's rise to world power. They did so by rejecting the city, and embracing a mysticism of the North and of the wild land that was the nineteenth century's final, crucial intellectual arrival in Ontario.

This is not—cannot be—the last story I tell. But the tale of the rise of a mysticism of the North in Ontario early in the last century is a story worth pondering, especially in a province where urbanization continues to intensify, the needle of our spiritual compass swings wildly and widely, and the steady pointing toward the North that Bucke believed in is past. In his brilliant book *Landscape and Memory,*

Simon Schama reminds us of the North and the venerable history of the forest, especially in the northern European lands from which Canada's founding peoples brought their myths and attitudes. "Religion and patriotism, antiquity and the future—all came together in the Teutonic romance of the woods," writes Schama of nineteenth-century Romanticism. Religion disappeared into patriotism, he explains, and the future was neutralized by antiquity. Bringing the point home to Canada in the early twentieth century, the painters of Ontario followed the lead of the nineteenth century's singers of the body electric—the technologists, as well as the official mystics and mystagogues—and found in the forests a deep reality that was neither Catholic nor Protestant, French nor English nor aboriginal. In the Northern wilderness, the uncertain future of a hectic, divided industrialized nation is left behind, as we descend into the primordial, embracing darkness. But we do not disappear there. We re-emerge renewed in an understanding of unities forgotten, or abandoned—of philosophy and science, faith and reason.

It isn't hard to understand the handiness of distinctive Canadian forest imagery in the fashioning of a mythology of unity circa 1920, given the powerful centrifugal forces at work in Ontario on the eve of the Great Depression. But even when one sees a myth for what it is— understands its limitations, its flaws and fragilities—it does not make the myth seem less powerful in its own time. The immense Ontario forest is a geographical fact, but not merely that. Even today, it remains as central to the popular imagination of the province as it did in 1920.

As the art of the Group of Seven and more recent landscape art reminds us—whether it is deployed as a vehicle for promoting a sense of national unity or a way to direct our attention to the ravaged Earth or a celebration of human unity with the world— such painting has lost none of its pathos or its power to compel, or its fascination for artists. We sense a timelessness and freedom in the woods that do not diminish when we learn, from books such as Schama's, that the idea has a long, complex history. Indeed, perhaps the enduring love for the forests, the notion that there we can find healing for the ills and divisions of civilization, is durable simply because we so deeply long for it to be true.

It is not. The earliest arrivals, thousands of years ago, in this place called Ontario pitched their seasonal camps along the edges of the waterways that define the south and southwestern limits of the land. When later civilizations—Indian, French, English—came here, they put down more durable roots by the water, then began the assault against the northern wilderness that has continued to this day. At first, the advance guard were farmers, clearing the land of trees to get down to the verdantly fertile ground below. Later, industrialists penetrated and domesticated the forbidding rocky expanse of the Canadian Shield. More recently, cottagers in search of the Group's sublime lakes and sunsets have transfigured the North yet more thoroughly, from

remote mystic source to summer getaway, quickly accessible from the densely populated south by high-speed expressways. There will always be a North in Ontario, of course; but it will not be there that Ontario's civilization will be built over the next hundreds or thousands of years.

That will happen, as always, along the great waterways of southern Ontario. And the culture that will arise—in varieties we can now only imagine—will be made by those who have come here in wave after wave, from the beginning: the arrivals.

Afterword
BUYING ON TIME

LIKE ANY BOOK OF STORIES about real people, this one has no real conclusion. It can only have an ending, and I have come to it.

But were I able, I would go on and on. There are wonderful tales to be told of the Italians of St. Clair West, the Hungarians and Portuguese, the Tibetans, Chinese, the Jews of Kensington Market and Bathurst Manor in Toronto, and men and women of myriad other tribes and tongues who have come here in flight from fear, political ruin or hunger, or out of the thirst for larger life. There is the story of Emma Goldman, the famous anarchist who fled J. Edgar Hoover's America, found refuge among the busy shops and tenements of Kensington Market, and died there. And there is the story of Jane Jacobs, who left the American cities at the height of their poisonous enchantment with Bulldozer Modernism, and stopped a Toronto expressway that would have wrecked the passionate richness of Ontario's most vibrant downtown forever.

There are the countless stories to be related about draft-dodging and war-resisting Americans who came to Ontario in the 1960s. Most of those Americans gradually became Canadians and melted into the downtown neighbourhoods and the suburbs, taking their tales with them. I would like to have found them all and gathered their narratives of voluntary exile from their native land into this book. But just before the completion of this writing, I received a copy of John Hagan's new work, *Northern Passage: American Vietnam War Resisters in Canada*, and felt a certain release from the burden of those untold tales and a new confidence that the necessary storytelling will continue.

Or it may not. As Rock told Orphan at the beginning of this book, some people will forget the old stories. A few will remember. But some will resist forgetfulness by carefully handing on what they remember. This book should surely end, not with despair about what we have lost, but with hope for the stories held in trust for the future, a few of which I have discovered and retold here.

Among contemporary tellers of tales who have given me high hope in this matter is the Toronto writer Antanas Sileika. Some years ago, he paused long enough in his career of novel-writing to give us *Buying on Time* (1997), a delightful and shrewd memoir of childhood in a family recently arrived in Toronto from Lithuania via occupied Germany after the Second World War. Like the English settlers in Ontario's British period, and the French before that—like the writer of this book, an American Southerner by birth and Canadian by choice—the Sileikas brought with them some of the Old World, and found themselves both enriched and displaced in the New. Perhaps this mixed sense of satisfaction and disquiet—irrational, especially after generations of settling in, but never quite extinguishable—has always been at the heart of Ontario's culture, from the very start.

I offer these passages from *Buying on Time* as a kind of grammar of this peculiar way of being here.

Imagine the place: Weston, Ontario, a small, once-prosperous Victorian village gobbled down and transformed into just another patch of endless cityscape by Toronto's abrupt twentieth-century sprawl.

Imagine the time: 1953.

Imagine the speaker: a grown-up much like Antanas Sileika, witnessing a collision of worlds in the little house his father built in Weston. Now imagine the Old Man, as Antanas calls the father.

Stan was a DP like my father, like the rest of us, but the outhouse in our back yard had made even him laugh. Not the outhouse itself, although it was the only one in the subdivision growing up in the old orchards, but the neat squares of newspaper my father had to stack beside the seat.

"You such fucking DP," Stan said to my father, and he held his sides as he laughed like a character out of a cartoon. Stan only swore when he spoke English, a language that didn't really count.

My father went out and bought two rolls of toilet paper, but for half a year we used them only as decoration, like twin flower vases. Stan's advice on toilet paper and anything else in this foreign land was reliable. As for what the locals advised, one could never be sure.

"A fool is always dangerous," my father told me, "but a foreign fool is worse. You can't tell if he's an idiot or simply a foreigner."

Those who came before—Indians before French, French before the English—have always been watched by the newcomers, with wariness or curiosity, fascination or dread or puzzlement. But *watched carefully,* always.

Mr. Taylor was a special kind of Canadian, an "English." They were the only kind who really counted, and observation of them could pay a dividend. Mr. Taylor was our English, the one who lived across the street and whose habits could be observed at will. We were astonished that he stayed in his dress shirt and tie as he read the evening paper in a lawn chair in his back yard. The lawn chair was just as astonishing. Who else but an English would spend good money on a chair that could only be used outside?

My father spat on the ground at this foolishness, but my mother sighed.

"These English are just like Germans," she said. She meant not like us, not DP. We belonged on the evolutionary tree with the Italians, Poles, and Ukrainians. Our knuckles scraped the earth.

"He's a banker," my mother told us, and the word was heavy with meaning. It explained how he lived in a house that not only had proper brick walls and a roof, but a lawn as well.

Our street had half a dozen other houses on it, but none of the rest were finished. People dug the foundations and laid the basement blocks. Then they waited and saved. When a little money came in, they bought beams and joists and studs. Then they waited some more. The Taylors stood out because a contractor had built their house from start to finish. We stood out too. We moved in before the above-ground walls went up.

"You want us to live underground?" my mother had asked. "Like moles? Like worms?"

"No," my father said, "like foxes."

Being here is always a matter of learning what it is to move here: the shortcuts to pleasure and to forbidden zones, routes to the edges and the centre, the correct path through the neighbourhoods where the *others* live, whether august or poor, wise or troublesome. It is learning the names of things.

The river marked the frontier of our town, and up on the opposite bank the world was more wondrous than ours. The banging and hammering that went on in our suburb was echoed there, but the houses that came up from the mud of Etobicoke were far more magnificent than ours. No little brick boxes rose up there, but wide-slung houses with only one storey that miraculously held three or even four bedrooms.

The Humber River valley was the no-man's-land between Weston and Etobicoke, a place where the locks had been cut off the grates of the storm sewers embedded in the banks. We hunted rats with slingshots deep into the drains, using candle stubs to light the way . . .

Gerry tied his shoelaces together and slung his shoes over his shoulder. He rolled up his pants, and I did the same. We carried sticks to brace us up in the water because the rocks on the bottom were slick with slime and we had to feel each spot with our toes before we put any weight on our feet. The bottom was littered with broken glass and crayfish snapped their tiny pincers on our skin if we disturbed their holes beneath the brown water.

The water hugged the steep river-valley bank on the other side, and there was barely room for us to sit on the bottom and put our shoes and socks back on. It was strangely cool in the shade of the West bank. There was little vegetation on the slope of broken shale above. Gerry had chosen a bad place to cross. The trestle abutment blocked us from searching for an easier way up unless we wanted to go back into the river, and there was no more forgiving slope upstream . . .

"Look at this." Gerry was holding a piece of shale the size of a cigarette package. It had a perfect outline of some kind of large water bug on it.

"It's a troglodyte," said Gerry.

"What's that?"

"A big old water bug. Say the word after me."

"What for?"

"Just say it."

I repeated the word.

"That's how you learn things. Improve yourself, or you'll end up like the Old Man."

In October, 1954, the immensely powerful tropical storm Hurricane Hazel swept across southern Ontario, leaving huge sorrow in its wake. Torrential rains sent Toronto's innumerable rivers, streams and underground rivulets surging from their channels in tides of death and destruction.

Understandably, the city moved rapidly to prevent any recurrence of uncontrolled torrents of water. A series of run-off channels and dams for flood control were built in the Toronto area in readiness for a similar disaster, which has never again (so far) struck the city. One result is a city with little to fear from any deluge short of Noah's. Another result is that few newcomers thereafter learned the high human price—some eighty people swept to their deaths—that was paid before the city became predictably safe and secure from rising water. At the time of this writing, those who remember vividly the terror of Hurricane Hazel are growing old and forgetting the facts, and the passion of human loss. It's the way of things. But people tend to forget calamity, unless someone tells a story about it.

They would not let us get close, but from the rise where we stood we could see that the entire valley was full of water. Whole trees floated by. We could not get close enough to see downstream to the curving bank where the Lotses had their house.

My father took us to a restaurant for the first time in my life. He ordered coffee for himself and soda floats for each of us, and he bought himself a newspaper. His lips moved as he mouthed the English words. Gerry looked over his shoulder, but I could not bear to look at the words on the paper. There was already too much talk around us.

"Any more survivors?" someone asked above the hubbub.

"Nope. Now they're just looking for bodies."

On the way back home, I asked my father what happened to Protestants when they died.

"They go to limbo," said Gerry.

I looked up the phone number for the Lotses and dialed it, but all I got was a repeated ringing that no one answered.

"Why don't you just look in the paper?" Gerry asked. "See if their name is listed."

Missing. Half of their street had been washed away in the night.

In the days that followed, I went down to the river to look over from our side. All the bridges were down, so there was no way to get across. Day after day, I phoned the number, but no one answered it. Gerry read the papers.

"Still missing."

It was all the papers wrote about for days. Houses were washed away. Five firemen died when their truck got swamped. Some people clung to trees for the whole night before they were rescued in the morning.

Then the talk stopped. People were tired of it.

Of course, things are different here. But not everything.

I kept phoning their number. One day between Christmas and New Year's, someone finally picked up the phone.

"Can I speak to Patsy?" I asked.

"I'm sorry, I don't know anyone by that name," a woman's voice answered.

"You're a liar!" I shouted, and I slammed down the phone.

My mother and father whispered together a great deal. That night at supper, my father would not let us get up from the table when we were finished.

"I have something to say to you."

He filled his pipe with great ceremony, and then lit it and filled the room with smoke. He leaned forward towards me.

"Listen. My father was shot," he said to me with no other explanation. "The farm where I grew up was burned down. Half my brothers are in Siberia. One of my sisters is dead. This is how life is. Get used to it."

He leaned back as if he had just finished a long speech.

"That's supposed to make him feel better?" my mother asked.

"Who said anything about feeling better? It's just the way things are."

In the early 1980s, the Old Man died. He had been born in a village in Lithuania when it was a province of Imperial Russia, worked as chief of police in his home town throughout the years that competing totalitarianisms traded Lithuania back and forth. He had worked and died in Ontario as a carpenter, though he had no formal training to be one. And after completing that astonishing trajectory, from a peasant village little changed since the Middle Ages to the house he built, basement up, in Weston, he went on living after death, in the way a dead man lives on: as a ghost haunting his son's house and car and mind, whispering reminders about the churn of comings and goings and changes, that eternal maelstrom of arrival.

I was driving through Weston on the way to my mother's house. The town had changed. When I was a kid, it had already stopped being a little town and become a neighbourhood on the edge of Toronto. Then the years passed and the edges of the neighbourhoods got smudged. The boundaries were gone. Now that there was a mall up by the highway for the carriage trade, the old main street was full of cheap discount stores. Soon the continent would be one big strip mall. In old downtown Weston, there were no more dress shops where my Aunt Ramona could mortgage her future, and no more appliance stores where my father could buy on time . . .

No trace of the old apple orchards remained when I turned onto my mother's street. In the early seventies, the city had put in sidewalks and planted trees. Maples on one side and dwarf cherries on the other. Twenty years before, the brick boxes still stood in the churned-up mud, and the whole place felt raw and new. It held some kind of promise then. It was a time when we had floated wooden boats on the water in the ditches. The city had paved over the ditches, but the water still ran down there, somewhere deep.

The geography of my childhood was changing, and the neighbours who had peopled it were disappearing. Where the Lymes had once lived in a concrete house with unstuccoed walls, a lawyer now resided with his family. Old man Lyme used to kick his daughters off the front porches if they were sassy and he was beered up, and now the house held a lawyer who sent his kids to private school. The Italian grocery, which had seemed so exotic with its olives and prosciutto, had become a West Indian grocery. We had turbaned South Asians, and former Vietnamese boat people stared out of picture windows as if they were marooned. We used to be the foreigners in the neighbourhood. It was enough to give me vertigo.

"So what did you expect?" the Old Man said from his place in the passenger seat.

CHRONOLOGY TO 1920

9000 BC: The continental ice sheet is retreating off Ontario, and the first visitors have arrived to hunt along the glacial margins.

5000 BC: Hunting peoples have spread into what is now northern Ontario and southeastern Québec.

AD 1100: Longhouse construction begins around Lake Ontario basin; earliest date for the founding of the League of the Long House People.

1453: Constantinople falls to the Ottoman Turks. Islamic traders gain monopoly over the West's Oriental trade routes.

1492: Supported by Isabel and Ferdinand of Spain, the Italian explorer Christopher Columbus embarks on an expedition to find an Atlantic route to the East. October 12: Columbus makes his first landfall in the Americas. In the course of this journey, and others in 1493, 1498 and 1502, Columbus explores the West Indies and Central America.

1497–98: On a transatlantic voyage underwritten by Bristol merchants, John Cabot (the Venetian Giovanni Caboto) makes the first landfall on the North American continent since the Vikings. Claims Cape Breton Island or Newfoundland—the location of his landing is not known for certain—for Henry VII of England.

1524: On behalf of François I of France, Giovanni da Verrazzano cruises along the continental shoreline from Florida to

Newfoundland and names the entire territory Francesca. The name Nova Gallia (New France) first appears on a map drawn by Giovanni's brother Girolamo.

1534: Jacques Cartier arrives in New France, visits Newfoundland and explores the Gulf of St. Lawrence.

1535: Cartier sails up the St. Lawrence River as far as the Indian towns of Stadacona (Québec) and Hochelaga (Montréal). His discovery of the St. Lawrence opens the way to French penetration of inner North America.

c. 1600: The Wendat are at the height of their power in French Ontario, with sixteen towns between Lake Simcoe and Georgian Bay.

1603: Champlain arrives in Canada, beginning his remarkable career of exploration and establishment of a vast fur trade with the nations of the Ottawa River and the Wendat of Ontario. From 1633, governor of New France.

1607: The first permanent English settlement in the Americas is established in Virginia.

1608: Champlain founds Québec on the site of the Algonkian town of Stadacona.

1609: Champlain supports the Algonkians against the Long House People at Lake Champlain. Henry Hudson and the *Half Moon*, sailing on behalf of the Dutch East India Company, enter the Hudson River in search of the Northwest Passage. He is set adrift by mutineers the following year on Hudson Bay. A formal trading alliance between the French and the Wendat is ratified, leading to the rapid growth of the fur trade.

1610: Étienne Brûlé goes to live among the Wendat and eventually becomes the first European to see Lake Ontario, Lake Huron and Lake Superior.

1615: Champlain and Brûlé explore southern Ontario as far west as Lake Huron. Franciscan missionaries attempt to establish a mission among the Wendat of south-central Ontario.

1617: Louis Hébert, an apothecary who had stayed at Port Royal twice, brings his wife and children to Québec. They become the first permanent civilian settlers of New France.

1619: A Dutch ship lands North America's first cargo of African slaves at Jamestown in Virginia.

1625: Charles I becomes King of England.

1626:   Jean de Brébeuf and his Jesuit companions found missions to the Wendat near Georgian Bay.

1627:   The Company of One Hundred (or Company of New France) is given a fur monopoly by Cardinal Richelieu and title to all lands claimed by New France. In exchange, they agree to establish a French colony of four thousand people by 1643, which they fail to do.

1628:   Prolonged warfare begins among the Wendat, Confederacy and other Indian peoples over domination of the beaver trade.

1634–40:   The beaver war, a devastating smallpox or measles epidemic and religious dissension among the Wendat severely reduce their numbers.

1635:   Samuel de Champlain dies in Québec.

1639:   The mission-fort of Ste-Marie-Among-the-Hurons is constructed by the Jesuits in Midland Bay, Ontario, and becomes the centre for Wendat mission activities.

1642:   Ville-Marie de Montréal is founded by Paul de Chomeday, Sieur de Maisonneuve, on the site of Hochelaga. Louis XIV (1638–1715) accedes to the French throne.

1645:   A peace treaty is struck between the French and the Long House Confederacy.

1648–49:   The war between the Wendat and the Confederacy over control of the fur trade reaches its climax. Some 1,200 well-armed Confederacy warriors sweep through Huronia, putting Wendat and Neutral to death, along with their Jesuit and French companions.

1649:   King Charles I of England is beheaded by Puritan revolutionaries.

1659:   Pierre-Esprit Radisson and Médard Chouart Des Groseilliers, pioneering fur traders, visit the western Great Lakes in search of business contacts with the Indians, reaching the west end of Lake Superior in 1658. The French peace with the League ends with the murder of a Jesuit missionary.

1664:   Peter Stuyvesant is forced to surrender Nieuw Amsterdam to the English. England installs a municipal government in the town, renamed New York. Father Jacques Marquette arrives in Québec from France.

1669:   The French explore the Ohio Valley for the first time.

1670:   The Hudson's Bay Company is founded by royal charter by Charles II.

1672:   Comte de Frontenac becomes governor general of New France.

1673:   Frontenac founds Cataraqui (near present-day Kingston). He sends Father Marquette and Louis Jolliet to explore the Great River presumed to lie in the west; they reach the Mississippi.

1680:   The Confederacy of the Long House reaches its maximum extent, from the Atlantic Ocean to the junction of the Ohio and Mississippi Rivers, and north to the south end of Lake Michigan, east across all of lower Michigan, southern Ontario and southwestern Québec.

1682:   René-Robert Cavelier, Sieur de La Salle, descends the full length of the Mississippi, claims all of the lands drained by the river and its tributaries for France and names it Louisiana.

1686:   La Salle is murdered by mutineers in present-day Texas.

1700:   French fur traders are operating along the Missouri River as far as the mouth of the Kansas River and perhaps beyond.

1701–13:   Louis XIV's last military venture, the War of the Spanish Succession (also known as Queen Anne's War), stems from his acceptance of the Spanish throne on behalf of his grandson, Philip.

1701:   Fort Pontchartrain du Detroit is founded by Antoine de la Mothe, Sieur de Cadillac.

1722:   The Confederacy incorporates the Tuscarora as its sixth member.

1730s: The Mississauga drive the Ontario Seneca south of Lake Erie.

c. 1750:   The Ojibwa begin to emerge as a distinct tribal amalgamation of smaller independent bands.

1754:   The French and Indian War begins, and the French and English struggle for control of inland North America. French America is at its apogee, with claims over the North American continent: from Hudson Bay to Louisiana, including a large part of what are today the Atlantic provinces, the entire St. Lawrence valley, the Great Lakes basin and the Mississippi valley.

1755:   Britain scatters the Nova Scotia Acadians throughout other North American colonies.

1756:   The Seven Years' War between Britain and France begins in Europe. France loses most of its overseas possessions to the British. The Marquis de Montcalm assumes command of French troops in North America.

1759:   The British capture Fort Niagara. Québec and Canada's fate are sealed on September 13, 1759, when British general James

Wolfe's troops climb cliffs thought unscalable to stage a surprise attack on the Plains of Abraham, a field adjoining the upper part of Quebec City.

1760: The British conquest of North America is complete. New France ceases to exist, and the final surrender of the continent to England, apart from La Louisiane, takes place in 1763. France will sell Louisiana to the United States in 1803. George III (1738–1820) comes to the British throne.

1763: A royal proclamation imposes British institutions on Québec.

1775: The American Revolution begins. Americans capture Montréal and attack Québec.

1776: Under Guy Carleton, Lord Dorchester, Québec withstands an American siege until the appearance of a British fleet. Carleton is later knighted for his resistance to the rebels.

1778: British regulars and Confederacy warriors under Joseph Brant attack American settlers on the western New York and Pennsylvania frontiers.

1779: Americans invade the League homeland in western New York, laying waste villages throughout the region and breaking the League's power.

1783: The American revolutionary war ends, and the settling of the U.S.-Canadian border begins. The process will take several years. The Long House Confederacy is reduced to only about eight thousand people.

1783–84: British Loyalists migrate from the United States to southeastern Ontario and Niagara, and Pennsylvania Germans move into southwestern Ontario.

1789: The French Revolution begins.

1791: With western Québec filling with English-speaking Loyalists, the Constitutional Act of 1791 divides Québec into Upper and Lower Canada (modern-day Ontario and Québec).

1793: John Graves Simcoe begins establishing York as the administrative capital of Upper Canada. In France, the Reign of Terror begins.

1794: Jay's Treaty, between the United States and Britain, permits peaceful British evacuation of the Ohio Valley forts and marks the beginning of international arbitration to settle boundary disputes.

1798: Joseph Brant decides to cede the Mohawk lands in New York to the United States.

1809–11:   Tecumseh, a Shawnee chief in the Ohio Valley, tries to unite Indian tribes and leaders (including Joseph Brant) to slow or halt the western expansion of the United States.

1812:   The United States declares war on Britain, beginning the War of 1812. Americans invade Canada from Detroit; Canadians victorious at the Battle of Queenston Heights.

1813:   Americans attack and occupy York. Tecumseh, brigadier general for the British, is killed in 1813, fighting for Canadian independence.

1814:   Victories alternate between U.S. and British forces until the Treaty of Ghent ends the war on December 24.

1824–9:   The first Welland Canal is completed, partly in response to American initiatives in building the Erie Canal.

1826–32:   Royal engineer Col. John By builds the Rideau Canal.

early 1830s: Immigration to Ontario rapidly advances. Upper Canada receives 193,000 people from Ireland, the United Kingdom and Europe. Their most common destinations are York (Toronto), London, Bytown (Ottawa), Hamilton, Cobourg and Kingston.

1833:   Slavery is abolished throughout the British Empire.

1834:   York, with 9,000 inhabitants, is incorporated and renamed Toronto. William Lyon Mackenzie becomes first mayor.

1837:   Victoria (1819–1901) becomes queen of the United Kingdom (1837–1901), later empress of India (1876–1901). William Lyon Mackenzie foments rebellion in Ontario, is defeated by loyal troops and escapes to the United States.

1838:   As governor general and high commissioner of British North America, Lord Durham arrives to investigate the circumstances behind the Rebellion. He recommends government reforms, and the union of Upper and Lower Canada to speed the assimilation of French-speaking Canadians.

1841:   An Act of Union unites Upper and Lower Canada as the Province of Canada.

1847:   There is a great influx of Irish immigrants in the wake of the potato famine.

1848:   Rebellions occur throughout Europe.

1849:   The boundary of the 49th parallel is extended to the Pacific Ocean. An Act of Amnesty provides for W. L. Mackenzie's return from exile in the United States.

1850: The site of By's headquarters during the construction of the Rideau Canal is incorporated as Bytown.

1851: The Great Exposition is held in London.

1855: Bytown is incorporated as Ottawa.

1856: The Grand Trunk Railway opens its Toronto-Montréal line.

1857: Queen Victoria designates Ottawa as capital of the Province of Canada.

1860: The cornerstone of the Parliament buildings is laid in Ottawa. Edward Albert, Prince of Wales (future King Edward VII), becomes the first royal visitor to Ontario.

1861: The American Civil War breaks out.

1864: Originally designed to discuss Maritime union, the Charlottetown Conference (September 1–9) takes the first steps toward Confederation.

1865: The American Civil War ends.

1866: The Fenians, a group of radical Irish-Americans organized to oppose British presence in Ireland, begin a series of raids on Canadian territory in the hopes of diverting British troops from the homeland.

1867: Confederation. Four of Britain's North American colonies are united by the British North America Act as the Dominion of Canada. Sir John A. Macdonald is Canada's first prime minister. Ottawa officially becomes capital of the Dominion.

1876: The Intercolonial Railway, growing out of the Halifax-Truro line, links central Canada and the Maritimes. The world's first long-distance phone call connects Brantford and nearby Paris, Ontario.

1885: The last spike of the transcontinental railway is put in place in the Eagle Pass, B.C.

1893: Water from Niagara Falls is diverted for generating hydroelectricity.

1903: Silver is discovered in northern Ontario.

1906: Sir Adam Beck succeeds in having the Ontario parliament establish the Hydro-Electric Power Commission of Ontario. Beck begins his campaign of absorbing private companies into the public utility.

1914: Britain declares war on Germany (August 4), automatically drawing Canada into the conflict. The first Canadian troops leave for England (October 3). Parliament passes the War

Measures Act, allowing suspension of civil rights during periods of emergency.

1916: The Parliament buildings are destroyed by fire.

1918: Armistice ends World War I.

1920: Canada joins the League of Nations at its inception. The Group of Seven holds its inaugural exhibition of Canadian landscape painting at the Art Gallery of Toronto.

SOURCES AND RESOURCES

Eᴀᴄʜ ᴏꜰ ᴛʜᴇ ꜰᴏʟʟᴏᴡɪɴɢ sᴇᴄᴛɪᴏɴs corresponds to a chapter in the book. If the same work has been used as a source in two or more chapters, the full bibliographical information appears in the first instance only.

I sincerely hope that these bibliographical notes will encourage readers to strike out on their own treasure-hunts for stories about Ontario, the history of which is really only in its beginning.

I. Origins

1. How the Stories Came

Clark, Ella Elizabeth. *Indian Legends of Canada*. Toronto: McClelland and Stewart, 1969.

Curnoe, Greg. *Deeds / Abstracts: The History of a London Lot / Greg Curnoe, 1 January 1991–6 October 1992*. London, Ont.: Brick Books, 1995.

———. *Deeds / nations*. Ed. Frank Davey and Neal Ferris. London, Ont.: London Chapter, Ontario Archaeological Society, 1996.

Curtin, Jeremiah. *Seneca Indian Myths*. New York: E. P. Dutton & Co., 1923.

2. The Woman Who Fell from the Stars

Hale, Horatio. "Huron Folk-Lore." *Journal of American Folk-Lore*, 1, no. 3 (Oct.–Dec. 1888).

Trigger, Bruce G. *Children of Aataentsic: A History of the Huron People to 1660*. Kingston and Montréal: McGill-Queen's University Press, 1987.

Wright, J. V. *Ontario Prehistory: An Eleven-thousand-year Historical Outline*. Ottawa: National Museums of Canada, 1972.

3. Ways Up and Down

Chamberlain, A. F. "Nanibozhu amongst the Otchipwe, Mississagas, and other Algonkian Tribes." *Journal of American Folk-Lore*, 4, no. 14 (July–Sept. 1891).

Hoffman, Walter James. "Pictography and Shamanistic Rites of the Ojibway." *American Anthropologist*, I (1888).

———. "The Menomini Indians." J. W. Powell, *Fourteenth Annual Report of the Bureau of Ethnology to the Secretary of the Smithsonian Institution*. Part I (1892–93). Washington: Government Printing Office, 1896.

Johnston, Richard B. *The Archaelogy of the Serpent Mounds Site*. Toronto: University of Toronto Press, 1968.

4. Flint's Work

Adams, Nicholas R. *The Prehistory of Ontario*. Newboro, Ont.: Adams Heritage, 1995.

Hale, Horatio. *The Iroquois Book of Rites*. Philadelphia: D. G. Brinton, 1883.

Hewitt, J. N. B. "A Constitutional League of Peace in the Stone Age of America: The League of the Iroquois and Its Constitution." *Annual Report of the Smithsonian Institution for 1918*. Washington: Government Printing Office, 1920.

———. "Legend of the Founding of the Iroquois League." *American Anthropologist*, V (1892).

Salvador, Ricardo J. "Maize." *The Encyclopedia of Mexico: History, Culture and Society*. Chicago and London: Fitzroy Dearborn Publishers, 1997.

5. The Great Peace

Cusick, David. *Ancient History of the Six Nations*. Lockport, NY: Niagara County Historical Society, 1961.

Murphy, Gerald. "Constitution of the Iroquois Nations: The Great Binding Law—Gayanashagowa." Cleveland: The Cleveland Free-Net, 1999.

Distributed by the Cybercasting Services Division of the National Public Telecomputing Network.

Parker, Arthur C. *The Constitution of the Five Nations, or the Iroquois Book of the Great Law.* Albany: The University of the State of New York, Bulletin no. 184 (Apr. 1, 1916).

6. Speaking a Little Differently

Coyne, James H. *The Country of the Neutrals: (as far as comprised in the County of Elgin), from Champlain to Talbot.* St. Thomas, Ont.: Times Print, 1895.

Kenyon, Walter Andrew. *The Grimsby Site: A Historic Neutral Cemetery.* Toronto: Royal Ontario Museum, 1982.

Le Clercq, Chrestien. *First Establishment of the Faith in New France.* Trans. John Gilmary Shea. New York: J. G. Shea, 1881.

Thwaites, Reuben Gold, ed. *The Jesuit Relations and Allied Documents: Travels and Explorations of the Jesuit Missionaries in New France, 1610–1791.* Cleveland: Burrows, 1897.

II. STRIFE OF EMPIRES

7. Roads to China

Columbus, Christopher. *The Voyages of Christopher Columbus.* Trans. and ed. Cecil Jane. London: The Argonaut Press, 1930.

Hughes, Robert, quoted in Kevin A. Miller, "Why Did Columbus Sail?" *Christian History,* 11, no. 3 (summer 1986).

Thwaites, *The Jesuit Relations.* 1642–43.

Verrazzano, Giovanni da, quoted in Donald Johnson. *Charting the Sea of Darkness: The Four Voyages of Henry Hudson.* Camden, ME: International Marine, 1993.

Wright, John Kirtland. *The Geographical Lore of the Time of the Crusades: A Study in the History of Medieval Science and Tradition in Western Europe.* New York: Dover Publications, 1965.

8. Fabulous Saguenay

Biggar, Henry Percival. *A Collection of Documents Relating to Jacques Cartier and the Sieur de Roberval.* Ottawa: Public Archives of Canada, 1930.

Burger, Carl. *Beaver Skins and Mountain Men: The Importance of the Beaver in the Discovery, Exploration, and Settlement of the North American Continent.* New York: Dutton [1968].

Cartier, Jacques. *The Voyages of Jacques Cartier*. Ed. Henry Percival Biggar. Ottawa: F. A. Acland, 1924.

Hakluyt, Richard. *The principal navigations, voiages, traffiqves and discoueries of the English nation*. 3 vols. London: George Bishop, Ralph Newberie and Robert Barker, 1600.

Innis, Harold Adams. *The Fur Trade in Canada; an Introduction to Canadian Economic History*. Toronto: University of Toronto Press, 1956.

Martin, Horace T. *Castorologia; or, The history and traditions of the Canadian beaver*. Montréal: W. Drysdale & Co.; London: E. Stanford, 1892.

Stewart, Alexander Charles. *The Beaver, and Other Odds and Ends*. Toronto: Hunter-Rose, 1918.

Taylor, Joseph Henry. *Beavers: Their Ways and Other Sketches*. Washburn, N.D.: J. H. Taylor, 1904.

9. Champlain's Knee

Bishop, Morris. *Champlain: The Life of Fortitude*. New York: Knopf, 1948.

Butterfield, Consul Willshire. *History of Brûlé's discoveries and explorations, 1610–1626*. Grand Rapids, Mich.: B. L. B. Black Letter Press, 1974.

Champlain, Samuel de. *Voyages to New France, being an account of the manners and customs of the savages and a description of the country, with a history of the many remarkable things that happened in the years 1615 to 1618*. Trans. Michael Macklem. [Ottawa]: Oberon Press, 1970.

———. *Voyages of Samuel de Champlain*. Trans. Edmund F. Slafter. Boston: The Prince Society, 1878.

———. *The Works of Samuel de Champlain*. Trans. Henry P. Biggar. 6 vols. Toronto: The Champlain Society, 1922–36.

Cranston, James Herbert. *Etienne Brûlé, Immortal Scoundrel*. Toronto: Ryerson Press [1969].

Davis, John, quoted in Johnson, *Charting the Sea of Darkness*.

Morison, Samuel Eliot. *Samuel de Champlain: Father of New France*. Boston & Toronto: Little, Brown and Co., 1972.

10. Black Robes

Burger, Carl. *Beaver Skins and Mountain Men*.

Gaither, Frances. *The Fatal River: The Life and Death of La Salle*. New York: Holt, 1931.

Jaenen, Cornelius J. *The Role of the Church in New France*. Ottawa: Canadian Historical Association, 1985.

————, ed. *The French Regime in the Upper Country of Canada During the Seventeenth Century*. Toronto: The Champlain Society and Government of Ontario, 1996.

Kennedy, J. H. *Jesuit and Savage in New France*. Hamden, Conn.: Archon Books, 1971.

O'Callaghan, E. B., ed. *Documents Relative to the Colonial History of the State of New York*. Vol. 9. Albany: Weed, 1856.

Russell, Osborne. *Journal of a Trapper*. [Portland]: Oregon Historical Society, 1955.

11. Again, the Beautiful River

Cox, Isaac Joslin, ed. *The Journeys of René Robert Cavelier, Sieur de La Salle / as Related by Henri de Tonty . . . [et al.]; Together with Memoirs, Commissions, etc.* New York: Allerton Book Co., 1922.

Gaither, Frances. *The Fatal River*.

Hennepin, Louis. *A New Discovery of a Vast Country in America*. Ed. Reuben Gold Thwaites. Chicago: A. C. McClurg & Co., 1903.

Saint-Simon, Louis de Rouvroy. *Memoirs of the Duke de Saint-Simon*. Trans. Francis Arkwright. New York: Brentano's [n.d.].

12. The Lost World

Hero, Alfred Olivier Jr. *Louisiana and Quebec: Bilateral Relations and Comparative Sociopolitical Evolution, 1673–1993*. Lanham, Maryland, and London: University Press of America, 1995.

Records of the Governor General of New France, 1728–1860. In *Collections of the State Historical Society of Wisconsin*. Vols. 17, 18. Madison: State Historical Society of Wisconsin, 1903–8.

Robinson, Percy James. *Toronto during the French Régime: A History of the Toronto Region from Brûlé to Simcoe, 1615–1793*. Toronto: University of Toronto Press, 1965.

Vachon, André, with Victorin Chabot and André Desrosiers. *Dreams of Empire: Canada before 1700*. Trans. John F. Flinn. Ottawa: Ministry of Supply and Services Canada, 1982.

III. THE WORLD UPSIDE DOWN

13. Miss Molly's War

Bazely, Susan M. "Who Was Molly Brant?" Paper presented to the Kingston Historical Society, April 17, 1996. http://web.ctsolutions.com/carf/document/brant.html.

Blakeley, Phyllis R., and John N. Grant. *Eleven Exiles: Accounts of Loyalists of the American Revolution.* Toronto and Charlottetown: Dundurn Press, 1982.

Green, Gretchen. "Molly Brant, Catharine Brant, and Their Daughters: A Study in Colonial Acculturation." *Ontario History.* 81, no. 3 (Sept. 1989).

Griffis, William Elliot. *Sir William Johnson and the Six Nations.* New York: Dodd, Mead, 1891.

Gundy, H. Pearson, "Molly Brant—Loyalist." *Ontario History.* 45, no. 3 (1953).

Holden, Mrs. John Rose. *The Brant Family.* Wentworth: Wentworth Historical Society, 1904.

Ke-che-ah-gah-me-qua. *Sketch of the life of Captain Joseph Brant, Thayendanagea.* Montréal: J. Dougall [1872].

Robinson, Helen Caister. *Mistress Molly, the Brown Lady: A Portrait of Molly Brant.* Toronto: Dundurn Press, 1980.

14. Muddy York

Benn, Carl. *Historic Fort York, 1793–1993.* Toronto: Natural Heritage/Natural History Inc., 1993.

Brode, Patrick. *Sir John Beverley Robinson: Bone and the Sinew of the Compact.* Toronto: University of Toronto Press, 1984.

David, Saul. *Prince of Pleasure: The Prince of Wales and the Making of the Regency.* Great Britain: Little, Brown and Co., 1998.

Dendy, William, and William Kilbourn. *Toronto Observed: Its Architecture, Patrons and History.* Toronto: Oxford University Press, 1986.

Fowler, Marion. *The Embroidered Tent: Five Gentlewomen in Early Canada.* Toronto: Anansi, 1982.

Fryer, Mary Beacock. *Elizabeth Posthuma Simcoe 1762–1850: A Biography.* Toronto and Oxford: Dundurn Press, 1989.

———. *John Graves Simcoe, 1752–1806: A Biography.* Toronto and Tonawanda, N.Y. : Dundurn Press, 1998.

Guillet, Edwin C. *Pioneer Settlements in Upper Canada.* Toronto: University of Toronto Press, 1933.

————. *The Lives and Times of the Patriots.* Toronto: Thomas Nelson and Sons, 1938.

Lunn, Richard and Janet. *The County: The First Hundred Years in Loyalist Prince Edward.* Picton, Ont.: Prince Edward County Council, 1967.

McBurney, Margaret, and Mary Byers. *Homesteads: Early Buildings and Families from Kingston to Toronto.* Toronto and Buffalo: University of Toronto Press, 1979.

Read, David Breckenridge. *The Life and Times of Gen. John Graves Simcoe, Commander of the "Queen's Rangers" during the Revolutionary War, and First Governor of Upper Canada, Together with Some Account of Major André and Capt. Brant.* Toronto: G. Virtue, 1890.

Riddell, James Renwick. *The Life of John Graves Simcoe.* Toronto: McClelland & Stewart, 1926.

Roberton, Thomas B. *The Fighting Bishop, John Strachan the First Bishop of Toronto: And Other Essays in His Times.* Ottawa: Graphic Pub., 1926.

Robertson, John Ross. *Landmarks of Toronto: A Collection of Historical Sketches of the Old Town of York.* Toronto: J. Ross Robertson, 1896.

Scadding, Henry. *Toronto of Old: Collections and Recollections.* Toronto: Adam, Stevenson & Co., 1873.

Scott, Duncan Campbell. *John Graves Simcoe.* Toronto: Morang & Co., 1910.

Simcoe, Elizabeth. *The Diary of Mrs. John Graves Simcoe.* Ed. John Ross Robertson. Toronto: William Briggs, 1911.

Simcoe, Elizabeth Posthuma. *Mrs. Simcoe's Diary.* Ed. Mary Quayle Innis. Toronto: Macmillan of Canada, 1965.

15. Handsome Lake

Parker, A. C. *The Code of Handsome Lake, the Seneca Prophet.* Albany: University of the State of New York, 1913.

Thomas, Jacob E. *Teachings from the Longhouse.* Don Mills, Ont.: Stoddart, 1994.

Wallace, Anthony F. C. *The Death and Rebirth of the Seneca.* New York: Knopf, 1970.

16. Serinette

Bernstein, Tamara. Review of *Serinette. The Globe and Mail,* 9 July 1990.

Dorland, Arthur Garratt. *The Quakers in Canada: A History.* Toronto: Ryerson Press [1968].

————. *Along the Trail of Life: A Quaker Retrospect.* Belleville, Ont.: Mika Pub. Co., 1979.

Everett-Green, Robert. Feature on *Serinette. The Globe and Mail,* 28 June 1990.

McIntyre, W. John. *The Early Writings of David Willson: A Forgotten Voice from Upper Canada.* Toronto: York Pioneer and Historical Society [1974].

————. *Children of Peace.* Montréal and Kingston: McGill-Queen's University Press, 1994.

Reaney, James. In conversation with Paula Citron, *The Toronto Star,* 6 July 1990.

Sandeen, Ernest R. *The Roots of Fundamentalism: British and American Millenarianism, 1800–1930.* Chicago: University of Chicago Press, 1970.

Willson, David. *The Collected Works of David Willson.* Sharon, Ont.: Sharon Temple, 1989.

17. John Toronto

Bethune, A. N. *Memoir of the Right Reverend John Strachan, D.D., LL.D., First Bishop of Toronto.* Toronto: Rowsell, 1870.

Boorman, Sylvia. *John Toronto: A Biography of Bishop Strachan.* Toronto: Clark, Irwin, 1969.

Strachan, John. *A Discourse on the Character of King George the Third: Addressed to the Inhabitants of British America.* Montréal: Nahum Mower, 1810.

————. *The John Strachan Letter Book: 1812–1834.* Ed. George W. Spragge. Toronto: Ontario Historical Society, 1946.

————. Letter to Thomas Jefferson, quoted in Raoul Renault. "Thomas Jefferson and the Loyal and Patriotic Society of Upper Canada." *North American Notes and Queries.* 1 (1901).

————. *Documents and Opinions: A Selection.* Ed. J. L. H. Henderson. Toronto: McClelland and Stewart, 1969.

18. Voyageurs

Osborne, A. C. "The Migration of Voyageurs from Drummond Island to Penetanguishene in 1828." *Ontario Historical Society Papers and Records.* 3 (1901).

Parkman, Francis. *The Parkman Reader.* Ed. Samuel Eliot Morison. Boston and Toronto: Little, Brown and Co., 1955.

Sandoz, Mari. *The Beaver Men: Spearheads of Empire.* New York: Hastings House, 1964.

IV. THE SETTLING

19. Mrs. Jameson's Wildest Tour

Coyne, James H. *The Talbot Papers.* Royal Society of Canada, Transactions. Series 3, Vol. 1, section 2 (1907–8). Ottawa, 1908.

Ermatinger, C. O. *The Talbot Regime; or, The First Half Century of the Talbot Settlement.* St. Thomas, Ont.: Municipal World, 1904.

Ermatinger, Edward. *Life of Colonel Talbot, and the Talbot Settlement, Its Rise and Progress, with Sketches of the Public Characters, and Career of Some of the Most Conspicuous Men in Upper Canada.* Belleville, Ont.: Mika Silk Screening, 1972.

Erskine, Mrs. Steuart. *Anna Jameson: Letters and Friendships (1812–1860).* London: T. Fisher Unwin, 1915.

Hamil, Frederick Coyne. *Lake Erie Baron: The Story of Colonel Thomas Talbot.* Toronto: Macmillan Co. of Canada, 1955.

Jameson, Anna Brownell. *Winter Studies and Summer Rambles in Canada.* London: Saunders and Otley, 1838.

Macpherson, Gerardine. *Memoirs of the Life of Anna Jameson, by Her Niece Gerardine.* London: Longmans, Green, 1878.

Paddon, Wayne. *The Story of the Talbot Settlement, 1803–1840: A Frontier History of Southwestern Ontario.* [n.p.] 1976.

Thomas, Clara. *Love and Work Enough: The Life of Anna Jameson.* Toronto: University of Toronto Press, 1967.

20. 1837

Arthur, Sir George. *The Arthur Papers: being the Canadian papers, mainly confidential, private and demi-official, in the manuscript collection of the Toronto Public Libraries.* Ed. Charles R. Sanderson. 3 vols. Toronto: Toronto Public Libraries and the University of Toronto Press, 1957–59.

Fraser, John. *Eminent Canadians: Candid Tales of Then and Now.* Toronto: McClelland and Stewart, 2000.

Martyn, J. P. "The Patriot Invasion of Pelee Island." *Ontario History,* Sept. 1964.

Raible, Chris. *Muddy York Mud: Scandal & Scurrility in Upper Canada.* Creemore, Ont.: Curiosity House, 1992.

Read, Colin, and Ronald J. Stagg. *The Rebellion of 1837 in Upper Canada.* Toronto: The Champlain Society in co-operation with the Ontario Heritage Foundation, 1985.

Salutin, Rick. *1837: William Lyon Mackenzie and the Canadian Revolution.* Toronto: J. Lorimer, 1976.

Traill, Catharine Parr. *The Backwoods of Canada.* Toronto: McClelland & Stewart, 1929.

Wait, Benjamin. *Letters from Van Dieman's Land: Written During Four Years Imprisonment for Political Offences Committed in Upper Canada.* Buffalo: A. W. Wilgus, 1843.

———. *The Wait Letters.* Ed. Mary Brown. Erin, Ont.: Press Porcépic, 1976.

21. Kindly Landings

Cameron, Wendy, and Mary McDougall Maude. *Assisting Emigration to Upper Canada: The Petworth Project, 1832–1837.* Montréal: McGill-Queen's University Press, 2000.

Gray, Charlotte. *Sisters in the Wilderness: The Lives of Susanna Moodie and Catharine Parr Traill.* Toronto: Viking, 1999.

Kenyon, Hugh. "Kirdford—Some Parish History" (1971). Quoted at www.surreycmc.gov.uk/re/whats_new/SHC/cranleigh_poor.htm.

Langton, Anne. *A Gentlewoman in Upper Canada: The Journals of Anne Langton.* Ed. Hugh Hornby Langton. Toronto: Clarke, Irwin, 1950.

22. The Coffin Ships

Whyte, Robert. *The Ocean Plague, or, A Voyage to Quebec in an Irish Emigrant Vessel.* Boston: Coolidge and Wiley, 1848.

23. Uncle Tom

Beattie, Jessie Louise. *Black Moses: The Real Uncle Tom.* Toronto: Ryerson Press [1957].

Henson, Josiah. *Uncle Tom's Story of His Life: An Autobiography of the Rev. Josiah Henson, 1789–1876; with a Preface by Harriet Beecher Stowe.* London: Christian Age Office, 1876.

24. The Last Invasion

Crawford, Michael, and Kenneth Armstrong, eds. *The Fenians.* Toronto: Clarke, Irwin [c. 1970].

Denison, George T. *History of the Fenian Raid on Fort Erie: With an Account of the Battle of Ridgeway.* Toronto: Rollo & Adam; Buffalo: Breed, Butler, 1866.

Macdonald, John A. *Troublous Times in Canada: A History of the Fenian Raids of 1866 and 1870.* Toronto: W. S. Johnston, 1910.

McKenzie, Thomas. *My Life as a Soldier.* Saint John, N.B.: J. & A. McMillan, 1898.

Neidhardt, W. S. *Fenianism in North America.* University Park and London: Pennsylvania State University Press, 1975.

Senior, Hereward. *The Last Invasion of Canada: The Fenian Raids, 1866–1870.* Toronto: Dundurn Press, Canadian War Museum, Canadian Museum of Civilization, 1991.

V. DOMINION

25. Niagara

Adamson, Jeremy Elwell. *Niagara: Two Centuries of Changing Attitudes, 1697–1901.* Washington: Corcoran Gallery of Art, 1985.

Plewman, William Rothwell. *Adam Beck and the Ontario Hydro.* Toronto: Ryerson Press, 1947.

Wells, H. G. *The Future in America: A Search after Realities.* London: Chapman & Hall, 1906.

26. Electric Empire

Edwards, W. F. L. *The Story of Jumbo.* St. Thomas: Sutherland Press, 1935.

Fessenden, Helen M. *Fessenden: Builder of Tomorrows.* New York: Arno Press, 1974.

Fry, Mervyn. "Radio's First Voice." *The Cat's Whisker—Official Voice of the Canadian Vintage Wireless Association.* 3, no. 1 (March 1973).

Grosvenor, Edwin S. *Alexander Graham Bell: The Life and Times of the Man Who Invented the Telephone.* New York: Harry Abrams, 1997.

Harding, Les. *Elephant Story: Jumbo and P. T. Barnum Under the Big Top.* Jefferson, N. C. and London: McFarland & Co., 2000.

Innis, Harold Adams. *Empire and Communications.* Intro. Marshall McLuhan. Oxford: Clarendon Press, 1950.

———. *The Bias of Communication.* [Toronto]: University of Toronto Press, 1951.

Mackay, James. *Sounds Out of Silence: A Life of Alexander Graham Bell.* Edinburgh and London: Mainstream, 1997.

Marchand, Philip. *Marshall McLuhan: The Medium and the Messenger.* Toronto: Random House, 1989.

Raby, Ormond. *Radio's First Voice: The Story of Reginald Fessenden.* Toronto: Macmillan, 1970.

Spencer, Robert H. *Alexander Graham Bell (1847–1922): A 125th Anniversary Address.* Privately published, 1972.

Withrow, John, ed. *Once Upon a Century: 100 Year History of the "Ex."* Toronto: J. H. Robinson Publishing, 1978.

27. The Swamp Murder

Birchall, Reginald. *The Story of His Life, Trial and Imprisonment as Told by Himself.* Toronto: National Pub. Co., 1890.

Murray, John Wilson. *Memoirs of a Great Detective, Incidents in the Life of John Wilson Murray.* London: Heinemann, 1904.

28. The Disenchantment

Carroll, John. *Past and Present: or, A Description of Persons and Events Connected with Canadian Methodism for the Last Forty Years by a Spectator of the Scenes.* Toronto: A. Dredge, 1860.

Dane, Barry, quoted in Allan Smith. "Farms, Forests and Cities: The Image of the Land and the Rise of the Metropolis in Ontario, 1860–1914." In David Keane and Colin Read, eds. *Old Ontario: Essays in Honour of J. M. S. Careless.* Toronto: Dundurn Press, 1990.

Mohr, Merilyn Simonds. "Stubborn Particularities of Place." *Treasures of the Place: Three Centuries of Nature Writing in Canada.* Ed. Wayne Grady. Vancouver and Toronto: Douglas & McIntyre, 1992.

Traill, Catharine Parr. *The Backwoods of Canada.* Toronto: McClelland & Stewart, 1929.

29. Cosmic Consciousness

Anonymous. "The Osler-Bucke Relationship and the Whitman Clutter," *Osler Library Newsletter,* no. 71 (October 1992). Montréal: McGill University.

Bucke, Richard Maurice. "Cosmic Consciousness: A Paper Read Before the American Medico-Psychological Association in Philadelphia, 18 May, 1894." Philadelphia: The Conservator, 1894.

———, ed. *Notes and Fragments: Left by Walt Whitman.* Privately printed, 1899.

———. *Cosmic Consciousness: A Study in the Evolution of the Human Mind.* Intro. George Moreby Acklom. New York: E. P. Dutton [1970].

———. *Letters of Dr. Richard Maurice Bucke to Walt Whitman.* Ed. Artem Lozynsky. Detroit: Wayne State University Press, 1977.

Cushing, H. *The Life of Sir William Osler.* Oxford: Clarendon Press, 1925.

Greenland, Cyril, and John Robert Columbo. *Walt Whitman's Canada.* Toronto: Hounslow Press, 1992.

Schmidgall, Gary. *Walt Whitman: A Gay Life.* New York: Plume, 1997.

30. The Mystic North

Armstrong, F. H., H. A. Stevenson and J. D. Wilson, eds. *Aspects of Nineteenth-century Ontario: Essays Presented to James J. Talman.* Toronto: University of Western Ontario and University of Toronto Press, 1974.

Bray, Robert Matthew, and Ernest A. Epp, eds. *A Vast and Magnificent Land: An Illustrated History of Northern Ontario.* Thunder Bay, Ont.: Lakehead University; Sudbury, Ont.: Laurentian University, 1984.

Clark, Christopher St. George. *Of Toronto the Good: A Social Study: The Queen City of Canada as It Is.* Montréal: Toronto Pub. Co., 1898.

Harris, Lawren S. "Creative Art in Canada." Bertram Brooker, ed. *Yearbook of the Arts in Canada, 1928–1929.* Toronto: Macmillan, 1929.

Hill, Charles C. *The Group of Seven: Art for a Nation.* Ottawa and Toronto: The National Gallery of Canada and McClelland & Stewart, 1995.

Maynard, Steven. "'Horrible Temptations': Sex, Men, and Working-class Male Youth in Urban Ontario, 1890–1935." *Canadian Historical Review.* LXXVIII (June 1997).

Nasgaard, Roald. *The Mystic North: Symbolist Landscape Painting in Northern Europe and North America, 1890–1940.* Toronto: University of Toronto, 1984.

Reid, Dennis. *The Group of Seven.* Ottawa: National Gallery of Canada, 1970.

———. *A Concise History of Canadian Painting.* Toronto: Oxford University Press, 1988.

Semple, Neil. "The Quest for the Kingdom: Aspects of Protestant Revivalism in Nineteenth-Century Ontario." In *Old Ontario: Essays in Honour of J. M. S. Careless.*

Smith, Philip. *Harvest from the Rock: A History of Mining in Ontario.* Toronto: Macmillan of Canada, 1986.

Strange, Carolyn. *Toronto's Girl Problem: The Perils and Pleasures of the City, 1880–1930.* Toronto: University of Toronto Press, 1998.

Afterword: Buying on Time

Hagan, John. *Northern Passage: American Vietnam War Resisters in Canada.* Cambridge and London: Harvard University Press, 2001.

Moritz, Theresa and Albert. *The World's Most Dangerous Woman: A New Biography of Emma Goldman.* Vancouver and Toronto: Subway Books, 2001.

Sileika, Antanas. *Buying on Time.* Erin, Ont.: The Porcupine's Quill, 1997.

ACKNOWLEDGEMENTS

T HE HAPPIEST MOMENT in the completion of any book comes when the author at last gets to thank the living, pay homage to the dead and acknowledge all who have contributed to the writing. I am especially indebted to my editor Cynthia Good, who hatched the idea for this book and, to my surprise, talked me into writing it, to Mary Adachi, Sandra Tooze, Liba Berry and Kathleen Richards. I appreciate Marie Day's willingness to adorn the book with her thoughtful drawings.

I wish to thank my superb literary agents, Jan Whitford at the beginning of the work and Helen Heller at the end; Robert Everett-Green, Antanas Sileika, Richard Handler, Anne Collins, Greg Gatenby, John Fraser, Ralph Spence, Vera Frenkel, Richard Rhodes, Matthias Mayer, Anne and Robert McPherson, Charlotte Gray, Michael Peterman, David Perkins, Brian Primeau, Anne Gibson and Ken Winters, my wife, Margaret Cannon, our daughter, Erin Anne Bentley Mays, and all others who encouraged and informed the writing.

I will forever be grateful for the example and vigorous creative intelligence of Greg Curnoe, to whom this book is dedicated.

ACKNOWLEDGEMENTS 409

The credit for all that is worthwhile in this volume should go to my editors, friends, supporters and sources. The blame for any errors or oversights must fall on me alone.

J.B.M.

COPYRIGHT ACKNOWLEDGEMENTS

The author gratefully acknowledges permission from the following publishers and persons to reprint material in their control:

Tamara Berstein for an excerpt from her 9 July 1990 *Globe and Mail* review of the opera *Serinette,* copyright © 1990 by Tamara Bernstein.

Canadian Institute for Historical Microreproductions for excerpts from "Letters from Emigrants Sent to Upper Canada by the Petworth Committee in 1832, 1833, and 1837" (CIHM/ICMH microfiche 59345) and "Instructions to persons intending to emigrate as to domestic articles they should take with them [etc.]" (CIHM/ICMH microfiche 63142), copyright © 1987 by Canadian Institute for Historical Microreproductions.

Paula Citron for an excerpt from her 6 July 1990 *Toronto Star* review of the opera *Serinette,* copyright © 1990 by Paula Citron.

Dundurn Press for excerpts from pages 78, 96, 100, 111 and 113 of *Old Ontario: Essays in Honour of J. M. S. Careless,* edited by David Keane and Colin Read, copyright © 1990 by Dundurn Press.

Faber and Faber and the Estate of T. S. Eliot for lines from "Little Gidding," in *Four Quartets from Collected Poems 1909–1962* by T. S. Eliot, copyright © 1963 by Faber and Faber.

INDEX

This index is a guide to the names of the principal persons, groups, historical events, ancient Ontario nations and places mentioned in this book, together with one glacier, one natural disaster and two animals: the beaver and Jumbo the elephant. In addition to the principal actors, I have included the names of historians and other authors who have invented or shaped the contemporary imagination of Ontario. The only frequently appearing topographical features omitted in this index are the most common ones: the Great Lakes and Georgian Bay.